An HS-2L is pictured flying majestically through the Cape Cod skies as it returns to the Chatham Naval Air Station from a routine patrol assignment. *Photo courtesy of the National Archives, Washington, D.C.*

WINGS

OVER

CAPE COD

The Chatham Naval Air Station

1917 - 1922

By Joseph D. Buckley

Library of Congress Control Number: 00-133197

ISBN 0936972-18-1

Printed in the United States of America by:
          Bookmasters, Incorporated, Chelsea, Michigan

Published By: Lower Cape Publishing, P.O. Box 901, Orleans, MA. 02653

HS-2L 1847 shown about to lift-off as it speeds down the channel between the Chatham Naval Air Station and Strong Island. *Photo from the Author's Collection.*

For my father

Dennis W. Buckley, Yeoman 2/c
(1892 - 1957)

and

all the other men of the United States Navy
who served at the Chatham Naval Air Station

``*You answered the call to the colors,*
You proved you were loyal and true;
And we – who can't go – will let others know
The debt that we owe to you!''

Anonymous - 1918

Above: An aerial view of the almost completed ``double'' seaplane hangar which was needed to house the large HS flying boats. To the right is the small original hangar designed for the older R-9 pontoon-type aircraft. **Below:** The dirigible hangar viewed from Bassing Harbor. Note the extensive number of windows used in its construction to admit as much daylight and ventilation as possible. *Photos courtesy of Robert S. Hardy and the Chatham Historical Society.*

Preface

My earliest recollections of the Chatham Naval Air Station are in the form of captivating bedtime stories my father would tell me when I was a very young lad in the late 1930's. War had just broken out in Europe, and the daily headlines apparently made him look back to 1918 and the time he spent as an enlisted man at that rather primitive aviation facility on lower Cape Cod.

They were simple stories he told, but I remember them to this day: sleeping by the window in the barracks and awakening one morning with snow on his bed; going up in a kite balloon and getting air sick each time the wind changed direction; having a sentry at the gate challenge him with a bayonet for not promptly supplying the password; and making the mail run into town in a motorcycle sidecar. But, most of all, how he loved to fly in the observer's cockpit of a flying boat, especially when the plane was accelerating across the ocean surface at time of take-off.

This youthful fascination stayed with me and, as I grew older, I began to collect everything I could related to NAS Chatham, always with the idea of writing in my spare time a history of the base. Spare time never came, but retirement did, and it was then that I began to fulfill my lifetime wish. One of the first hurdles I recognized was that a person does not write a book without the aid of others, and I am thankful that so many came forward with their full support in my times of need.

Among those to whom I am indebted for giving me both their encouragement and professional expertise are Joe and Lannie Liggera of the Western Front Association; Stanley Tzeski, Senior Archivist at the National Archives-Northeast Regional Office in Waltham, Massachusetts; Richard Peuser, Archivist in the Old Navy-Maritime Records Division of the National Archives in Washington; Mary Sicchio, Special Collections Librarian of the Nickerson Memorial Room at Cape Cod Community College; and Phil Hunt, Museum Specialist at the Boston National Historical Park.

Once the research was completed, then came the writing. I here extend my gratitude to those additional people who generously offered editorial comment as the manuscript was being developed: Noel Shirley, Associate Managing Editor of *Over the Front Journal;* the late Dick Layman, noted author on the subjects of early airships and vintage military aviation; Marion Vuilleumier, well known Cape Cod writer and local television personality; and especially to my editor and publisher, William P. Quinn, who put it all together.

Others to be mentioned are those who granted me interviews and allowed me to draw upon their personal knowledge of specific people and certain events. These include Paul G. Brown of Duxbury, Donna Lumpkin and her parents of Chatham, Joe Nickerson of the Chatham Historical Society, Ralph Cashen of Harwich, Bill Deane of the Massachusetts Aviation Historical Society, and Bill Strohmeier of South Dartmouth. All of you have by sincerest appreciation.

Lastly, but most important of all, I am forever grateful to three special individuals who assisted me from the start and continued their unwavering help until the book was finished. First, Bob Hardy - retired airline pilot, member of the Chatham Historical Society, and lifelong resident of Chatham. A virtual storehouse of information on the Chatham Naval Air Station, he shared with me everything he knew about the base and furnished me with many appropriate photographs from his vast collection. Second, Ellen Sullivan - typist extraordinaire, friend, and master of the personal computer. She had no idea what she was getting involved with when I first asked if she would "do a little typing for me". Owing to her enduring patience and professionalism, the preparation of the manuscript, along with its countless rewrites, was a true joy and adventure. Not one of the frustrations I had dreaded early on ever surfaced. Third, and foremost in my thoughts, my wife Eileen - dedicated mother, devoted grandmother, skilled homemaker, former schoolteacher, and part-time proof reader. She unselfishly allowed me all of the research, writing and travel time I needed and never complained that my chores around the house were sometimes dramatically falling behind. Without the continued commitment of any one of these three, this history would never have appeared in print.

J. D. B.

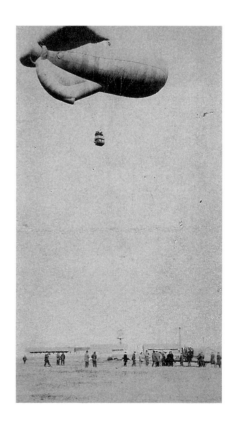

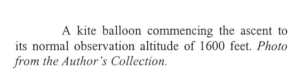

A kite balloon commencing the ascent to its normal observation altitude of 1600 feet. *Photo from the Author's Collection.*

Contents

Introduction

In August of 1914 the diplomatic tensions existing in the Balkans had erupted into an armed conflict that quickly, through alliances, engulfed all the nations of Europe. History would later identify this massive disruption of global peace as "The Great War" as so many other countries would eventually participate. The fighting, as it progressed, was continually being monitored by both civilian and military leaders who quickly observed the unexpected successes of the new weapons that were expanding the dimensions of warfare.

One of these which attracted more and more American attention was the German submarine. The sinking of the *Lusitania* on May 7, 1915 recalled to mind the destructive capabilities of undersea attack and re-emphasized how effective the U-boat had become in destroying Allied vessels. This was followed on July 9, 1916 by the merchant submarine *Deutschland* arriving at Baltimore with commercial cargo to prove Germany had an advanced type of submersible that could span the Atlantic. The *Deutschland* then made a second such trip across to New London on November 1, 1916 showing its continued reliability. Additional concerns also had come on October 7 when the fully armed *U-53* appeared unexpectedly at the Newport Naval Base apparently for propaganda purposes as neither supplies nor services were requested. It stayed only three hours then departed to sink one Norwegian, one Dutch, and three British steamships off the New England coast.[1] Any doubt that a U-boat could make a trans-Atlantic crossing, carry out military operations and return to Germany had been eliminated.

Congress was well informed on all this activity at sea and the possible threat the situation held to our national security. Even before the sinking of the *Lusitania* committees were established to look into the whole concept of war preparedness. One in particular was the National Advisory Committee for Aeronautics created by Congress in March of 1915. This committee sought input from the Army and the Navy on many issues including the use of the airplane and the airship in the protection of our coastline. Several general responses were made over a two year discussion period, but it was not until early Spring of 1917 that the Joint Army and Navy Board of Aeronautic Cognizance made final recommendations to establish several combination seaplane and blimp bases. The following locations on the East Coast were put forth: Provincetown, Montauk, Rockaway, Cape May, Hampton Roads, Savannah, and Key West. The actual acquisition of an appropriate site and the development of each into an operating air station became strictly a Navy undertaking. The only changes the Navy made to the suggested list concerned Provincetown and Savannah. In the first case, no satisfactory beach could be found except at great cost and modification expense, so Chatham, on the elbow of Cape Cod, was substituted as an alternative site. The Savannah area was dropped altogether for lack of any suitable thirty-five acre parcel of flat waterfront property.[2]

Despite these re-occurring board discussions and Congressional hearings, entrance of the United States into the war on April 6, 1917 found the fleet's air arm with only a single, inadequate training facility at Pensacola, 48 officers, 239 enlisted men, 54 airplanes, 1 blimp, and 3 balloons.[3] This, supported by the small Massachusetts Militia site at Squantum, the New York Militia site at Bay Shore, Long Island, and the First Yale Unit training at the Wanamaker estate in West Palm Beach, constituted the extent of naval aviation at that time.[4]

Above: Nickerson Neck in Chatham circa 1916 showing the Nickerson Farm. **Below:** Nickerson Neck circa 1919 showing part of the Chatham Naval Air Station. The large building in the background is the dirigible hangar. *Photos courtesy of Robert S. Hardy and the Chatham Historical Society.*

Chapter One

The First Months

The Navy department had acquired at Chatham a thirty-six acre tract of land adjacent to the shore on what was known as Nickerson Neck. The site selected was ideal for a combination seaplane and blimp base, as it was clear of trees and buildings with only a minimum amount of ground leveling needed. Equally important, it also had the required length of sheltered sandy beach.

The Beginnings

Construction of the Chatham Naval Air Station commenced on August 29, 1917, almost six months after our involvement in the war when Coleman Brothers Company of Boston was chosen as general contractors under contract No. 2552 on a cost-plus basis. The contract specified building living quarters, hangars, a gas holder, a boat house, a dispensary, a pigeon loft, repair shops, and other small associated structures necessary for operation. It also included the creation of a septic system and bringing in water from the nearest point 3 1/2 miles distant thru pipes laid in trenches which had to be dug and back-filled by hand. Speed was necessary so high wages were offered. Carpenters earned $.75 an hour with a big bonus for overtime, and laborers were being paid the unheard of rate of $4.50 a day. Electricity was provided by the Buzzards Bay Electric Light Company which had to obtain permission to place its poles and run its wires through a section of Harwich to deliver the product. Heating was in the form of low pressure steam generated from two central locations, one serving the eastern group of buildings and the other the western group. Both power plants had furnaces that burned bituminous coal.

Initial progress during the fall was rapid, and by mid-October quarters were ready with furniture and galley equipment in place for about one hundred men.[1] The flag pole had also been erected so on Sunday, October 28, the general public was invited to celebrate the first raising of the American flag on the site. One of the largest crowds ever seen in Chatham, about 3,000 people, came "afoot, by teams and in hundreds of cars" to gather outside the open fence to watch the proceedings, to hear the speeches, and to enjoy the martial music of the Bay State Brass Band of Middleboro.[2]

The dirigible hangar[3] was progressing on schedule with sub-contractor Daniel Marr & Sons completing the steel frame on December 6. The installation of wooden panels overlaying this frame was finished just a few days later, and then the cold weather set in. The winter of 1917-1918 was one of the coldest ever experienced in this area with Buzzards Bay, Vineyard Sound, Nantucket Sound, and the waters around the Elizabeth Islands frozen solid while heavy, icy winds caused extensive property damage as far east as the end of Provincetown.[4] Concreting the floor of the hangar had to be done by heating the materials for pouring and then protecting the poured mix against freezing with tar paper and hot sand. The installing of the sliding hanger doors took from January 24 until February 28 - twice the normal length of time.

COASTAL AIR STATION CHATHAM MASS DIRIGIBLE HANGAR FROM E DEC 8,1917
CONT 2552 COLEMAN BROS.
3154

Above: A front view of the dirigible hangar taken on December 8, 1917 showing the building just about completed except for the installation of its massive sliding doors. *Photo courtesy of the National Archives, Washington D.C.* **Below:** Two floating pile drivers at work building a cofferdam in front of Building #42, the new seaplane hangar, to allow construction of the concrete apron to extend into the water. *Photo from the Author's Collection.*

Above: A shore-side view of the boathouse with Strong Island in the background. *Photo courtesy of Robert S. Hardy and the Chatham Historical Society* **Below:** A Sea Sled underway at cruising speed in quiet coastal waters. These speedy rescue craft were capable of skimming the surface at 42 miles per hour when necessary. *Photo from the Author's Collection.*

The wooden seaplane hangar took eight weeks to erect but was ready for use by the end of February. The boat house, 75 feet wide by 60 feet in depth, was designed with its front open to the ocean and stood on pilings in deep water at the end of a 240 foot pier. Inside were four equal sized covered slips sufficient in length and width to accommodate, among other water craft, a 32 foot Sea Sled which was used primarily for high speed rescue work. These small Sea Sleds could carry from two to twenty-four people and still maintain a speed of 42 miles per hour at full throttle, a performance impossible for any other type of boat of that period.[5] The final contract put out at this time was for an above-ground, windowless concrete powder magazine at a remote section of the landing field.

Placed in Commision

To go back a bit, construction had progressed by the end of 1917 to the point that the base was considered livable though not operational. Consequently, the Navy with appropriate ceremony placed Chatham in commission on January 6, 1918. At the time of commissioning there were 87 enlisted men and five line officers attached to the station. Now that the construction site was officially accepted by the Navy, the contractor's employees from that point on had to show their badges to gain entrance, while naval personnel had to give the appropriate password. The rifle-carrying sentries turned all others away at the gate except people on business who could request a special pass from the officer-of-the-day.

A front view of the new seaplane hangar during its construction. *Photo courtesy of the Boston National Historical Park, Charlestown, Massachusetts.*

The first commanding officer was Lieutenant Edward H. McKitterick (Naval Aviator 39). McKitterick came to Chatham from MIT where he had served as Commandant of the recently established eight-week Aviation Indoctrination and Ground School for future naval pilots. He, therefore, brought with him not only flight experience, but the expertise that was needed to get a new facility to function smoothly. About the same time, the First Naval District assigned Ensign Fred C. Burris, (Pay Corps) to develop the supply department and Dental Surgeon Samuel Kalison to work with the dispensary personnel. Also during January, the first detachment of Machinist Mates arrived and installed the equipment in the now completed machine shop. They placed in operation the temporary lighting unit, the pump house, and the power plant as well.

Aircraft were in such short supply that the Navy had two obsolete Burgess hydro-pushers, A-55 and A-56, shipped to the station late in the month. Once they were uncrated however, both were declared to be "of no use to anyone and not worth the cost of returning them or sending them elsewhere for duty".[6] They stayed unassembled until October when they were stricken from the Navy's list. February saw no other planes delivered; so, the Machinist Mates spent time on maintaining the stationary equipment and giving the two vehicles the station had at the time, a 3½-ton Service truck and a 12-passenger open Rainer bus, a complete overhaul.

The Equipment and Plant Report of the First Naval District dated February 27, 1918 listed the following fourteen buildings as erected and ready for occupancy.[7]

1. One dirigible hangar, 122' x 250'
2. One hydrogen generator plant, 45' x 63'
3. One pump house, 30' x 27'
4. One officers quarters, 30' x 115'
5. Two mens quarters, 40' x 90'
6. One mess and recreation building, 40' x 90'
7. One dispensary, 30' x 90'
8. One heating plant, 40' x 30'
9. One truck shed, 45' x 40'
10. One machine shop, 75' x 30'
11. One store-house, 75' x 30'
12. One sea-plane hangar, 100' x 120'
13. One boat-house, 60' x 75'

There were also two streets in place. The first ran from the main gate to the officers quarters almost parallel to the barbed wire fence on the boundary to the north. The second was from the main gate to the dirigible hangar and hydrogen building parallel to the barbed wire boundary to the west. Both were well lighted by electric incandescent lights.

Staffing

With the first construction contract about completed, Rear Admiral Spencer S. Wood, the Commandant of the First Naval District in Boston, then turned his attention to obtaining well qualified pilots and to pinning down the delivery date of the aircraft. A letter he wrote to his friend, Captain Nathan Irwin, at the Navy's aviation desk in Washington expressed his thoughts:

Above: A close-up view of a thirty-two foot Sea Sled with its unique concave bow clearly visible. *Photo courtesy of the National Archives, Washington, D.C.* **Below:** The main gate in the early morning hours. The small one-story building in the center is the radio shack and the twin buildings behind it form the new barracks. Behind the fence to the right is the new large mess hall. *Photo courtesy of the Boston National Historical Park, Charlestown, Massachusetts.*

My dear Irwin:

Learning that the planes for Chatham are so far advanced that we may hope to get them very soon, might I ask you to take up the subject of the detail of personnel for duty at Chatham? Young Backus has reported and is down there now and after consulting with McKitterick as to another likely young man, I have learned that one Ensign Lingard, who has just been commissioned would be very valuable to the Station because of his professional attainments, of which McKitterick speaks in the highest terms. If you could see your way clear to let us have this man, we would be very glad to get him.

Please do not find fault with me for striving to get good men, for you, of course, know how much interested I am in the success of this Station up in this blustering region, and I believe we should have some of the best men in the Service up here where a good deal of good horse sense will be very necessary in meeting the winds and fogs.

Have you any news of when our planes are to be started on their journey for Chatham?

With kindest regards, believe me,

(signed) Spencer S. Wood[8]

The First Planes Arrive

Coincidently, about the same time that Wood was writing his letter to Washington the first four seaplanes, Curtiss R-9's, arrived in crates at the local rail depot. They were 913, 914, 915 and 916. Each had to be assembled then have its engine tested and installed before patrol duty could begin. The initial flight was made by Lieutenant McKitterick on March 25 in 914. Later that spring eight additional R-9's were received, four in April (931, 932, 965 and 967) and four in May (991, 992, 993 and 994). With the increase in the number of aircraft, it became easier for the pilots to maintain a regular patrol schedule, for now there were sufficient planes available when some required repairs or were undergoing routine maintenance. None of the R-9's was equipped with a bombsight; so, one of the pilots assigned to Chatham, Ensign Waldo H. Brown (Naval Aviator 458), designed and constructed a temporary one to use until those the Navy had developed were distributed for general usage. The accuracy of these substitute instruments attracted the attention of the Bureau of Ordnance which then circulated Brown's blueprints as well as his compensation tables for wind, speed, and altitude to the other air stations.[9]

Once the base had become operational, a committee of enlisted men sponsored a dance for everyone on Friday evening, April 5, at the Chatham Town Hall with all proceeds going to buy athletic equipment. The community, anxious to assist their new neighbors, responded in good fashion by filling the ground floor as well as the balcony to capacity. In addition to the dancing, there was entertainment consisting of a soloist from the base and a special drill-team

Above: The dirigible hangar from the northwest with the huge doors closed. *Photo courtesy of the Boston National Historical Park, Charlestown, Massachusetts.* **Below:** The dirigible hangar with the doors open exposing a blimp's rudder and tail assembly. *Photo courtesy of Robert S. Hardy and the Chatham Historical Society.*

exhibition by enlisted men. Recognized among the guests that night were some chaperoned young ladies from the Wide-awake Club who, the previous week, had held an introductory social for thirty-six of the sailors at the Woman's Club hall in Hyannis. The fund-raiser was a total success and all present, including the Commanding Officer, looked forward to having a similar such event in the near future.[10]

Flight Instructor Murphy

Although Chatham was getting active with patrol missions, the men were never too busy to try and accommodate a fellow pilot, especially one on his way overseas. Ensign Thomas H. Murphy (Naval Aviator 51) had been a flight instructor at Pensacola for some time and was now visiting in Provincetown with his family. He was on a reassignment leave and was about to depart for Killingholme, England to become a squadron commander at the U. S. Naval Air Station there.

Murphy wanted to fly over the house where his wife and two children were staying; so, he drove to the air station on April 8th and renewed some old friendships as he had been one of the first enlisted men selected to become an aviator. With the best wishes of all, he was permitted to take an R-9 on a test flight which allowed him 20 enjoyable minutes performing above Provincetown and its harbor. Many people witnessed this unscheduled aerial exhibition including a correspondent from the Sandwich Independent who wrote about it in the paper's April 11 edition. The article concluded with the sentence, "His circling and speed were wonderful.".

The R-9 was actually a training plane that had been adapted for anti-submarine warfare. It was a two-seat tractor-type bi-plane on twin floats. The crew sat in a tandem arrangement with the pilot in the forward cockpit and the mechanic/observer in the after one. This plane was powered with a single Curtiss V-2 engine of 200 hp giving it a maximum speed of 82 mph. It could remain airborne about four hours at cruising speed. Armament consisted of an air-cooled Lewis machine gun fed by a 97-round replaceable drum-type canister whose cartridges lay inside in radial positions. The gun was mounted on a Scarff ring swivel in the rear seat and manned by the mechanic/observer. The R-9 could also carry two Clarke Mark IV bombs attached to the underside of the fuselage, but usually only one was taken aloft to keep the weight down.

Third Liberty Loan

All of the flights were not patrol orientated. One in particular involved a request by the people of Nantucket to have Navy planes help in the island's efforts to publicize the Third Liberty Loan Drive. This they happily did on April 17 by first dropping leaflets on those assembled at Brant Point and then landing near the beach for close-up viewing. The airmen came ashore for several hours, mingled with the residents, and answered all their questions before returning to the air station later in the day. Many they learned had never previously seen a plane. One of the four R-9's participating, 932, struck the shoal water of Coatue Flats and had to be returned by boat to be repaired. On May 2 the planes came back to the island so that the aviators could see the movies which had been taken of their involvement in the Liberty Loan events of two weeks previous.[11] On both occasions the pilots involved, in addition to Lieutenant McKitterick, were Ensign Edward P. Brennan (Naval Aviator 406), Ensign Thomas Durfee (Naval Aviator 415), and Ensign Edward M. Shields (Naval Aviator 452).

Above: Two R-9's on the beach at Nantucket helping to publicize the Third Liberty Loan Drive, April 17, 1918. *Photo Courtesy of the Nantucket Historical Association.* **Below:** A front view of an R-9 seaplane with Strong Island in the background. *Photo from the Author's Collection.*

Above: Building number 4, The officers quarters from the west with the station pick-up truck to the right. Note that the steering wheel is on the right in Ensign Lange's Stutz automobile. **Below:** Building number 7, the recreation building, looking south. *Photos courtesy of the Boston National Historical Park, Charlestown, Massachusetts.*

Above: Tents were used for a brief period along the northern boundary of the property to help house the continuous influx of enlisted men being assigned to the air station before sufficient barracks space became available. **Below:** One of the B-class blimps approaching the station for a landing. The buildings to the right are the officers quarters and the original enlisted men's barracks. *Photos from the Author's Collection.*

Medical Emergency

The medical staff was also in place by April of 1918 and experienced its first emergency on April 29. An accident occurred on a patrol boat, the *USS Nelansu (SP-610)*, which was out of the water, at the time, undergoing hull repairs on a marine railway at Stage Harbor. An enlisted member of the crew, Chief Machinist Mate Robert B. Hoxie, was aboard the vessel working in the open cockpit while it was pulled up on shore. Also on shore, about 100 feet away, a shipmate of his was testing a rocket gun by firing signal rockets into the water until one of them skimmed the surface and ricocheted upwards hitting Hoxie in the head. He was rushed to the air station still alive but with little chance of surviving. Although every effort was made it was too late and he died in the emergency room a few hours after being admitted.[12]

Highlights of May

That the R-9's were fragile was demonstrated on Thursday, May 9, as recorded in the log of the Pamet River Life Saving Station at Truro. An entry at 10:00 A.M. states that R-9 916, piloted by Ensign W. H. Brown, landed in the water in front of the station and came to anchor just off the beach. Brown quickly waded ashore and received permission to telephone Chatham to send a boat to assist R-9 932 which was being flown by his partner on patrol, Ensign Eric Lingard (Naval Aviator 540), and was now down at sea with engine trouble eight miles from the base. Then, returning to his own plane, Brown climbed back into the cockpit via a pontoon and took off at 10:40 A.M. to resume his mission.[13]

As the base was now flying many aircraft patrols, Admiral Wood felt an official inspection was warranted; thus, he conducted one in mid-May accompanied by Captain Charles G. Marsh, his Chief of Staff and Ensign C. H. Crosby, his Aide. At the time of his visit 157 enlisted men were assigned to the station. A month later the complement had risen to 250, but even with overcrowding the barracks and converting the recreation hall to berthing space, only 180 could be accommodated.[14] The remaining were billeted outside the base, mostly at the Marconi Radio Station which had been taken over by the Navy in April.

War Comes Closer

Sunday, June 2, brought the war closer to Chatham and the whole eastern seaboard when the Ward liner *Mexico* radioed it had picked up fifty survivors from various vessels sunk by a German U-boat off the coast of New Jersey. The flying personnel at all the east coast air stations, disappointed at not having been assigned to bases overseas, suddenly found the same shooting war they longed to be involved in now on their own shoreline. Chatham cancelled all leave and liberty until further notice and put all of its available R-9's into the air, but to their disappointment and concern the submarine was not located.

The next day the intensive search effort initiated by the First Naval District was still in effect; so, shortly after daylight, five planes lifted off the water at the air station to continue the hunt. Only four returned. The fifth R-9, flown by Ensign Louis T. Rouleau (Naval Aviator 453) with Machinist Mate Harrington as his mechanic/observer had been forced down by engine failure and was last seen on the surface, south of Nantucket, drifting out to sea. Several patrol vessels that were dispatched to the last known position had no success. However, that very

The wreck of R-9 seaplane 916 on the deck of the work boat *Oriole* at a Nantucket Wharf. *Photo courtesy of the Nantucket Historical Association.*

evening a Nantucket fishing boat, the *Sadie A.*, spotted the men and their aircraft ten miles southwest of Sankaty Head Light. Once the flyers were safely aboard and fed by the fishermen, the battered plane was taken in tow, but the sea became so rough after midnight that continued towing threatened further damage. The wreck was then cast off, anchored in 30 fathoms of water and buoyed until another vessel could retrieve it in calmer weather. The *Sadie A.* sailed on with the rescued aviators and arrived at Nantucket Tuesday about 5:00 A.M. The work boat *Oriole* was then sent out to the buoy location, and what was left of the plane was brought back early Wednesday morning, hanging over the starboard side apparently a total loss. The two airmen, shaken up but uninjured, were subsequently returned to Chatham.[15]

The increased number of patrols continued for several days with exhausted flight crews performing beyond expectations. Another mechanic/observer, Chief Machinist Mate Edward R. Jason, summed up the heightened activity by telling how he was in the air a total of 25 hours within a three-day period. He further mentioned that during that time aloft he had passed over his home town of Cohasset on two different mornings at 4:00 A.M., thus indicating some rare night flying was included in the overall endeavor.[16] Also amid this frenzy, the planes often flew above the outer beaches of Gloucester to assure the fishing industry that every type of protection was being given to the coast. Those watching from the shore could see the R-9's circle high above Bass Rocks and Brier Neck as they made wide turns at the northern end of their sector to go back out over Stellwagen Bank and Massachusetts Bay to continue reconnoitering. The hostile submarine that everyone was searching for, the *U-151*, never came to the New England area. Her sister subs would come at a later date, however, and raise their own brand of havoc.

16

Change of Command

Shortly afterwards, on June 19, 1918, Lieutenant Phillip B. Eaton (Naval Aviator 60), a former Coast Guard aviator and most recently Executive Officer of the Montauk Naval Air Station, relieved Lieutenant McKitterick as Commanding Officer. McKitterick, who made Chatham operational, had been reassigned to command the Naval Air Station at Lough Foyle on the northern coast of Ireland. The solemn tradition of the relieving ceremony was impacted somewhat by a report that an R-9 out on patrol was down 1½ miles northeast of Wellfleet. The initial anxiety turned to relief when it was located intact. The surfmen from the Cahoons Hollow Life Saving Station had spotted it, and had launched their boat at 9:30 A.M. in spite of deteriorating weather conditions. They rowed to the stricken craft and found both airmen, Ensign Edward M. Shields and Petty Officer W. J. Jenkins, sitting in their cockpits with the engine running but unable to lift off. While waiting for a patrol boat to assist them, the motor gave out, and the plane came ashore through the now rough surf, fortunately in a surprisingly good condition! The aviators could see little chance of being towed off any time soon; so they, with the surfmen, secured the craft by burying anchors in the sand, and all walked the beach to the life saving station to wait out the storm.[17]

Flying Boats Added

One week later four new Curtiss HS-1L flying boats were delivered in packing crates at the in-town railroad freight yard, trucked to the base, assembled, and put into service as rapidly as possible. These were 1693, 1694, 1695 and 1696 which had been shipped direct from the Curtiss Aeroplane and Motor Corporation plant in Buffalo, New York. The HS-1L had a crew of three with the pilot and assistant pilot, usually commissioned officers, sitting side by side just forward of the overhead power plant. The third member of the crew was positioned in the bow cockpit complete with the Lewis gun on a Scarff ring mount. He frequently was an aviation machinist mate or other rated man, who tended to temporary repairs and functioned as the combination signalman, gunner, observer and bombardier. When acting as bombardier and using the bombsight on a bombing run, the bow cockpit man communicated necessary course variations to the pilot by hand signals and/or head nods. Each plane was propelled with a single American-designed pusher-type 12 cylinder Liberty engine of 360 hp. This was felt by many to be the finest airplane motor manufactured in the war. It produced a maximum speed of 88 mph for the HS flying boats and gave them endurance for four hours of flight at cruising speed.

Patrol Areas

With the HS flying boats added to the R-9's, a new level of energy was introduced into the patrol assignments flown each day from dawn to dusk when weather permitted. The designated zone to be covered extended from Cape Ann on the north to Nantucket Shoals on the south and out to the western limits of Georges Banks. This designated zone was operationally divided into two distinct patrol areas, AREA "A", or the northern patrol, and AREA "B" or the southern patrol. AREA "A" was approximately 25 miles wide with the inshore boundary being an imaginary line from Chatham to Thatcher's Island off Cape Ann, a distance of 61.8 miles. It comprised about 1500 square miles. AREA "B" was different in that it was triangular in shape

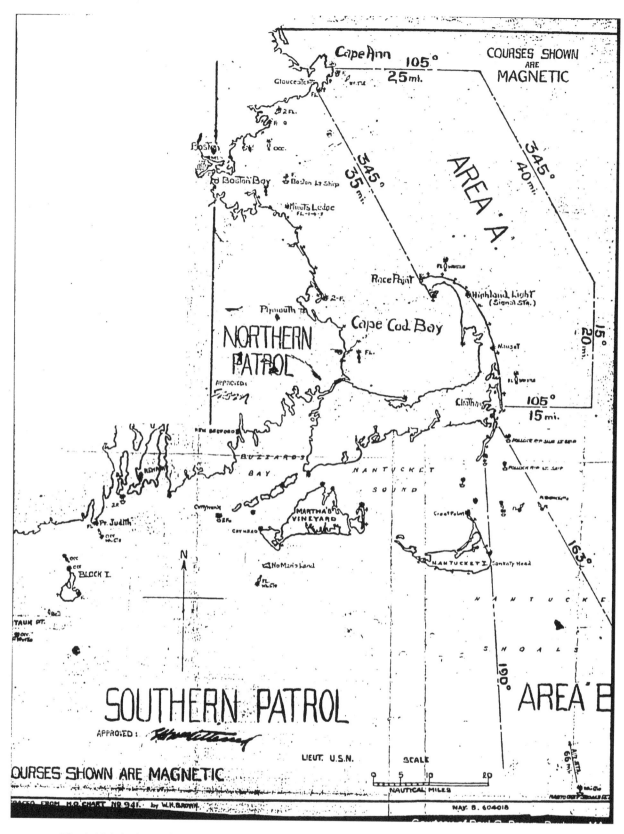

The initial designated zone to be covered by patrol planes out of Chatham was divided into ``Area A'' (the Northern Patrol) and ``Area B'' (the Southern Patrol). They are here shown drawn on H.O. Chart No. 941 by Ensign Waldo H. Brown during the early months of 1918 when Lieutenant McKitterick was the Commanding Officer of the air station. *Courtesy of Paul G. Brown, Duxbury, Massachusetts.*

The boathouse showing an R-9 on the beach in the foreground and an HS-2L in the distance to the right. *Photo from the Author's Collection.*

with the air station at the apex of a 27° angle. The western boundary line extended from Chatham, south through Sankaty Head for 66 miles to Nantucket Shoals, then east about 40 miles to the western limits of Georges Banks, and then northwest back to the station.[18]

Planes always went out in pairs with only one carrying a radio transmitter, but both having two homing pigeons for emergency communication with the base. The birds had been trained for either the north patrol area or the south patrol area and could not be interchanged between the two. Each patrol was required to report its current position every ten minutes during the flight, but neither had a radio receiver with which to get an acknowledgement as nothing could be heard over the noise of the Liberty engine. All planes were supplied with emergency rations and water for three days, a flashlight, a Very pistol with red and green cartridges, flares, a sea anchor, life preservers, a signal book, and local charts. The standard patrol was flown at an altitude of 1000 feet.[19]

The primary purpose of the patrol was to protect shipping within the defined area. The planes would pick up a vessel at a predetermined geographical position, and keep flying continuous circles over it watching for submarines while the ship proceeded on its course. If no ships were in the zone, the planes went out on submarine search following a "spider web" pattern developed by the British at the Felixstowe Naval Air Station. Besides having planes engaged in routine patrols and escort duty, two additional aircraft, if available, were anchored off the beach with their flight crews standing by ready for immediate take-off in case of emergency. The success of their mission would depend upon how fast they could get aloft with complete and accurate courses to intercept the target. Seven minutes was considered a good time for a plane to become airborne after the initial alert or "allo"[20] was received.

Auxiliary Bases

As the construction at the various naval air stations advanced with the good weather, and the number of assigned aircraft increased by the month, the Navy, in June of 1918, also directed its attention to creating convenient unmanned auxiliary bases to be known as ``rest and refueling stations.'' These were positioned to enable pilots and planes to prolong their patrols and thereby cover a greater expanse of ocean. Each had a small sandy beach and was provisioned with a supply of fresh water, some lubricating oil, essential spare parts, basic hand tools, and at least 5,000 gallons of gasoline. Rest and refueling stations serving Chatham were planned for Gloucester and for a location on the island of Nantucket. The Nantucket facility was created in the summer at Nantucket Village and assisted the planes from Montauk as well when they were at the northern end of their designated coverage zone.[21] The Gloucester site never materialized although an extensive survey of the Stage Fort Park area was made by Lieutenant Godfrey L. Cabot (Naval Aviator 1339) of the First Naval District Staff in Boston.[22]

Honor Shield

On Saturday, July 13, 1918, the air station experienced a different type of mission when two of its planes and their crews provided flying demonstrations in the skies over a crowded Martha's Vineyard. The entire island that day was celebrating the award of the Honor Shield to the little town of Gay Head, located at its southwestern tip and inhabited mainly by Native Americans.

The Honor Shield concept originated in the editorial office of the Boston Post, ``The Breakfast Table Paper of New England.'' The Post had announced it would recognize with a handsome bronze plaque that New England township which, one year after our entry into the war, had the largest proportion of its population serving in the armed forces of the United States. When the statistics were gathered, Gay Head stood out from all the rest with an amazing 10.4% ratio, 17 out of 162 residents.[23] The Honor Shield committee chose the date for the award ceremony and developed the agenda which featured the Governor of Massachusetts making the presentation. The Navy agreed to transport the entire official party to the island from near-by Woods Hole.

On the day of the event Governor Samuel McCall made an unforgettable voyage from the mainland to Vineyard Haven on board the flagship of the First Naval District, a 260-foot converted yacht now known as the *USS Aztec (SP-5900)*. The *Aztec* was accompanied all the way by a guard of honor composed of several submarine chasers and a pair of seaplanes from Chatham. These made continuous circles above until 12:30 P.M. when the dignitaries disembarked for the motor trip to Gay Head. The planes then returned to the air station but reappeared over Edgartown at 5:15 P.M. to conduct low-level flyovers as well as landings and takeoffs in the harbor for those attending the Governor's reception at the Home Club.[24]

Fatalities

Unfortunately, the outstanding record at Chatham of no fatalities or serious injury related to flying came to an end that same Saturday morning, July 13, 1918, at 11:26 A.M. The first fatal accident occurred when R-9 913 crashed at the waters edge two miles from its base near the Old Harbor Coast Guard Station. The plane burst into flames the instant it struck the ground, and about one minute later the pressure tank, under the pilot's seat, exploded. The pilot, Ensign Junius F. Andrews (Naval Aviator 413) was killed instantly and his body burned beyond recognition while the observer, Lieutenant J. K. Parks, survived the crash but received serious burns on the face and the hands.[25] Parks was not attached to the air station. He was assigned to the aviation recruiting and public affairs office of the First Naval District in Boston, and his job this day was to be a part of the Woods Hole to Vineyard Haven honor guard flight. It is thought they encountered so much fog that they were obliged to turn back and, while commencing to descend near their home station, experienced some unexplained loss of power.

One of the B-class blimps ascending at the edge of the dirigible field. The building at the lower right is the officers quarters. *Photo courtesy of the National Archives, Washington, D.C.*

Blimps on Cape Cod

After the completion of the dirigible hanger, two B-class blimps, the Goodyear B-7 with gondola car A-241 and the B. F. Goodrich B-12 with gondola car A-246 arrived at the end of March in crates. They remained unassembled for several weeks however until officers and men who knew how to erect them were assigned to the air station. This delay would prove providential, for it allowed the designated landing field to be seeded and gave the grass ample time to mature into sod. Grass was the choice at these coastal air stations to provide the firm footing the ground crew needed when line-handling the blimps. In addition, it kept down the amount of sand being blown around by gusty winds and spinning propellers. Also grass was non-abrasive and, unlike the asphalt macadam or cement, would not produce sparks when struck by a heavy object.

The first officer to arrive for lighter-than-air duty was Ensign Karl L. Lange (Naval Aviator 547) who reported in April as Chatham's initial LTA Squadron Commander. Finally, on May 22, 1918, the first lighter-than-air flight was made in B-7 with Ensign Walter B. Griffin (Naval Aviator 544) as pilot. This test flight high above Massachusetts Bay was announced in advance in all the newspapers at the request of the naval authorities. They wanted the public advised that what they might soon see flying in the distance was a friendly craft and not a German Zeppelin bringing devastation to the area. Later, a few trial runs were made closer to shore, and one over Plymouth on June 1st received front page coverage in the Old Colony Memorial of June 7, 1918. This was probably the earliest write-up of an actual blimp sighting ever to appear in the Greater Boston press:

> "Those who were on the outlook to seawards on Saturday had a good view twice that day of a big dirigible balloon voyaging about in the air off the water front. It first appeared late in the forenoon coming from the haze which covered the bay and took a turn or so about the harbor and going to North Plymouth circled over the plant of the Plymouth Cordage Co. several times and then buzzed away to seaward going out of sight a little north of the Gurnet. Along in the afternoon it showed up again over the harbor and then disappeared in a southeasterly direction. The gas bag was sausage shaped and was estimated to be about 150 feet long. The machine seemed to be under perfect control and made good speed. It is believed to have been a machine from the Chatham aviation station on a tryout and is probably the same one which has been announced to voyage to Boston this week."

That it circled several times above the Cordage Plant was understandable as that company was manufacturing and supplying hawsers to the Navy, as well as all the lines used in handling blimps, kite balloons, and free balloons.[26] In the meantime, between these appearances at Plymouth, it flew to Nantucket where it passed and re-passed over the harbor at 300 feet shortly after noontime. During this part of the flight B-7 was observed frequently changing its altitude and speed, as the crew conducted various experimental maneuvers off Brant Point to familiarize themselves with the craft's capabilities.[27]

The typical B-class blimp was 163 feet long with a rubberized cloth fabric envelope whose diameter of 31.5 feet held 80,000 cubic feet of hydrogen. The blimp's width was 36.2 feet measured tip-to-tip at the protruding tail fins. The gondola was a modified Curtiss aircraft fuselage suspended from the envelope by cables with a Curtiss OXX-8 100 hp engine attached to the forward section. It carried the three-man crew seated on the centerline with the mechanic in the front seat, the pilot in the middle, and the assistant pilot in the rear. A maximum speed of 47 mph was obtainable, but normally the 35 mph cruising speed was used to extend its range to 900 miles. Like the seaplanes, blimps saw little action along the coast, though they had an advantage in that they could stay aloft all day on longer scouting missions, going beyond the defined zone while the shorter range planes of that period had to come back every few hours to refuel.

Above: One of the B-class blimps with its rudder and portside aileron clearly visible. *Photo courtesy of Robert S. Hardy and the Chatham Historical Society.* **Below:** A close-up view of a B-class blimp's gondola car. Note the grassy landing field surface in the foreground. *Photo from the Author's Collection.*

Above: A work detail surveying the wreckage of the B-12. It crashed on June 16, 1918 at the rear of the Cashen Property on Pleasant Bay Drive in Harwich. **Below:** The salvaged parts of the B-12 on the way back to the Chatham Naval Air Station for repair. The station truck carried the gondola while the trailer contained the envelope neatly rolled in strips. Note the solid rubber tires on both vehicles. *Photos courtesy of Robert S. Hardy and the Chatham Historical Society.*

This advantage, however, was offset by the limited prior exposure the United States had with airship design and construction. These first airships were small, slow, lacked expected range, and developed unforeseen mechanical problems. Training was provided by the Goodyear Tire and Rubber Company at the Wingfoot Lake Naval Lighter-Than-Air Station. This had been established on May 28, 1917 on part of a 720 acre site that Goodyear owned in Suffield, Ohio, twelve miles from their plant in Akron. However, no amount of instruction could anticipate all of the control problems that the crews would encounter with the sudden wind changes along the Atlantic Coast.

This was borne out at Chatham as B-7 served the air station from only May 22 to June 8 when, returning from a flight, it struck overhead wires at the station causing the airship to loose steering and be blown out to sea, fortunately without loss of life or injury. The blimp eventually came down 10 miles off shore and was towed to South Hyannis by a patrol boat. It was there placed aboard a large navy truck plus an attached 4-wheeled trailer and taken to the air station for the mechanics to attempt repairs. Her value was placed at $40,000.[28] The best description of the incident and the problems the crew had to face are found in the unnamed pilot's official account:

"When off Highland Light, the wind, which had been blowing from approximately North by 1/4 West, shifted suddenly to the Southwest and increased in force. The return to the station was begun at 4:28 P.M. Heavy puffs were encountered and the ship just made headway. At 6:25 P.M. the station was made. Owing to the wind direction, the landing had to be made by coming in over the electric wires to the North of the landing field. Just before crossing these wires, the ship was caught in a down current and nosed sharply. The pilot immediately gave the ship hard up-flipper. The ship itself cleared the wires but the tail handling line was fouled. This tail line came free with a fast upswing but put both the flipper and rudder controls out of commission as well as ripping a small hole in the bag. The ship was then out of control so the motor was throttled and the ship operated as a free balloon. The assistant pilot threw ballast and the ship cleared the buildings to the east of the field by a slight margin. As soon as the ship was clear of the obstructions she was valved and started to drag across the flats east of the station.

The assistant pilot made every effort to pull the rip panels without success, due to the construction of the panels themselves and the flabby condition of the bag. As a final resort he tied the rip cord under his arms and jumped clear of the fuselage. This did not rip the panels but tore a slit in the bag about ten feet long, where the rip cord came through the envelope. This ship was traveling with the wind at about twenty-five or thirty miles per hour and, as every effort had been made to save her without result, she was abandoned before she went to sea."[29]

On June 6, two days before the B-7 was wrecked, the B-12, also delivered in March, was given its test flight and incorporated into the long range scouting schedule. All went well with the second one until Sunday, June 16, when a "leaking gas pipe" caused it slowly to descend and come down in a wooded area of East Harwich at the rear of the Cashen property on Pleasant Bay Road. Fortunately the two aviators still on board were not injured, and neither was the third member of the crew who swam to a boat after falling out of the gondola into the water as it passed low over Pleasant Bay. A working party with a truck and trailer arrived from Chatham and brought the craft back to the air station in pieces.[30] Once repaired, it flew regular patrols as weather permitted but suffered more mechanical problems on a July 19th mission, causing it to lose power and be blown north toward Nova Scotia, out of control and out of communication. Aboard it as crew were Ensign William C. Briscoe (Naval Aviator 1070), pilot; Ensign Griffin, assistant pilot; and Chief Machinist Mate Eben A. Upton, mechanic.

After the accidents of June 8 and June 16, the Squadron Commander for blimps placed an order for seven parachutes with the Follmer-Clogg Company of Lancaster, Pennsylvania[31] but they had not arrived at the time this latest lighter than-air patrol took flight.

German Strategy Altered

When the United States came into the war in the spring of 1917, the monthly tonnage of ships sunk by German submarines decreased sharply from 875,023 tons in April of that year to 292,769 tons by the following November.[32] The major reason for this was the reduction of individual merchant ship sailings, and the institution of the convoy system with American destroyers serving as shepherding escorts. Such a plan had not been successfully executed prior to our entry because the naval vessels of our Allies were continually needed in more vital areas to carry out offensive operations. If Germany were to regain control of the sea lanes with her U-boats, she had to, in some way, busy the American destroyers to prevent their being used for convoy protection.

The German Admiralty, in its attempt to accomplish this, altered its existing strategy and included U-boat activity along the East Coast of the United States. To implement this expansion it requisitioned their long-range commercial submarines into naval service and modified them with mine laying equipment, torpedo firing systems, and armament for surface action. Their mission would be to proceed directly to the North American eastern seaboard to lay mine fields and to harass coastwise shipping. The idea behind the plan was to attract enough attention to force the American destroyers to be reassigned to defensive coast patrol, leaving the trans-oceanic merchant ships once again unescorted. Thus the four Deutschland-class cargo carriers became *U-151, U-152, U-155* and *U-156.*

These converted submarines had a length of 213 feet, an outer hull beam of 29 feet and an 18.5 foot draft. Displacement on the surface was 1512 metric tons (about 1673 short tons) and each carried a complement of fifty-six men under normal wartime conditions. The propulsion units were two M.A.N. diesels which gave a maximum speed of 12.4 knots on the surface and four electric motors which allowed up to 5.2 knots submerged. Surface range was 25,000 nautical miles at a 5.5 knot cruising speed. They were equipped with two 19.7-inch torpedo tubes in the bow only and carried approximately 40 mines in addition to 12 torpedoes. Armament consisted of two 5.9-inch deck guns, two 3.4-inch anti-aircraft guns, and one machine gun plus 400 rounds of fixed ammunition for each weapon. Realistically, each vessel was fueled, armed and provisioned to stay at sea for up to five months. All were destined to cross the Atlantic to try to disrupt the convoy system.[33]

Chapter Two

U-boat on the Prowl

One of the units designated to effect this new German strategy was the *U-156* which left her home port of Kiel on or about June 15, 1918 under Kapitanleutnant Richard Feldt.[1] She was on the second of what ultimately would be seven long range submersible missions that would depart for American waters during the war. Contrary to standing orders, her Atlantic crossing was anything but one of complete secrecy and evasion.

Active in the Atlantic

She torpedoed and sank the British steamer *Tortuguero* of 4,175 gross tons on June 26, northwest of Ireland. She then disguised herself as a merchant ship by erecting a false funnel, by elevating her two 43 foot hinged masts, and by utilizing her smoke generator. Appearing in this fashion on July 5 near the 43rd meridian, she engaged in an unsuccessful gun attack on the *USS Lake Bridge*, a small, converted naval collier of 1,984 gross tons now used to transport mines from Norfolk, Virginia to Scotland for the North Sea mine barrage. On July 7, 750 miles from the coast of New Jersey, she fired a warning shot, boarded, and then blew up the Norwegian bark *Marosa* of 1,987 gross tons. She did likewise to the Norwegian schooner *Marx King* of 1,729 gross tons the next day in the same region. Between July 9 and July 16, *U-156* reached the vicinity of Fire Island and, sometime during that period, laid her mines in the general area. It is believed to have been one of these which later sank the cruiser *USS San Diego* ten miles from the Fire Island lightship. On July 17, the submarine was sighted on the surface about 400 miles due east of Sandy Hook by the *USS Harrisburg*, a thirty year old troopship of 10,499 gross tons carrying two 6" guns, two 4" guns and two 1-pounders. *U-156* made no effort to attack, thereby confirming that she intended her principal targets to be unarmed and poorly armed vessels of commerce. She submerged and was not heard from for four days at which time she appeared off Orleans.

Attack off Orleans

On that Sunday morning, July 21, 1918, the Lehigh Coal & Navigation Company's steel ocean-going tug *Perth Amboy* and her tow of four barges were leisurely steaming in a southerly direction within sight of the outer beaches of Cape Cod. The *Perth Amboy* had been built by the Staten Island Shipbuilding Co. in Port Richmond, New York in 1912 and had a displacement of 452 gross tons. She was one of the newest tugs in their fleet. Three of the barges, No. 766, No. 703[2] and No. 740 were of steel construction and were under the same ownership as the tug. The other was the Lehigh Coal Company's wooden barge, Lansford. The tug had left Portland Harbor at 2:00 P.M. on Friday, July 19 with the Lansford and No. 766. The Lansford, now empty, had been to the Kennebac River and was on her way back to Elizabeth, New Jersey. Barge No. 766, on the other hand, was loaded with granite for New York which had been taken aboard at Long Cove, Maine. Saturday afternoon the tug put into Gloucester to pick up No. 703 and No. 740, both in ballast, before continuing her trip to deliver all four to the New York/New Jersey area.

Above: Late on the morning of July 21, 1918 a periscope broke the calm surface of the Atlantic, three miles off Cape Cod and the German submarine *U-156* began shelling a tug and four barges in tow near Orleans. The barges were sunk and the tug set on fire. The day after the attack, another tug, the *Lehigh* came to the aid of the smouldering *Perth Amboy* and towed it to Vineyard Haven. Later the *Lehigh* towed it to New York to be rebuilt. *Photo from the collection of William P. Quinn, Orleans, Massachusetts.*

She stood out of Gloucester sometime that evening and rounded the tip of Provincetown Sunday morning on the way to Vineyard Sound.

The routine of the voyage suddenly terminated at 10:30 A.M. within sight of Orleans when a submarine emerged from a fog bank to the east and opened fire on the tug. There were several flashes from the enemy's deck gun, and one shell tore apart the pilothouse, severely injuring the helmsman. By the time the *Perth Amboy*'s captain, J. P. Tapley, ran from his cabin out onto the exposed deck, the maurading *U-156* had become completely visible. The unfamiliar sound of gunfire attracted the attention of a large number of locals and summer visitors who helplessly witnessed the one-sided engagement from the beach. Several shells landed on the shore at Orleans. Whether accidently or intentionly is not known, but they were the only enemy shells to fall on United States soil in World War I, and the first to do so since the War of 1812. Fortunately, no onlooker was injured.

Shortly after the encounter began, the deliberate though somewhat erratic shelling caused fire to break out on the unarmed tug. There was no choice for her crew and those on the drifting barges but to abandon ship. All eventually reached land including the wounded.

When the submarine saw that the *Perth Amboy* was turning into an inferno and lying dead in the water, she broke off the attack to go after the now unmanned tow. While raking the barges with continuous gunfire, *U-156* spotted the Boston seiner *Rose* passing through the area two miles to the east. The undersea raider trained one of her deck guns on this newest contact and discharged several poorly aimed rounds in her direction. The fishing boat hurriedly opened the range and easily escaped from the non-pursuing aggressor without being hit. Once again the main battery was concentrated on the barges and soon No. 766, No. 740 and No. 703 were on the bottom, while the wooden Lansford with five shell holes in her hull was sinking by the bow. The *Perth Amboy* continued to be ablaze but would survive to be rebuilt and sail another day.[3] This was the situation as it existed when the planes from Chatham arrived to commence their first air attack on a known enemy submarine.

The shelling had started at 10:30 A.M. and nineteen minutes later, when the Executive Officer at the air station, Lieutenant (jg) E. E. Williams, was notified he ordered all available planes into the air. The only aircraft still at the base, however, were three flying boats that were not in service. One was from Rockaway undergoing repairs, while the other two were recent arrivals and had not been thoroughly tested. The rest were either out searching for the overdue blimp or on routine patrol. Ensign Thomas Durfee, the Squadron Commander, had no alternative but to have the new ones armed with bombs and hope for the best. Then, with Ensign Frederick B. Hicks (Naval Aviator 729) as assistant pilot and Petty Officer Cleary in the observer seat, he taxied out into the bay in HS-1L 1693 only to develop a spark plug problem that forced his return to the beach.[4]

Chatham Responds

The first plane off the water and at the scene was HS-1L 1695 piloted by Ensign Eric A. Lingard with Ensign Edward M. Shields as assistant pilot and Chief Special Mechanic E. H. Howard in the bow cockpit at the bombsight. According to Chief Howard, the plane made its first bomb run coming in on the beam at an altitude of 800 feet. The sight was lined up directly on the amidships section when he pulled the release and it failed to function. Lingard then made a second pass, this time approaching stern to bow at 400 feet. Howard again pulled the release and when it did not function a second time, he leaped out of the bow seat, crawled to the lower

Above: On the day following the attack, the Boston Globe published a cartoon lampooning the event off Cape Cod. *Illustration from the Boston Globe of July 22, 1918.* **Below:** The survivors from the attack rowed ashore in lifeboats and landed on Nauset Beach in Orleans. *Photo from the collection of William P. Quinn, Orleans, Massachusetts.*

wing, and while holding a strut with one hand, released it with the other. The bomb dropped within a few feet of the sub and failed to explode. As these Mark IV bombs were designed to do fatal damage within a 100 foot radius of the target, this one would have destroyed the U-boat had it operated properly. Lingard continued to keep the *U-156* in sight despite anti-aircraft fire until he saw another plane from Chatham approaching the scene. It was Lieutenant Eaton flying alone in R-9 991 straight for the submarine and coming in low through the smoke of the blazing tug. Eaton dropped his bomb at 500 feet and although his release worked the bomb did not and it too splashed as a dud about 100 feet off the starboard quarter of the target.[5] This time the submarine dived and stayed down as other seaplanes arrived from the naval air station. To understand just how determined these pilots were for a kill, operating procedures specified a plane fly no lower than 1000 feet in a bombing run, as an exploding Mark IV with its 120 pounds of TNT was capable of tearing the fabric from the wings below that altitude.

The search for the sub turned up nothing the rest of the day though Ensign Waldo Brown, in another R-9, dropped a bomb about noon on what was thought to be a periscope. This bomb also failed to function. A fourth Mark IV was dropped on an oil slick in the early afternoon on a second trip made by Lingard and Shields, but with Chief Quartermaster William Donnelly as the observer/bombardier. It also did not explode.

In the meantime the *U-156* was proceeding north and sank a large fishing boat the next morning near Gloucester then continued along the coast to Maine and Nova Scotia primarily shooting up the Grand Banks fishing fleets. She was lost on her return voyage to Germany, apparently striking a mine in the North Sea near the Faroe Islands in late September.[6]

The stern of the barge Lansford after being sunk by shell-fire from the *U-156* on July 21, 1918 off Nauset Beach in Orleans on Cape Cod. *Photo from the collection of William P. Quinn, Orleans, Massachusetts*

Faulty Bombs

The fact that these bombs did not function was no surprise to the personnel at Chatham. Before the *U-156* incident, from June 9 through July 17, the station had dropped thirteen bombs which did not explode, and also fired two on the beach by direct drive to the detonating device. The device was faulty in every test, and the ordnance department in Washington was so apprised.[7] Chatham was not the only base with this problem. Lieutenant (jg) Wells Brown, an officer stationed at Rockaway, has written "We had a great deal of trouble with bombs supplied by the ordnance department. It was always a gamble whether they would explode when dropped. The affair at Chatham, where planes from that station dropped them within effective distance of the German Submarine which had shelled and sunk several ships, was a glaring example of the unreliability of the fuse mechanisms."[8]

To further indicate that the bomb problem was far reaching, Lieutenant Albert J. Ditman (Naval Aviator 108), attached to the ordnance department in Washington, said "At Cape May we installed and instructed the ordnance officer in the handling of the Davis gun and also tried to make their bombs operate. There was a great deal of question at all these stations as to whether the Mark IV would go off or not and I was out to show them that it would. This was a rather difficult job because everyone in the department felt pretty certain that the Mark IV was a failure."[9]

In addition, the Chief of the Bureau of Ordnance acknowledged in an August 22, 1918 report to the Chief of Naval Operations that the bureau had been aware since June 8 that the Mark IV had certain shortcomings which they had been working to overcome. Paragraph No. 7 of that report is quoted below in its entirety:

7. The Bureau now believes that its Mark IV bomb is an efficient bomb when properly cared for and properly operated, but that its mechanism is too complicated for the average personnel in whose charge it is placed. This is stated in no spirit of criticism, but is a frank statement of what is believed to be the fact. It cannot be expected that the average personnel can be as well versed in the mechanism of these bombs as the officers of the Bureau who have been intimately connected with its manufacture and development. The performance of this bomb in service has shown that a simpler design is necessary, and the Bureau inaugurated plans for a new design upon the failure of the first bombs, June 8, 1918. The incorporation of essential safety features require no small degree of design ingenuity. These safety features contribute largely, if indeed they are not the sole contributors, to the complicated character of the mechanism, and the Bureau now, in the process of its new design, is experiencing difficulties, which may be insurmountable, in retaining these safety features, or at least all of them, in a more simple mechanism.[10]

The forward part of the *Perth Amboy's* deck house after the battle. The tug's Captain, J.P. Tapley, reboarded his vessel at Vineyard Haven and retreived several battered pots and pans from the galley. He later auctioned these off and gave the entire proceeds to the local Red Cross Chapter. *Photo courtesy of the Peabody Essex Museum, Salem, Massachusetts.*

Lastly, there is the statement of the Commandant of the First Naval District in Boston as it was given to the press:

"I want to correct the impression given currency by certain published stories that the Chatham aircraft were late in getting to the scene of the attack or were not otherwise 'promptly on the job'. They were there and dropped two bombs, the explosion of either one of which might have been effective in destroying the hostile craft."[11]

The night following the attack on the *U-156* a new shipment of bombs was hurried to Chatham which tests proved would explode properly.

Warning the Fishing Fleet

In addition to trying to locate the submarine, the pilots had the further responsibility of warning the fishing fleet and other small craft of the marauder's activity in the area. As none carried radios, communication had to be by signal buoy. A signal buoy was a watertight paper box with a wood staff running through the center of it, weighted on one end and with a red pennant on the other. The message was written on the top of the box and, when the seaplane was in the proper position, well ahead of the vessel, the buoy was dropped for a surface recovery. One such communications drop was made to the schooner *Natalie J. Nelson* advising "German U-boat sinking ships. Better go home." The ship's captain, Antone White, adhered to the suggestion, returned to Provincetown, and had the buoy displayed in the front window of A. W. Fuller's store where all could see how naval aviation was interacting with the fishermen.[12]

33

Above: A Goodyear kite balloon on its tether above the dirigible landing field. The building at the left of center is the magazine, isolated from the other structures for safety reasons. *Photo courtesy of Robert S. Hardy and the Chatham Historical Society.* **Below:** An observer descending to the landing field from the basket of a kite balloon at the completion of a mission. *Photo courtesy of the National Archives, Washington, D.C.*

Kite Balloons

Another event occurring at Chatham on the same day as the submarine attack was the first flight of a manned kite balloon from the air station landing field. A kite balloon was designed to go aloft on a cable controlled by a special high-speed anchored winch which could send it up and pull it down at a rapid rate of speed. They usually operated at an altitude of 1600 feet although the reel held 2500 feet of line. Communication between the crew of two in the basket and handlers on the ground was maintained via telephone with the cord in the core of the tether. Motion sickness could be a problem for the occupants during periods of wind changes or at times of too rapid an ascent or descent.

Two French Caquot-type kite balloons,[13] A-725 and A-726, both manufactured by the Goodyear Tire and Rubber Company had been shipped to the station and assembled for flight by the end of June. Unfortunately, the anchor winch, used to raise and lower the craft, had not been included in the shipment and was to arrive at a later date. On July 21, with an attacking U-boat in the area, orders were given to somehow get a kite balloon aloft for observation reports. With no available winch, the ground crew improvised a rather rudimentary mechanism which served as a satisfactory substitute. Using a truck at the end of the tether cable, and a pulley block attached to a "dead man" in the center of the dirigible landing field, they were able to control it although it was a very gradual ascent and descent. Later when the winch had arrived and a Cleveland tractor had been acquired, the process was much simpler. The tractor would tow the winch assembly with the balloon on top of it to the desired site and then remain as an additional anchor while the winch controlled the launch, the flight and the recovery.

The kite balloon's primary purpose at Chatham was to observe activity over a considerable area of ocean adjacent to the station. Secondary uses were for pigeon training and parachute practice. Statistically each was 93' long by 28' wide at its greatest diameter and contained 35,000 cubic feet of hydrogen. A third kite balloon, A-2756, was assigned in August of 1918, and later a second Cleveland tractor was delivered in error but allowed to remain.

A small Cleveland tractor. Two of these were at the Chatham Naval Air Station; one was assigned to the seaplane hangar while the other worked with lighter-than-air operations. *Photo from the Author's Collection.*

Above: The bow of HS-2L flying boat 1848 showing a Davis gun on its swivel with a Lewis gun affixed to the top for sighting purposes. A sailor is shown holding a shell for the Davis gun. *Photo courtesy of Robert S. Hardy and the Chatham Historical Society.* **Below:** A Davis gun on an HS-2L with the gunner/observer standing in the proper position to fire the weapon. *Photo courtesy of the National Archives, Washington, D.C.*

Chapter Three

Flight Activity Intensifies

As a result of the *U-156* incident, three changes for the better immediately took place, all of which should have happened earlier:

First, to further protect shipping against enemy action off the coast, President Wilson ordered the Federal Railroad Administration, on July 23, to take over the privately owned Cape Cod Canal. Once under government operation, rate inducements were offered which were attractive to both the toll-conscious coastwise shipping and to the tug and barge trade bringing vital coal to New England ports.[1]

Second, to augment Chatham's patrol capabilities, the Navy assigned ten new HS-2L flying boats to the air station which the Curtiss Company sent by rail from their Buffalo plant on July 25. Added to the flight line were 1847, 1848, 1849, 1850, 1851, 1852, 1853, 1854, 1855, and 1856. The HS-2L was similar to the HS-1L, the main difference being it had additional footage on each wingspan and a larger rudder surface to allow for an increased load.

Third, newly modified Davis guns were shipped to Chatham and, by the end of August, all of its HS flying boats were equipped with one in the bow cockpit position. The Davis gun was a recoil-less cannon designed to get heavy fire power aloft, to conduct air-to-land or air-to-sea actions, and to attack enemy airships. The gun had two barrels on reciprocal headings with a common chamber. When the trigger was pulled the forward barrel fired a conventional 6-lb. projectile at the target while the rear barrel simultaneously fired off into space a counter shot of the same weight made of grease and lead pellets. This created off-setting recoils thus maintaining stabilization of the plane in flight. Because the Davis gun was not equipped with a gunsight, a Lewis gun was affixed to the top of the forward barrel and the machine gun's sighting mechanism was used for accurate firing.

Safe in Nova Scotia

On the day following the submarine incident, word was received at Chatham that the overdue blimp, B-12, had been located 10 miles off the coast of Nova Scotia by the Swedish freighter *Skagern*. It was in a partially deflated condition but with its flight crew in good spirits. The vessel then took the men and their airship on board and proceeded to Halifax, its next scheduled port of call. Upon arrival and debarkation, the aviators registered at the Queen Hotel and contacted their Commanding Officer to report and to obtain further instructions. They then went to see the sights of the city but only one crewman had on a regulation uniform. The other two aroused a great deal of curiosity wearing leather flying coats and fur caps in the month of July.[2] The official report filed by the blimp's pilot after his rescue best explains the problems encountered since it departed on routine patrol on July 19, 1918:

> "The patrol was made to the North and at 3:30 P.M. a transport was sighted off Highland Light. We convoyed the transport until 4:00 P.M. at which time the heel brace on the vertical stabilizer broke off at the rudder gudgeon. The direct cause of the break was the high winds which had been encountered and made the ship hard to handle. The break caused the rudder to

drop and jam to the left. At the time of the accident the ship was in plain view from at least two life saving stations as well as from the transport, two tugs with barges and two seaplanes. The ship could only be circled to the left and this was done repeatedly in the hope of attracting attention. This circling continued for 3/4 of an hour. The Very pistol was also fired at one minute intervals, nine rounds. The ship was drifting to the North during these maneuvers. The motor was then cut off to save the gasoline for ballast and the ship operated as a free balloon. The drift at this time was North at about 25 miles per hour. The ship was flying at 200 feet altitude. When the drag rope paid out, the sea anchor caught and dragged about ten feet, then the rope parted. Every conceivable plan was worked out in an attempt to counteract the wind by the torque of the motor. A schooner was sighted about twenty-five miles East of Cape Ann at 8:30 P.M. The Very pistol was again fired at one minute intervals about six rounds. Our signals could be easily seen and apparently were, as the schooner altered course to bear down upon us, but shortly swung back to her original course and passed upstern by not more than three miles. While the ship was approaching the motor was again started and the ship circled to the left in order to hold position. During these maneuvers the lead from the emergency oil tank broke and the contents of the tank were lost before it was discovered. The ship attained an altitude of 3,000 feet and continued rising. The mechanic crawled out on the landing gear and blocked the lead with wood and tape. It was necessary to valve continually to bring the ship to a lower altitude in order to be picked up more easily.

This was the last vessel sighted until Sunday as fog shut in and only lifted occasionally for a few minutes. At 2:00 A.M. Saturday, July 20th, the bag buckled and the horizontal fins dropped to a vertical position. At 11:30 A.M. July 20th, in view of the lightness of the ship and the hot sun, it was decided to bring the ship to the water as all available ballast for descending, had the ship risen, has been expended. The atmospheric conditions had been very unstable due to the lifting and settling of the fog, and in consequence all gasoline, sand, water and one bomb had been used for ballast up to this time. From 11:30 A.M. July 20th until 9:00 A.M. July 21st the ship was kept from sinking by discharging the following as ballast:

> The blower motor
> The other bomb
> The bomb launching gear
> The radio outfit (or such part as was aboard)
> Other movable articles such as pyrene, batteries, etc.

It is estimated that the change in temperature from mid-day to 2:00 A.M. was 40 to 45 degrees. At 9:30 A.M., July 21st, a vessel was sighted and signaled to. She hove to and sent a small boat alongside and arrangements were made to take aboard the dirigible and crew.

The sun was quite strong at this time, and the gas remaining in the bag was expanding, consequently giving more lift. This made it possible to land the dirigible on the deck of the steamer. This maneuver was successfully carried out and the rip panels were pulled, although the right longeron was cracked on the forward hatch combing. However, the tail of the airship was suspended partly over the port side of the vessel and some gas was trapped there. In order to take it aboard quickly, one panel was cut with a knife for a distance of 8 inches. This enabled the crew to entirely deflate and secure the bag to the deck. The vessel was the Swedish ship Skagern belonging to the Transatlantic Company of Gothenburg, Sweden, Captain Bror Rudenburg. The director of the company is G. Carlsson of Gothenburg. The location of this rescue and salvage was North Latitude 42° 18", West Longitude 65° 50". The steamer was bound from Hampton Roads, Virginia to Halifax, Nova Scotia and proceeded on her course when the dirigible was secured, arriving at Halifax at about 2:00 P.M. Monday, July 22, 1918."[3]

Ensign Briscoe further commented that during their long ordeal, none of the three men even had his feet get wet while awaiting rescue. The blimp was later returned to Chatham by rail, where it was repaired and served throughout the rest of the war.

The *SS Skagern*, the Swedish freighter which picked up the partially deflated B-12 with its crew at sea and landed them at Halifax on July 22, 1918. *Photo courtesy of the Peabody Essex Museum, Salem, Massachusetts.*

A Damaged Cargo Ship

Also on July 22, sounds resembling gunfire were heard to the east northeast by those on the Pollock Rip Lightship. At this same time a plane from Chatham landed at the village of Wauwinet on the eastern side of Nantucket. Coming ashore the pilot said he had seen in the haze a badly shot-up steamship all by itself and dead-in-the-water near Great Round Shoal about six miles away. It was assumed that *U-156* was still active in the area; so, the owner of the Wauwinet House contacted Lieutenant Thomas J. Prindiville who commanded the section base at the harbor, and *SC-166* was sent out to investigate. The Lieutenant then went out himself in a private speedboat driven by its owner, William Wallace, but nothing was found. The haze turned to fog as evening approached and the search was temporarily suspended.

The next day the captain of the *Sankaty*, an island steamer from New Bedford, reported passing a four-masted steamship mid-way between the Cross Rip Lightship and Tuckernuck Shoal in tow of a tug bound westward. He noticed it had a shattered stack as well as holes in the superstructure and appeared to be a wreck of some sort. On the side were the words "BELGIUM RELIEF" in large white letters. Planes from Chatham flew to investigate only to find that the vessel was a damaged freighter being towed by the Merritt-Chapman Company's salvage tug *Resolute* to New York for repairs. Further communication determined it to be the *Imo*, a Norwegian bulk cargo carrier chartered to the Commission for Relief in Belgium. It had collided with the French ammunition ship *Mont Blanc* in Halifax Harbor on December 6, 1917 creating one of the most catastrophic man-made explosions in history. The original sighting from the air that claimed the ship was not underway was accurate. The tug, with the fog settling in, had anchored the tow in the vicinity of Great Round Shoal not wishing to proceed through the Sound under adverse weather conditions at night.[4] The gunfire sounds were simply other units from the air station testing modified aerial bombs in a somewhat distant area.[5]

Nantucket is Popular

The pilot who came ashore at Wauwinet on Monday, to report the sighting of the *Imo*, was just the first of several to visit the island that week. Nantucket, in the next few days of stepped-up search activity for both a U-boat and a damaged cargo ship, was host to multiple seaplane landings at various locations much to the delight of the summer folk who found them exciting to watch.

On Tuesday morning, July 23, a plane from Chatham landed at Brant Point where the aviators met with Lieutenant Prindiville to develop a coordinated air/sea plan to find the vessel reported in danger. It returned across the Sound about an hour later. That same afternoon three R-9's, running low on gasoline, set down near the harbor, filled their tanks, then flew to the mainland after the refueling was completed. Another, a HS-flying boat flown by Ensign Lingard, arrived at Steamboat Wharf in tow of the Gloucester fishing boat, *Florence Marchant*, and remained overnight while repairs were made to correct an engine condition that had forced it down 20 miles off Provincetown. The next day at 2:00 A.M. a plane appeared at Low Beach once again for fuel and, receiving as much as was needed from the Surfside Coast Guard Station, continued on its way heading eastward out over the Atlantic. Later in the day two more came over the northern coast, landed near Hussey Shoal buoy and taxied through the moored boats to the end of "Thousand-dollar-road" for gasoline. All of the planes that came Wednesday were from Montauk while the Monday and Tuesday callers were Chatham based. Nantucket was proving itself as an excellent site for rest, refueling and other types of assistance.[6]

On the 23rd as well, R-9 994, which had come down at sea near the Great South Channel with engine trouble, was under tow back to Chatham at 8:00 P.M. when the towing vessel, *SP-614*, ran aground on Handkerchief Shoal. The plane was cast loose but managed to limp to Monomoy under its own power, where it was beached by the men of the Monomoy Point Life Saving Station. The pilot, Alfred W. Hudson (Naval Aviator 490), and the observer, Quartermaster 2nd Class R. S. Thrift, stayed overnight with their rescuers. At 9:00 o'clock the next morning, after a Sea Sled had arrived, the 994 was refloated and continued its journey on a towline.[7]

Additional Acreage

The events of the weekend gave rise to a thorough inspection of the air station on August 3, once again by Admiral Wood, but this time he was accompanied by an extensive technical staff. These men were Captain James P. Parker, his Military Chief; Captain John M. Edgar, District Senior Medical Officer in charge of all medical, sanitation and hygienic work; Civil Engineer Homer R. Stanford, from the Charlestown Navy Yard; Lieutenant Harold C. Van Valzah (Naval Aviatior 665 1/2), Commanding Officer of the Naval Aviation Ground School at MIT; and Lieutenant Godfrey L. Cabot, District Aviation Aide.[8] It should be noted that being inspected for the first time were the 9.83 additional acres of adjacent land recently acquired by lease from the Great Point Golf Club to allow for base expansion. Ordnance experts the previous week had checked all the bombs, weapons, and ammunition and made their report separately.

New Construction

As the air station received more and varied types of seaplanes and began housing lighter-than-air craft, a greater number of patrol missions were assumed, and increased personnel were necessary to bring the station up to full operating capability. All of these additions required further construction, and a new round of contracts were originated in the summer of 1918 to be completed by early fall. Added to the station were a dirigible storehouse, a fabric shop, two blower houses, a compressor house, a hydrogen cylinder storehouse, an oil reclaiming plant, a motor testing shed, and various improvements to the hangars. Also, a conduit system for telephone and electrical cables was installed to avoid the overhead obstructions that interfered with the handling of blimps.[9]

Social and Welfare Services

Two other single story buildings erected on base property, but at private expense and staffed by uniformed civilians, were the "huts" of the Young Men's Christian Association (YMCA) and of the Knights of Columbus (K of C). Both of these national organizations, because of their past achievements during the Mexican Border campaign of 1916, had been selected by the government to look after the social, physical, informational, and moral welfare of armed forces personnel at the various Army camps and Naval stations.

The YMCA, in addition to making religious support available to the various Protestant denominations, operated the base canteen or post exchange, maintained a general library with books supplied by the American Library Association, and provided reading rooms. Other areas were set off for writing letters and for consultations. The K of C, in turn, focused its religious support toward Roman Catholics. Their "hut" was equipped with moving picture equipment, musical instruments, a large hall having a stage at the rear, and a technical library featuring manuals to study for advancement in rate. It too had its areas of quiet for reading, writing, and spiritual development. This division of social welfare offerings had been agreed to in advance to provide maximum efficiency and to avoid costly over-lapping. All personnel, including officers, were encouraged to make use of all the material services and facilities regardless of sponsorship. Sports organization and distribution of athletic equipment was a joint endeavor, as was the planning of dances, shows and boxing matches. The person in charge of each "hut" was given the title of "Secretary" and was identified as a Welfare Officer. The YMCA was represented by George J. Voltz who had been transferred from a similar assignment at Fort Andrews in Boston

Above: An aerial view of the southwest part of the Chatham Naval Air Station. The building shaped like an ``H'' was the new barracks. The two buildings to the right of the road were, from top to bottom, the ``Y'' and the ``K of C'' respectively. **Below:** A close-up view of the ``K of C'' building. *Photos from the Author's Collection.*

Harbor,[10] while the K of C position was filled by Howard E. Gamble,[11] a newcomer to this type of work.

A small station like Chatham, which did not have a Chaplain, was fortunate to have the services of these organizations. There was a shortage of Navy Chaplains caused primarily by the age limit being set at thirty. This was especially true in the Catholic faith where many diocesan Bishops would not honor the enlistment requests of their young priests, believing that this special ministry required men of experience and maturity.[12]

Aerial Tributes

With the increased number of planes and pilots now available, occasionally a special mission would be assigned which went beyond the usual patrol or training flight. One of the more interesting of these occurred on August 4 at which time Chatham was asked to send aircraft to fly over Cambridge. The main reason for this stems back more than a year earlier when, just after the United States came into the war, a rapidly expanding Navy found itself confronted with a situation it was not equipped to handle.

Once new recruits completed boot camp, the small radio training program at Pensacola was unable to accommodate all those selected for special instruction in the use of wireless and Morse code. The solution was to quickly find a college with a decline in wartime enrollment that resulted in a number of under-utilized classrooms, lecture halls, dormitories, and dining areas. Harvard was just such an institution and an agreement was executed on May 1, 1917 for the lease of ten university buildings which provided the Navy with the facility it was seeking. The school started small with just 50 men, but by mid-1918 it had expanded to 3,000, and the projections based on continuing demands were for the enrollment to go higher. The existing Harvard site soon reached its capacity so an additional thirteen temporary wood structures were constructed on adjacent Cambridge Common to accommodate another 1,800 trainees.[13]

Dedication of this new cantonment took place on Sunday, August 4, 1918, with appropriate ceremonies capped off by two HS-flying boats from Chatham circling overhead. Under orders from the Commandant of First Naval District they departed the air station for Boston Harbor, then followed the course of the Charles River to Cambridge, where they commenced performing low altitude maneuvers above the College and the Common.

Upon completion of their aerial salute to the highly successful radio school, they flew to Quincy to perform above the Bethlehem Fore River shipyard which was launching the *USS Mahan (DD-102)* that same day. This event also invited special recognition as a record had been set by the workers in sending a destroyer down the ways only 92 days after laying the keel, when the usual period was almost five months.[14] The planes afterwards continued their flight to a new Bethlehem plant on 70 acres of government-owned land located in the Squantum section of the city, where another unique occurrence was about to happen. This flyover at the so-called Victory Plant was in tribute to that yard preparing to launch, two days later, its second destroyer, the *USS McDermut (DD-262)*, despite the launching site being nothing but a grassy marshland ten months previous. Not only had this committed company built two destroyers at Squantum in less than a year with several more under construction, but it had actually built the shipyard at the same time during the coldest winter on record.[15] Finally, with fuel getting low, the planes and crews headed for Chatham, rewarded with a day of welcome change from the continuous submarine searches. Both aircraft returned without incident.

The Forgotten Man

On August 7 a fairly common occurrence took place involving another of the planes which, before it was over, was to turn out rather memorable for one of the crew. About 5:00 o'clock in the evening a fog set in along the coast of Cape Cod causing a seaplane, on its way back to the air station, to lose direction and land about 1½ miles south of Life Saving Station 42 at Chatham. The surfmen went down the beach with their equipment but were unable to assist as the tide had gone out, leaving the craft high and dry on the sand. At the time of stranding, one of the aviators, not knowing help was on the way, walked in the other direction to notify Life Saving Station 43 at Monomoy which responded by sending men as well. Upon arriving at the plane's location, they found not only the personnel of Station 42 already there but also Lieutenant Williams with a working party from the base standing-by offshore in a Sea Sled. At 11:00 P.M. the plane refloated itself on the incoming tide and, although operational, was towed back to Chatham because of darkness and fog. What made this incident different from the others was that the gunner/observer on the flight, Quartermaster 2nd Class M. D. Cavin, was overlooked in the excitement by all these rescuers and was left behind on the beach. He walked to Station 42 with the lifesavers, remained overnight as their guest, and was picked up by his embarrassed colleagues at 10:00 o'clock the next morning.[16]

Camp Quanset

The following Saturday, August 10, one of the summer boarding camps for young girls in Orleans, Camp Quanset, put on a pageant created especially for the sailors. Camp Quanset enjoyed a fine relationship with the air station, and earlier the girls had auctioned off several pieces of discarded plane wreckage they had obtained, netting the local Red Cross Fund the tidy sum of $25.00. One item that was cherished and not put to the gavel was a large two-bladed propeller which lay on the mantelpiece in the central dining room.[17] There it served to remind them, three times each day, of their friends in uniform stationed a short distance away on Nickerson Neck.

Mechanical Problems

The good weather of summer saw construction progressing on schedule, and the increased personnel and equipment provided for more realistic and organized air patrol coverage. This was further enhanced by the arrival of four more HS-2L's (1915, 1916, 1917 and 1918) which were assembled in late August and incorporated into the flight schedule early the following month. No longer were there only eight pilots, with a few R-9's and overworked mechanics, trying to cover the 12,000 square mile area daily from dawn to dusk as in the days of April, May and early June. The base was approaching full complement and planes were continually in the air. Also the two basic patrol sectors, "A" and "B", had been expanded geographically and now extended further out to sea. With such activity aloft it was inevitable that there would be an increase in the number of mechanical failures and several involving flying boats took place in September.

At 6:50 A.M. on Sunday, September 8, the regular 4-plane morning patrol took off from Chatham searching for submarines and anything else of interest to a nation at war. Included in the pair that went to AREA "A" was HS-1L 1693 flown by Ensign Thomas T. Hoopes (Naval

A new draft of enlisted men about to depart for duty at the Chatham Naval Air Station. Note the patriotic phrases such as ``Berlin or Bust'', ``Aviators'', and ``Look out U-boats'' chalked on the side of the railroad car. *Photo courtesy of Robert S. Hardy and the Chatham Historical Society.*

Aviator 1094) with Ensign John C. Flood (Naval Aviator 921) as assistant pilot, and Gunner's Mate Bouchard in the forward seat. At 9:00 A.M. 1693 was down in Broad Sound off Winthrop with an engine problem, but the crew from the Nahant Life Saving Station spotted it, towed it to shore, and pulled it above the high water mark. The aviators contacted the air station by phone while two lifesavers served as guards to prevent people from coming close or taking pictures. The men stayed overnight at Nahant and were met in the morning by their executive officer, Lieutenant Williams, plus four mechanics who had come over the road to make repairs. However, it was found that replacement parts were necessary, so on the 10th these were flown up by HS-1L 1694 which hit Black Rock Point Wharf upon arrival and smashed both wings on one side. The next day two planes came and delivered additional parts without incident. On the 14th, 1693 was able to fly back to the air station in the late afternoon, while the repair party left the following morning in a Sea Sled towing 1694 to the Cape. No one was injured in either mishap, but the two aircraft were out of service during a period when every one was needed. To make the situation even worse, once 1694 was inspected at Chatham, it was determined to be beyond repair.[18]

On September 11, one of the R-9's became disabled and landed in a rough sea about 2 miles northeast of Nauset. The crew of Nauset Life Saving Station, spotting distress signals, started down the beach with a horse-drawn wagon which carried a surfboat and some assorted rescue equipment. The plan was to arrive at the scene and row out with an anchor to hold the plane offshore until a Sea Sled came to retrieve it. Everything was going smoothly until the horse gave out on the way, and the lifesavers themselves had to help pull the wagon through the sand, proceeding at a greatly reduced rate of speed. By the time they reached their objective, the plane was already in the surf so the men from Nauset brought the flyers ashore then beached the craft using planks and rollers. An extended period of bad weather then set in. This prevented the R-9 from being moved until September 18 for the tow back to Chatham, meaning one more plane was out of service for more than a week at this time.[19]

Above: An HS-2L being pulled onto the beach by a Cleveland tractor. *Photo courtesy of Robert S. Hardy and the Chatham Historical Society.* **Below:** The *SS Parina*, the Canadian freighter that rescued Ensign Lingard who had been forced down in HS-1L 1696 near the Nantucket Lightship on September 27, 1918. *Photo courtesy of the Peabody Essex Museum, Salem, Massachusetts.*

In the middle of these incidents, HS-2L 1849, flown by Ensign Robert H. Staniford (Naval Aviator 967) with Ensign Frederick C. VanDusen (Naval Aviator 937) and Radioman 2nd Class R. G. Jeffers, came down on the 12th at about 10:00 A.M. 2½ miles north of Life Saving Station 37 at Pamet River. The men from Station 37 got a line aboard and once again with the use of rollers, planks, some rigging and a horse, hauled it above the high water mark. This great effort took until almost one o'clock in the morning. The next day men arrived from the air station and, with bad weather imminent, removed the wings to prevent their being damaged by the wind. After several days of unsuccessful beach repair, 1849, the fourth plane disabled that week, was pulled off the beach on September 19 and towed to Chatham for a major overhaul.[20]

Another well documented mechanical breakdown happened to a morning patrol on the 27th of September. The report of the pilot of the downed plane, Ensign Louis J. Rouleau, reads as follows:

"A patrol consisting of two HS-2L seaplanes, 1852 and 1850, left the naval air station at 10:00 A.M., Friday, September 27, 1918. The motor of the seaplane 1852 died down suddenly while flying at an altitude of 1800 feet. A good landing was affected in a 14-ft. choppy sea without damage to the plane or hull. The wind velocity was 40 knots blowing from the southeast. The position at landing was Longitude 61° 25' West, 41° 38' North Latitude. The motor was idling on one bank and upon examination the left hand distributor was noticed to vibrate severely. On taking off the distributor block the aluminum housing was seen to be broken nearly all the way round. This bank of cylinders was rendered useless. The motor was quickly started and maintained at about 370 r.p.m. in order to keep the plane into the wind. Ensign Rouleau, pilot, became indisposed during the afternoon and after leaving orders to keep the plane headed into the wind, he retired. It is suspected that the right lower aileron and the right wing-tip pontoon were damaged by whales disporting about the plane during the afternoon. At 1:00 A.M. SC-265, a rescue ship, approached the plane and launched a wherry in which the crew transferred. A line was fastened to the gun-mount so that in case the plane should capsize the gun could be hauled aboard. The SC then started to tow the seaplane but owing to the high seas and wind the plane was so damaged that she sank before reaching port and was abandoned."[21]

Rescue

One of the planes trying to locate the missing 1852 was piloted by Ensign Lingard, who himself was forced down during the search and remained on the water five hours before being spotted by the *Parima*, a freighter of the Quebec Steamship Company, enroute from New Brunswick to South America via New York. He and his crew were rescued, but he asked that the vessel not proceed until the plane's engine was taken aboard also. This unusual request was caused by a Navy directive stating that when a wreck occurs a pilot's first duty after saving lives, was to save valuable government property, and the new Liberty was considered a priority item. He obtained a line from the ship's crew, swam back to his plane, secured the line to the engine and had it hoisted onto the deck before he reboarded. For this feat, Lingard was recommended for promotion to the next highest rank by his Commanding Officer at Chatham.[22] The plane, 1696, was so badly damaged by wave action it later sank. A statement filed by the Captain of the

Parima, Charles M. Gladwin, in March of 1919 gives some indication why he agreed to allow Lingard the time to retrieve the Liberty engine:

"It was the fear of the seaplanes that kept the Germans away and made coast-wise shipping possible. If we had not had them, the Germans would have made a clean sweep of the coast. About two weeks before the Chatham U-boat attack, the Routing Officer at St. Thomas, in the Virgin Islands, warned me about what was going to happen. He said: 'Look out for U-boats, as the probablity is that they will start somewhere near Cape Cod and make a clean sweep down the coast.' And they would have done it too, if they hadn't been met and driven away at their first attack which was off Chatham. I made nine round trips to South America (from Canada) during the last year and as I got up along these waters, I used to be mighty glad to hear the hum of those planes coming. There was hardly an hour of the day when we wouldn't see the airplanes hovering around and we used to see them far out to sea. I have heard several Merchant Marine skippers say the same thing. It was just by a shake of luck that we picked up Ensign Lingard's wrecked seaplane. We were on return from New Brunswick and as we passed Nantucket Lightship, the setting sun struck the sinking plane which was tilted at an angle in the waves. The regulations for Merchant Marine were at that time very strict: that a vessel should not stop for any purpose whatsoever; not to give help no matter what conditions of distress, and not even to rescue crews or passengers in open boats where a ship had been sunk, because this would just give the rescuing ship to the torpedo of the U-boat as one more victim. We had got a wireless that same morning from St. John's that a U-boat was operating off the vicinity of Cape Cod, but just the same we decided that if this was really a sea-plane we would stop and pick her up, as we had a great admiration for the U.S. Air Patrol and considered them our main protection."[23]

Captain Gladwin's decision to save the aviators, in spite of standing regulations and at the risk of his own ship, indicates how effective the submarine patrol was considered by coast-wise sailors and the affection they had for the men who flew the planes.

Veteran Pilot Dies

Another aircraft malfunction occurred on October 10, 1918 when Chatham received a "SOS" from a South American steamer reporting it was about to be attacked by a submarine. At 11:45 A.M. the fully-armed stand-by plane, HS-1L 1693, responded with Ensign Shields as pilot, Ensign W. James Shilling (Naval Aviator 951) as assistant pilot and Ensign Lingard in the bow cockpit. Lingard had volunteered to go as gunner/observer/bombardier in hopes he would have the opportunity to once again engage the enemy. This time he was equipped with a new Davis gun which had not been available at the time in July when he made the ineffective bomb-drop on the *U-156* off Orleans.

Ensign Shields flew a course-to-intercept of 75° T from the mouth of Chatham Harbor, but was forced to come down at sea after 45 minutes due to a cracked camshaft housing on number one cylinder. Heavy wave action prevented taxiing to safety with an engine not producing full power. By 4:30 P.M. the lower right wing was almost underwater so Lingard and

Shilling when out on the end of the left wing to try to compensate the plane back to an even keel. In the meantime, Shields had shifted his position to the bow cockpit to better signal with the Very pistol and noticed the hull had commenced to leak. At 8:30 A.M. the next morning the seas had subsided, and Ensign Brown appeared overhead then landed alongside the stricken craft, but could do little except check the condition of the personnel and the status of the plane. At 3:30 P.M., *SC-166* arrived, lowered a boat and took aboard Ensign Shilling, who had to be carried and could hardly speak. Shields and Lingard remained, trying to remove the Davis gun and finally succeeded just before the plane sank about four miles east of Pollock Rip Lightship.[24] When Shields filed his official report saying no one suffered physically from the experience, he apparently was premature, as Lingard soon came down with pneumonia which was attributed to his 27 hour experience on the cold October waters of New England. He died at Chatham on October 29, 1918 and was interred at Mount Adnah Cemetery in Annisquam, Massachusetts with full military honors, including a two-plane flyover by his fellow pilots casting flowers from the air on the solemn event. An earlier tribute had been made by 200 officers and men of the air station, who marched the five mile distance to the local funeral home, escorted the casket to the rail depot, and stood at attention while taps was played. Lieutenant Williams the Executive Officer, Ensign Shilling who flew with him on the last flight, and Ensign J. R. Pringle accompanied the remains on the train trip and attended the burial service joining some 250 other mourners.[25] The "SOS" Shields and his crew were responding to must have been a false sighting as German records made available after the war indicated no U-boat was in the area on the date in question.

Uncommon Assistance

Sometimes just a routine patrol would develop an unexpected amount of drama when the surface navy came to the assistance of a plane forced down at sea. One of the more uncommon rescues involved Ensign Brown and his mechanic who had landed with engine problems and were adrift off Cape Cod. In the late evening the downed plane was sighted by the *USS Bassen*, a War Shipping Board naval auxillary, which came alongside and took Brown aboard via a Jacob's ladder. Then in the dark of night, near Peaked Hill Bars, Brown transferred to the minesweeper, *USS East Hampton (SP-573)*, by jumping to the quarterdeck from the *USS Bassen's* bridge. Later that same night he jumped from the deck of the *USS East Hampton* to the deck of the *USS Actus (SP-516)*, a patrol vessel, which took him and his mechanic to its home port of Provincetown with the disabled plane in tow. In one night he had been aboard three United States naval ships underway on the high seas without utilizing a small boat or a transfer line. The timing of the rescue was fortunate as the repairs made at Provincetown allowed him to fly back to Chatham the next day and return the much needed plane to active service.[26]

The *USS East Hampton.* A Maine fishing vessel, she was acquired by the Navy in 1917 for patrol, minesweeping, towing, and icebreaking duties in the waters around Cape Cod. *Photo courtesy of The Mariners' Museum, Newport News, Virginia.*

Above: HS-flying boats parked on the platform in front of the small original hangar. To the right is a rear view of the framework used to support a hangar door that has been slid open. *Photo from the Author's Collection.* **Below:** The new barracks for three hundred men looking southeast. The hydrogen storage tank in the rear indicates it is about half filled with gas. *Photo courtesy of the Boston National Historical Park, Charlestown, Massachusetts.*

Chapter Four

A Busy October

Although our armed forces in France were fighting effectively by September of 1918, the end to hostilities was hardly visible to the average American at home. The coastal population, for instance, had become incensed at the Navy and demanded that something be done about the on-going German submarine activity just off our coast. The *U-156* might have come and gone but she had been replaced with several other long range U-boats that continued to harass our fishing and shipping industries from Maine to Cape Hatteras.

More Construction

Therefore, during the month of October, two additional construction contracts were awarded to further expand the existing facilities at the air station, in spite of reports that the enemy was weakening. The first, contract No. 3405, awarded to Frank A. Days & Sons on October 2, was a small one calling for an enlarged concrete seaplane hangar platform to give more off-beach parking for the flying boats.[1] The second, contract No. 3474, entitled "Additions to Naval Air Station", went to Coleman Brothers Company on October 22 and was to greatly increase the number of buildings and capabilities at the base. It covered the construction of two barracks for 300 men each, one mess hall for 600 enlisted men, an oil reclaiming plant, a gate house for the guard at the main entrance, a combination carpenter/electrical/copper shop, a lumber storehouse, a photo laboratory, a power house for heating the new barracks, an addition to the existing dispensary, a fresh water pump house, and alterations to the existing living facilities.[2] Over and above that, under a separate agreement, a 3,200 foot section of entrance roadway was to be rebuilt with asphalt macadam at a cost of $13,800 shared jointly by the government, the State, and the Town of Chatham.[3]

Flight to Philadelphia

With the upgrading of the station and the arrival of blimps and additonal HS-flying boats for patrol work, some older R-9's were now considered excess. Orders were shortly received to fly four to Philadelphia and transfer them over to the relatively new Naval Aircraft Factory located there. Upon receipt of the planes the NAF was to dismantle them and place them in storage at the Gloucester Naval Aviation Storehouse across the Delaware River in Gloucester City, New Jersey. The following flight report filed by Ensign Adams, the flight leader, is quoted in its entirety as it gives an insight into what pilots at that time could expect to experience on a typical "long distance" flight:

> "I have the following report to make of the trip with four type R-9 seaplanes from Chatham, Mass. to Philadelphia, Pa. on October 4, 1918. At 6:27 A.M. all seaplanes were in the air at Chatham and at 6:30 A.M. all were flying at about 900 ft. altitude in a diamond shaped formation with plane No. 991 containing Ensign Durfee and MM1c McCabe leading. Plane No. 965 with Ensign Hudson

and Ensign Adams to the right, plane No. 994 with Ensign Walker and MM1c Cosgrove to the left and plane No. 967 with Ensign Shields and MM1c Huso following. Several camouflaged steamers and barges were passed through Vineyard Sound and at 7:53 A.M. Block Island was passed. At 8:03 A.M. the formation circled over the Naval Air Station at Montauk at an altitude of 1200 ft. and headed along the shore. At 8:07 A.M. one machine was seen to land in a small pond. Ensign Durfee flew back to it and after circling twice we continued according to instructions towards Bay Shore with the other plane. Owing to the fact that the sun was directly behind us it was impossible to tell the number of the plane which landed or the one which continued with us. We only knew that it was Ensign Durfee who went back because he was ahead of us in the formation. The flight was continued without incident save that at 8:53 A.M. when flying toward Bay Shore at an altitude of 1400 ft. a bit of bumpy weather was encountered. At 9:25 A.M. a landing was made at the Naval Air Station at Bay Shore and while getting out I saw the two planes which had landed near Montauk come in. Walker had merely landed to oil his pressure pump, had not stopped his motor and had continued the flight in less than four minutes. While at Bay Shore it was found that one magneto on plane No. 965 had burned out and could not be repaired. After discussing whether or not it was advisable to wait for the arrival of a new magneto it was decided to take a chance and the planes were made ready to get away. Officers at Bay Shore seemed surprised that we had come from Chatham, and more surprised when we told them we were going to Philadelphia. They told us of a restricted area off Sandy Hook and advised us to follow the shore to Rockaway Beach. When we told them we expected to fly an outside course direct for Barnegat Light, they evidently thought we were crazy and offered no more advice. Owing to the difficulty in obtaining fuel and attention at Bay Shore, it was 12:19 P.M.before all planes were in the air and headed for Barnegat. At 12:40 P.M. we were out of sight of land and flying at about 1050 ft. in a haze. At 12:55 P.M. we circled once to make sure that plane No. 967 was in sight. At 1:45 P.M. there was a thick haze at 1100 ft. altitude and at 2:06 P.M. we were directly over Atlantic City, N.J. At 2:40 P.M. we sighted the Naval Air Station at Cape May, N.J. and landed there are 2:44 P.M. The USS Savannah and a destroyer were anchored off the station while a submarine had run aground and was being pulled off by an SP boat. We did not stop for luncheon, but obtained fuel and oil. While this was being done, I telephoned the Naval Aircraft Factory at Philadelphia and reported that we would probably get away from Cape May about 4:15 P.M. While at Cape May it was discovered that plane No. 994 had four broken valve springs, so after being told by a chief that only about two planes could be beached at a time at the Naval Aircraft Factory we changed planes and at 4:25 P.M. Ensign Durfee and MM1c McCabe in plane No. 991 and Ensigns Shields and Adams in plane No. 967 left Cape May, leaving Ensigns Walker and Hudson to follow as soon as valve springs could be replaced. At 4:37 P.M. we had turned around the Cape and were flying up the Delaware River at about 2000 ft. elevation. Going up the river it was a bit colder and quite hazy. We climbed to about 3500 ft. and sighted the Naval Aircraft Factory at 5:36 P.M. where we landed at 5:41 P.M. I immediately reported to Lcdr. Colburn, the manager of the Naval Aircraft Factory , and at 6:25 P.M. Ensigns Walker and Hudson landed in planes No. 994 and No.

965. I obtained a receipt for all four planes from Lcdr. Colburn and immediately reported our arrival to the Commanding Officer at the Naval Air Station, Chatham, Mass. by telephone. Upon reaching Boston on October 7th, I reported to the Commandant, First Naval District, and Captain Parker, the Military Chief. The trip throughtout was made in a manner which reflects much credit on the ability and good judgment of the pilots and the skill and willingness of the enlisted men. I recommend that a notation to this effect be entered in their enrollment records."[4]

Repairs at Plymouth

October also saw, on Wednesday the 23rd, an R-9 land off Plymouth near Gurnet Light to wait out a fog bank settling in over the bay. Once on the surface, leaks developed in the pontoons, forcing the pilot to skitter the plane to the shore at Saquish Cove to prevent sinking. It seemed a good location but, in coming onto the beach, the pontoons became further damaged by contact with sharp rocks protruding through the sand just below the water. Fortunately, some members from the near-by Gurnet Coast Guard Station appeared on the scene, one of whom was able to make temporary repairs. He did this by covering the breaks in the 3/16" mahogany planking with canvas and then applying a coat of white lead paint to insure the patches were waterproof. The plane took off the following day at 3:00 P.M. after being pulled from the beach by a power surf boat.[5]

Submarine Chaser

Many of the reports filed by downed aviators at Chatham refer to a ship identified as an "SC", coming to their rescue. SC stood for a class of wooden submarine chaser; 110' in length, 15' 5" in the beam, and drawing just under 6' of water. They were driven by triple screws each directly connected to its own 220 hp gasoline engine manufactured by the Standard Motor Construction Company of Jersey City, New Jersey. Maximum speed was about 17 knots, but they normally operated at 12 knots which gave them a range of 1000 nautical miles.[6] Each had a complement of 19 men.

The submarine chaser was designed to be mass produced quickly at several shipyards to offset the ever increasing number of U-boat launchings. They were the solution to the need for an anti-submarine type vessel, falling between small former non-military ships which were usually inadequate when converted to naval use (SP's), and destroyers (DD's) that were effective but expensive and took a relatively long time to build. Their armament consisted of a stub-nosed 23-caliber, 3" dual purpose Poole gun with a range of 5000 yards mounted on the forward deck, and two 30-caliber Browning or Lewis model machine guns, one on each wing of the bridge. Amidships on the afterdeck stood their most formidable weapon, a Y-gun capable of firing two, 300 pound Mark II depth charges simultaneously a distance of 50 yards off the port and the starboard quarters. In addition, racks on the fantail allowed Mark II's to be manually rolled over the stern to complete the depth charging ability of each vessel.[7]

SC's usually worked in hunting units of three and attacked in a triangle formation with the lead ship, once at the contact's estimated position, firing her depth charges while maintaining course, as the two trailing "wing boats" turned 90°, one to port and one to starboard, dropping their patterns in order to expand the area of underwater detonations.[8] Their effectiveness was further enhanced by their being a class of vessel equipped with radio telephones, giving them voice communications not only with each other, but with the blimps and the shore establishments

A typical one-hundred and ten foot wooden submarine chaser (SC). On many occasions these small sleek vessels came to the assistance of downed Chatham flyers and their fragile planes. *Photo from the Author's Collection.*

within a range of 20 miles. However, the SC's did not have any way of talking with the seaplanes. Their only contact occurred when a pilot would hand-drop a signal buoy containing a written message inside. The pilots, though, had become quite adept at this procedure as they had developed it earlier communicating with the offshore fishing boats. The submarine chasers which operated with the seaplanes and blimps from Chatham were assigned to section bases located at Boston, Provincetown and Nantucket.

Lost in the fog

Another down-at-sea situation involving a patrol flight and surface ships occurred when Ensign Robert Jordan (Naval Aviator 924) piloting HS-2L 1848, became lost in the fog over Cape Cod Bay on Saturday, October 26, 1918. The official report of the aborted mission filed by Ensign Jordan is quoted in its entirety. No summary could do justice to the series of situations that developed and the continuing decisions that confronted the pilot when he was lost in fog with only a limited supply of fuel:

"On October 26, 1918, two HS-2L's left Chatham on patrol at 10:15 A.M. and we headed North. It was a rather hazy day with a slight Southeast wind, but not an unusual day for this region. At 10:40 A.M. we changed our course to 300° heading for Boston Harbor. After we had been running on the course about ten minutes, we sighted a vessel heading Southeast. I changed my course slightly to about 290° to get a good look at the vessel, and found that it was an SC heading for Provincetown. I then resumed my course of 300° and sailed for forty minutes until I picked up land at the entrance of Boston Harbor. By this time it had become very hazy, and the visibility was exceedingly poor. After picking up land at Boston Harbor, I ran into a very heavy fog in which you could not see more than fifty yards. From five hundred feet I could make out certain buildings on the land but further inside the harbor was very heavy fog so I decided to turn back. Just before I turned back I lost my companion to the right of me apparently steering a parallel course. Then my machine gradually drew away from him and I took the lead. The other machine was in back, and slightly below me, so that I could not see him but my observer in the front cockpit would turn every few seconds and signal me that the other plane was in sight. After I had been running my course for about forty-five minutes my observer signaled he did not see the other plane. I immediately turned back on my course thinking the other plane might have been forced to land on account of motor trouble. I circled back and forth for nearly fifteen minutes, and not being able to locate him, I decided to continue on my course until I struck the northern end of Cape Cod, at Provincetown, put in there, land, and inquire if he had landed there and notify Chatham. Consequently, I continued on my previous course of 120° and failed to pick up the end of the Cape when I should. Just at this time I sighted a steamer in the distance about Southeast of me, so I headed for her to get my bearings. I landed near her and taxied close to her within hailing distance. She slowed down and swung head into the wind. I pulled alongside as close as I dared and tried to get my bearings, but being a Norwegian steamer with all Swedes aboard, they could not understand me and just stood there looking at one another, wondering what sort of queer thing I was. I then took off and headed SWxW thinking that I would strike land on that course because the steamer was fairly good size and was headed South, so I figured I was outside the course and had gone North of the end of the Cape. I sailed the course for half an hour and then as I was getting low on gas, and visibility was poor, I decided to head due West figuring that if I didn't strike land I would at least be inside the bay where the water would be fairly smooth and I would have a good chance of getting some gas from the numerous fishing vessels in that vicinity. I ran due West about ten minutes when my motor began missing and finally cut out. I nosed her over and cut out my windmill pump to cut in on the gravity tank, although front port tank indicator registered five gals. The motor then picked up although sputtering quite a bit, and I ran on for about twenty-five minutes more when the motor stopped entirely and I landed. It was then 2:40 P.M. and the water was smooth with a slight S x SE wind. The sky was clear the fog had lifted by this time so the visibility was good. We made a sea anchor by taking some canvas, then sewed it with copper wire into a bag shape and we took off a couple of boards from the seat rack and crossed them, fastening them together and to the bag with copper wire. We put this out with about five fathoms of line and it seemed to retard our drift quite a bit. When no vessel or plane had come in sight by 5:30 P.M. we got ready to prepare for the night. We got out our Very Light and emergency rations, covered over the motor and front cockpit, and as the fog had settled again, we put up a canvas cover over the rear cockpit to protect us from the mist. We fastened this to the lower part of the radiator and to the lead wire on each side of the motor so that it formed a shield like a lean-to shanty, only we could see out on both sides and also the front by stretching our necks a bit. About 7:30 P.M. it started to rain, not a really heavy shower, but enough to have gotten a good wetting except for our shelter. It rained for about an hour and then stopped although the air was still hazy and damp. My observer and myself kept a sharp lookout on all sides and I fired my Very pistol about every hour from 8:30 P.M. to 6:00 A.M. the following morning, but we saw no light all night due to the heavy fog. On Sunday morning the fog still hung heavy so we busied ourselves about the plane. I was curious about the gas tank that registered five gallons so we screwed off the dial and took out the whole apparatus and there looked to be about five or six inches of gas in the tank. We tried to get the gas up to the gravity tank by using the hand pump but could not so we disconnected the line leading up to port rear engine strut and took our bilge pump and pumped the gas from the tank up to the gravity tank. We got all except perhaps a quart or so. We then tried the other tanks although the indicators registered zero. We got about two gallons more from the starboard tank in the same way. We decided we would wait before using this until the fog had lifted, or in case we should drift near shore or rocks, we could start our motor and get away from it. We waited until 10:15 A.M. of the 27th when we thought we heard a fog horn about due West of us, so decided to try to taxi toward it. We listened carefully and determined as nearly as we could the bearing of the sound although we could not see more than one hundred feet. We started the motor and she took the first shot so I got her up on the step and we both kept a sharp lookout and I taxied about twenty-five minutes, but of course with the motor running could not hear anything. I then stopped as I did not want to use up all my gas, but when I stopped I could neither see nor hear a thing. We then put out our sea anchor again, and got ready for dinner, our first meal since Saturday morning at 6:00 A.M. Neither of us felt very hungry, but we opened a can of brown bread and we each had a slice, which was enough for me, although I guess my observer had two. After the lunch we sat up on deck and played checkers for a couple of hours, making the checkers out of the paste board boxes of the Very lights. Along about 5:30 P.M. the fog started to lift and we could see the blue sky overhead, but no sign of any ship. It was 6:45 P.M. before we made out a light South of us, and I started shooting my Very rockets, but the light failed out in the darkness. At 8:00 P.M. I saw another light due East of us, and I started shooting my Very light again. This vessel seemed headed in our direction because the light, dim at first, now became clearer and clearer. I shot off my Very light at about fifteen minute intervals. I finally saw the red port light of the steamer and his masthead light very distinctly. I got on deck and lighted one of my flare lights to show him my position as I thought he had seen my Very lights, and was heading for me. We waited and waited, but instead of coming towards us, he changed his course, headed North, and then swung around West in back of us, giving us a wide berth. Half an hour later I saw four lights about West of us and tried to attract their attention. I again fired a Very light. Almost immediately one of the lights suddenly went out as if by magic, and just a few moments later the other two. I thought that rather queer, but supposed that these two and the other had become frightened, thinking I was a sub perhaps, and put out their lights to give me a wide

Above: An unusual view of the air station showing the barbed wire fence which surrounded the property. *Photo from the Author's Collection.* **Below:** An aerial view of the Chatham Naval Air Station showing the almost completed ``double'' hangar which was needed to house the large HS flying boats. To the right is the small original hangar designed for the older R-9 pontoon-type planes. *Photo courtesy of the National Archives, Washington, D.C.*

berth. I did not see anything then for probably half an hour when I caught the sound of an engine or propeller. I would hear it for a few minutes then all would be quiet again. I shot off another Very light and showed them my position, but did not use the flare, because I carried a Davis gun, and thought that if they saw that they would think I was a sub for sure. Finally the sound during the interval became more distinct, and I thought it sounded like that of a sub-chaser. Finally I heard it real distinctly, and saw the SC approaching me about three points off my starboard beam. I was afraid he was going to run me down so I fired another Very light. He was very close to me then and either he swung to starboard or I was drifting for we saw him about one point forward off my starboard beam. Someone helloed but I could not make out what was said because he immediately ducked away as quickly as he could and I answered and shouted, but he was away in the darkness again in a jiffy and probably could not or did not hear me. Then I did not see or hear a thing again for probably ten or fifteen minutes, when I saw three blinks going. They were all three blinking at once, and I could not make them out and thought they were blinking to each other giving orders. I had previously taken the light over my compass, and punched a hole in the thin copper disk in the bow, and run the wire up through. My observer was on deck holding the light towards them which I operated with the push button as a blinker sending "Seaplane, out of gas-give us a tow". This light cast a ray of light out to the end of the wing, and I supposed they could see it. While I was operating this blinker, all of a sudden a shot was fired, like a bolt out of a clear sky and landed at the end of the outer or port wing, and sent a column of water into the air and came down on that wing like a cloud burst. Then four other shots were fired in rapid succession. My observer, who was on deck, dropped the light and jumped into the cockpit where I was. I jumped up on deck and started shouting at the top of my lungs, and frantically waving the little light. By this time two of the boats were right on top of me, one directly in front and the other a little off my starboard beam. The one in front, SC-138, finally put her search light on me, and told the other, SC-276, to take me in tow. I fastened a line to the plane, and the observer and I went aboard SC-276. They towed us into Boston Harbor, where about 8:00 A.M., Oct. 28th, a sand schooner named Eureka rammed the plane in the fog, and stove a hole in her, low down to the water line. The plane was towed to Battery Wharf where the engineering officer of Boston Section patched her up with canvas, and Wednesday morning, October 30th, at 9:00 A.M. we started in tow by SC-268 for Provincetown. We reached there at 2:30 P.M. leaving for Chatham Friday morning. When we got outside of Race Point, the water was pretty rough so we put back into Provincetown. Saturday morning we started off again at 6:00 A.M. and got as far as Coast Guard Station No. 35 when the seaplane nosed in sticking up bow first at an angle of 25°. She started to fill and gradually partially submerged. We stood by from 9:30 A.M. until 3:30 P.M. when SC-341 came by and put the plane aboard. We made

Provincetown around 8:30 Saturday night and Sunday morning SC-341 came alongside the wharf, and put the plane on the dock. The plane after she sank was pretty badly damaged by the water, and putting her aboard SC-341 and taking her off on the dock she was smashed."[9]

Considering what they went through, Ensign Jordan and his crew were lucky to have survived such an ordeal without injury or exposure It was unfortunate never-the-less, that after such a valiant 8-day effort by so many people, the HS-2L 1848 was declared a total wreck and never flew again.

Decoy Vessel

One ship the flying boats saw with some frequency out in their patrol area, but were instructed to totally ignore, was the *USS Arabia (SP-3434)*. The *Arabia* was a 113' auxiliary fishing schooner built in 1903 and taken over by the Navy on August 13, 1918. Because the U-boats had been so active in boarding and blowing up fishing vessels, the Navy wanted to have one of its own to use as bait. Manned by a naval crew clothed as fishermen, the unarmed *Arabia* cruised Georges Banks as a decoy for the submarine *USS N-1*, which traveled with it but at some distance away. The plan was to torpedo the U-boat when it stopped to launch a boarding party, but no encounter ever occurred although many "fishing" trips were made between August 15 and the armistice.[10]

On October 29th the Commandant of the First Naval District made his quarterly inspection. Admiral Wood's inspecting party this time included Captain Charles G. Marsh, his Chief of Staff; Captain John M. Edgar, District Senior Medical Officer; and Chaplain Henry VanDyke. Lieutenant Commander VanDyke later addressed an assembly of all officers and men that were not on duty about the conditions he experienced on a recent three month observation tour of the trenches.[11]

A Wayward Balloon

Three weeks later, on November 10, all naval facilities on Cape Cod received a somewhat urgent message informing them to be on the lookout for a wayward balloon. Early in the morning of the previous day, a Navy Type-M Caquot kite balloon had come loose from its control winch at the Wingfoot Lake Naval Air Training Station near Akron. The balloon was the property of B. F. Goodrich Company and was at the time being demonstrated to an officer of the Royal Air Force. There were no crew members or observers on board, but 10 bags of ballast had been placed in the basket to substitute for human weight. The bag was up some 1100 feet when the cable parted at the ground end, and the winds immediately started it on an unscheduled flight toward western Pennsylvania. All stations to the northeast of Ohio that could be reached by phone were alerted and instructed to report its estimated course and altitude if it were spotted.[12]

Once being apprised of this, the pilots of Chatham reacted with great interest as they thought, if it were to pass out to sea over their patrol area, they would be ordered to pursue it and shoot it down for a surface recovery. Time went by, however, and no sighting was ever reported within the First Naval District. Four different possibilities for this were advanced: first, that the automatic release valve on the bag had let sufficient gas escape to bring the balloon to earth before it reached the coast; second, that the balloon was drifting low enough so that its 1,100-

foot tether had become entangled with some object which stopped its flight; third, that it had crossed overhead either at night or in a period of poor visibility and escaped detection; and fourth, that those on watch had missed it in the excitement created by the signing of the armistice on the 11th of November.

Also during November, only thirteen months after Coleman Brothers Company received the first construction contract, the air station was just about at its operational potential. The total complement of 41 officers and 398 enlisted men[13] was staffing and maintaining more than 45 buildings while operating 12 seaplanes, 1 blimp and 3 kite balloons. The daily average complement of the station during the fiscal year, July 1, 1918 to June 30, 1919, was about 375 officers and men. The highest number at any one time was 450, and the lowest was 123 which occurred on June 30, 1919.[14]

An aerial view of Chatham Naval Air Station, looking west to east. In the upper left area of the photograph is Strong Island. *Photo courtesy of the National Archives, Washington, D.C.*

Chapter Five

Chatham by Departments

In order to fulfill its primary mission of patrolling the approaches to Boston Harbor and Nantucket Sound, Chatham, like every other naval air station, was organizationally divided into several departments, each one of which, in its own way, existed to support flight operations.

Engineering Department

The engineering department, accounting for 75 men and 3 officers, continued to maintain the planes, keep current the engine logs, operate the stationary machinery, supply personnel to fly patrols in the gunner/observer/bombardier position, and include one man on each boat crew. Since September, the department had also assumed the operation and maintenance of the power plant at the Marconi Radio Station located near-by.[1]

In addition to these regular duties, engineering took part in several experiments which led to correcting operating problems or improving efficiency. As each is technical in nature it is best, for the sake of accuracy, to quote directly from the official reports the Commanding Officer of the air station made to his superiors during October and November of 1918:

1. "Considerable difficulty has been experienced in HS-2L planes by having gasoline supply run out when machine was nosed over. This was remedied by loading gasoline from the fan pump to the carburetor directly and allowing the excess supply to overflow into the gravity tank. This arrangement functions while there is gasoline in the main tanks. At one time a spiral was made from 8,000 feet and motor still idled when machine landed. To use gasoline in gravity tank with fan pump operating, the pump valve should be closed."

2. "It has been found that when an excessively hard landing was made in the HS-2L's and HS-1L's the upper wing tended to drive forward, carrying with it the radiator and braces to the engine bed and consequently throwing the machine out of alignment. The stay wire leading from the outrigger at the tail to the wings did not furnish enough tension to hold the wing back. Two additional wires were stretched from the outrigger to the struts nearest the hull on either side. These wires took care of extra strain and no further trouble has occurred."

3. "Ensign Waldo H. Brown and Ensign Leon Freudenhein, the latter attached to the Bureau of Construction and Repair, completed a set of speed tests with HS-2L No. 1917 over a course of one knot at Provincetown, Mass. The boat was fully loaded, carrying three men and all necessary accessories. Conditions for the tests were not perfect, a heavy sea was running, and the wind blowing 5 (Beaufort Scale) up and down the course. The results, however, were satisfactory showing about a three percent maximum error in the reading of the air speed indicator which read slow. Specimen results follows:

A.	With wind	r.p.m.1800
	Speedmeter read -	69.70 knots
	Time	38 sec.
	Course	1 knot
	Wind	27 knots (up and down course)
	Ground Speed	94.7 knots
		27
		67.7 knots
		69.5 average
	Error	1.8 knots fast

B.	Against wind	r.p.m.1500
	Speedmeter read -	55 knots
	Time	1 min. 52 sec.
	Course	1 knot
	Wind	27 knots (up and down course)
	Ground speed	32.1 knots
		27
		59.1 knots
		55 average
	Error	4.1 knots slow

4. "An interesting experiment was tried on an HS-2L plane. Graphite was painted on the bottom and the plane took the air appreciably quicker than usual, but not enough difference was noticed to warrant its general use."

5. "A careful examination of the equipment carried by HS-1L and HS-2L planes has been made by Ensign Hudson, and the following proposals made for a much needed reduction in weight, in order to increase patrolling radius. At the present time three and one-half hours is the maximum average safe patrolling time, flying at over 1500 r.p.m. The principal saving recommended is to reduce the crew from three to two, saving 180 lbs.. Further saving in weight is advocated by taking a 15 lb. emergency tool kit instead of a complete set, omitting three motor and hull covers totaling 25 lbs., substituting for a 10 lb. tow line and 3½ lb. safety belt, a sea anchor and line totaling the same. Total equipment now carried 639.5 lbs. Equipment suggested 446 lbs. saving of 193.5 lbs. resulting. A possible further reduction is suggested by fitting the bilge pump with a special "intake" hose, small and flexible enough to be capable of sucking water from the odd corners, reducing the weight from 20 to 10 lbs. By using unsweetened chocolate bars and "pemmican" instead of canned goods, a greater concentration of nourishment might be obtained for the same weight. The gasoline supply cocks leading to the lower tanks (except the cock shutting off the supply from the fan pump) are never used at this station, and their elimination would make an appropriate reduction in weight."

6. "On Tuesday of this week Ensigns Pardee and Barnes from the Bureau of Steam Engineering, Washington, D.C. reported at Chatham to superintend the installing of an Ingersoll Rand hydrogen compressor. This is the first compressor of the vertical type to be installed at any of the Naval Air Stations. It is driven by a gasoline motor and has a 1500 cu. ft. per hour capacity. A charge of about 3000 feet of gas was run into a nurse balloon, which served as a container to suck the gas to the compressor. The gas passes from the compressor to cylinders

which are attached to a manifold, and is compressed to 1800 lbs. per square inch, each bottle containing approximately 180 cu. ft. of gas. The compressor was very successfully operated and good results were obtained."[2]

Communications Department

While the engineering department was maturing into an effective component of the air station, wireless was developing its ability to provide information, as technology in communications continued to reach new levels. In the early days of Chatham the radio division was limited because of a general lack of equipment and technicians throughout the Navy. With only Chief Electrician (RO) William J. Corbett and two other enlisted men assigned, many obstacles had to be overcome just to equip three planes with transmitters and maintain a small receiving set in a corner of the barracks. In the summer of 1918, however, personnel specially trained in wireless began to arrive in numbers and additional supplies soon followed. By the middle of October, a well-equipped receiving station was operational with every plane having a

The Duty Officer in the radio shack at Chatham Naval Air Station in 1919. *Photo courtesy of Robert S. Hardy and the Chatham Historical Society.*

transmitter, and two planes testing experimental airborne receivers. All planes could now contact the base, and each had one crew member trained as a wireless operator. Position and weather reports were still being made every ten minutes, and a simple code was devised for reporting unusual events. As many as fifty-one messages had been successfully received in a single day from the planes, but the average number was closer to thirty-five.[3] The various model types of radio equipment in use were:[4]

Transmitters

SE 1200
SE 1100
CP 1110
CAG 1295 (blimps)

Receivers

CE 937
SE 950

Message transmission from the planes was of maximum importance so records were kept as to the reliability of the various transmitters. The following report from Lieutenant Commander Chase to the Bureau of Steam Engineering indicated that tests found the CP 1110 to be the most trustworthy:

From: Commanding Officer
To: Bureau of Steam Engineering.
Subject: SE 1300 Radio Transmitters.

1.   Since August 4, 1918, we have carried out two hundred and seventy-five patrols with either Cutting and Washington CP 1110 transmitters, or International SE 1300 transmitters aboard, operated by radio electricians. Of this number, one hundred and fifty-nine were with SE 1300 sets, and one hundred and sixteen with CP 1110 sets.

2.   Of the one hundred and fifty-nine patrols with SE 1300 sets, forty-one times no results were obtained, due to the fault of the set. Of the one hundred and sixteen times with CP 1110 sets, only once did we have any trouble.

3.   It is requested that the five SE 1300 sets be turned in, and that five CP 1110 sets be sent to this station to replace them.[5]

In addition, radio telephone equipment was placed in one of the blimps with the receiver located in a section of the gondola that had been made soundproof. Under this arrangement both transmitter and receiver worked satisfactorily, but only one test was made as the blimp crashed on its next flight with the units on board.[6]

The radiomen by now had a building of their own, plus two 100' aerial towers acquired in June of 1918 from the Marconi Wireless Company. Much later, a frame building with a radio compass transmitting unit was located on the Fox Hill section of the property to send out signals to assist with navigation.

During the daytime, guard was kept on 378 meters and 600 meters, the former used by the seaplanes and the latter being the commercial frequency, but during the night the watch shifted to 600 meters and 4000 meters. The shore station would receive messages from other coastal facilities, from abroad, and from vessels at sea to keep the patrol office informed of any submarine activities. All reported positions were plotted and maintained on a current basis using Hydrographic Office Chart No. 5125, which was posted on the wall of central flight operations. This office also had direct telephone lines to the First Naval District in Boston, to the submarine chaser section base at Provincetown, and to Highland Light at Nauset Beach for fast coordination if U-boats, floating mines, or downed planes were reported.[7] The main telephone trunk line coming into the base led to a switchboard which had 26 internal extensions connected to it.

When it was necessary to transmit classified information the messages were encoded from a naval cipher book that contained groupings of three letters, each group or combination of groups having a special translation. An example of one directed May 22, 1918 to bases on Cape Cod came through as follows: "EFC-XBH-TWV-CNO-CMA-WRN-YHB-JUH-XBH-INK". Decoded this read: "American submarine proceeding to this area under convoy of submarine chaser".[8] As the code was an alpha type, classified information could be sent via radio, telephone, flag hoist, semaphore, or wig wag as the situation demanded.

A view of the air station from Bassing Harbor looking northwest. At the base of the 100 foot radio antenna to the left of the picture is the approximate location of the station's main entrance and gate house. *Photo courtesy of Robert S. Hardy and the Chatham Historical Society.*

The phonetic alphabet used in radio telephone communications was as follows:[9]

ABLE	BOY	CAST	DOG	EASY	FOX
GEORGE	HAVE	ITEM	JIG	KING	LOVE
MIKE	NAN	OBOE	PUP	QUACK	RUSH
SAIL	TARE	UNIT	VICE	WATCH	X-RAY
YOKE	ZED				

But the communications department was not confined to wireless operators. Another important division was composed of the pigeon men who had responsibility for training and taking care of the homing pigeons, as well as maintaining the station loft. Two pigeons were carried on each plane that went out on patrol and each bird, as has been mentioned, was trained specifically for either the Northern Area or the Southern Area. These swift and silent messengers had, strapped to one leg, a light aluminum container into which a note was inserted when the pilot wished to communicate with the base. The usual homing pigeon could be trained to travel with accuracy up to two hundred miles the first year, and up to more than twice that distance after two years on the job. However, there was a limitation to this method of sending messages in that pigeons could not be used after dark or in dense fog, as they needed light to guide their flight.[10]

Occasionally these little warriors would get lost especially during their training phase and would fail to return to the air station. Instinct would usually steer them toward the land, however, and they would come to roost on other parts of Cape Cod and the Islands. This prompted the Navy to run occasional notices in the various local papers reminding anyone seeing or finding a pigeon with a metal tag marked "N.A.S." to please notify the newspaper or naval authorities at once.[11] At least one known response was elicited by these ads. Mrs. Isaac H. Valler, who lived on the shore road 10 miles south of Plymouth Center, notified the Old Colony Memorial that a carrier pigeon had come to her home about five weeks previous. The bird was tired and hungry upon arrival, but she cared for it and returned it to a healthy state. She then liberated it to fly to its owners, only to have it come back and insist on remaining at her property. It had an empty message tube on one leg and an aluminum band on the other marked "N.A.S. 19 CH 44".[12]

By January of 1919, the existing loft was full so with the spring breeding season ahead, funds were requested to purchase materials to build a second one using station personnel for labor. This approach circumvented the bureaucratic bidding process with civilian contractors, which occasionally resulted in unforeseen delays that could not be tolerated in this instance.

Responsibility for the radio division and the pigeon men was assigned to the communications officer who also oversaw all official photography and the safekeeping of classified publications. The first communications officer was Ensign Waldo Brown.

Ordnance Department

Engineering and communications, however, were not the only so-called "line" departments at these coastal air stations. A third one was the ordnance department with accountability for the performance and storage of explosive devices. Specifically, at Chatham, the ordnance department was responsible for the Lewis guns, the Davis guns, the small arms, the bombs, the pyrotechnics, and the magazine. The first ordnance officer was Ensign Lingard who served in that capacity until his untimely death just before the armistice.

The Lewis gun, invented in 1911 by Colonel Isaac N. Lewis of the United States Army as a land weapon, had been adapted for airborne use by eliminating the heavy air-cooling chamber around the barrel, and substituting the cooling wind from the speed of the plane to prevent it from overheating.[13] Although considered reliable in 1918, the gun was sensitive and still subject to frequent jams when in continuous operation. It was installed, never-the-less, with a Scraff ring mount on every R-9 and on every flying boat until the Davis gun replaced it on each HS-1L and HS-2L at the base.

The Davis gun, thought ideal for use on patrol aircraft though still in a semi-experimental stage, was actually a small cannon which fired a 6-lb. shell that could fatally damage a surfaced U-boat. These guns arrived at the air stations too late in the war to be battle-tested, but target shooting demonstrated that caution was needed to insure that the pellets discharged out the rear barrel would not hit the engine or hole the wings. Pilots also noted that its forward location somewhat impaired their visibility, while the weight of the unit and the 70 lbs. of compensating sand in the tail section made the plane "cranky" in turns.[14] This type of recoil-free gun was developed in various sizes in 1910 by Commander Cleland Davis of the United States Navy for shipboard installation, but only the 6-lb. shell version was considered light enough to be adapted for use in the air.[15]

The small arms available were standard bolt-action 30-caliber Springfield rifles, Colt 45-caliber automatic revolvers, and Colt 38-caliber double action revolvers. These were issued from the small arms locker when needed for guard duty, the mail run, target practice, official ceremonies, and for such local events as Liberty Loan parades.

The bombs used at Chatham throughout its existence were the Mark IV type manufactured by Clarke & Company of Ardmore, Pennsylvania, and as previously mentioned they experienced many detonation problems. The Mark IV was composed of 120 pounds of cast TNT in a 26-pound casing, 10" in diameter and 55" long. It had a small wind-driven propeller at the tip which activated the fusing mechanism as it fell from the plane.[16] Bomb tests, field modifications, and filing reports to the Bureau of Ordnance in Washington accounted for much of the time of the department personnel.

In addition, small practice bombs of a sub-caliber type were also maintained to train the observer/bombardiers properly, and were adapted for use in the standard bomb-release mechanisms. These practice or "smoke" bombs, made of cast iron in a teardrop configuration with four fins, had an overall length of eight inches and weighed less than three pounds. To obtain the smoke puff upon impact with the target, an ordinary 10-gauge shotgun shell, loaded with 8 drams of black powder, was fitted into a cavity in the bomb's head one inch in diameter, and held in place by a cotter pin.[17] In addition, concrete "dummies" were stocked which had the same size, shape, weight, and center of gravity as the actual Mark IV bomb they represented. The practice bombing range was at Billingsgate Shoal off Wellfleet where the shallow depth of the water made retrieval for reuse relatively simple.

The pyrotechnics consisted of bombs and ammunition cartridges filled with chemicals for producing smoke or light as the situation required. If a certain spot had to be marked at sea in daylight, a smoke bomb was dropped to pinpoint the location. If a plane were down on the water at night and in distress, several red star shells were periodically fired at one minute intervals from a hand-held Very pistol in the hopes of bringing assistance.

Above: An HS-2L just after releasing a Mark IV bomb from under the lower starboard wing. The bomb carried beneath the port wing can be seen in this picture still attached to the plane immediately below the rudder post. **Below:** An R-9 seaplane on a concrete pad in front of the hangar. Note the two Mark IV bombs strapped under the lower wing beneath the forward seat. *Photos courtesy of the National Archives, Washington, D.C.*

The station's daily Material Status Report of November 3, 1918 indicates the typical amount of ordnance on hand during wartime:[18]

	Number	Type
Guns	2	Davis non-recoil 6 pdr.
	23	Lewis aircraft guns
	2	Colt Automatic Revolvers 45 cal.
	4	Colt Double Action Revolvers 38 cal.
	17	Very's Night Signal pistols
Bombs	53	Mark IV
Ammunition	60 rds.	6 pdr. ammunition
	18,000 rds.	30-30 Lewis Guns
	500 rds.	Colts Automatic 45 cal.
	950 rds.	Colts Double Action 38 cal.
	275 rds.	Very Night Signals (Green)
	520 rds.	" " " (Red)
	275 rds.	" " " (White)

Right: Machinist Mates can be seen working on the gondola of a B-class blimp inside the dirigible hangar. *Photo from the Author's Collection.*

Supply Department

Another integral part of the air station was the supply department which handled the business and fiscal transactions as well as the feeding of the personnel. It was responsible for the ordering, reception, storage, care, custody, transfer, shipment, and issue of most all supplies from food to fuel. In addition it operated the base post office, the ship's store, the supply office, the commissary, and the clothing and small stores area. Accounts not coming under its jurisdiction were those relating to medicines and medical equipment. The department numbered at its peak about 40 people including commissary stewards, storekeepers, cooks, bakers, and yeomen. The kind of work each performed is apparent except for that of the yeomen who handled all the correspondence and prepared all the reports including the official or "smooth" logs of the station. These typed logs contained the major happenings that took place during the six daily watch periods listed below:[19]

Commences	to 4:00 A.M.
4:00 A.M.	to 8:00 A.M.
8:00 A.M.	to Meridian
Meridian	to 4:00 P.M.
4:00 P.M.	to 8:00 P.M.
8:00 P.M.	to Midnight

Pay accounts of the officers and men were kept by the disbursing office of the First Naval District in Boston and checks were forwarded to Chatham for distribution every two weeks.[20] The following table condensed from the Bluejackets Manual of 1918 gives some idea of the enlisted men's monthly pay scale during the final year of the war:

Rate	Seaman Branch (Boatswain's Mate) (Gunner's Mate)	Artificer Branch (Machinist's Mate) (Electrician)	Special Branch (Yeoman) (Pharmacist's Mate)
Chief	$55.00	$77.00	$66.00
1st Class	44.00	60.50	44.00
2nd Class	38.50	44.00	38.50
3rd Class	33.00	33.00	33.00
Entry Level			
Seaman	17.60	--	--
Fireman	--	24.20	--
Landsman	--	--	17.60

As of August 3, 1918, Ensign H. M. Jackson (Pay Corps) relieved Ensign Fred C. Burris (Pay Corps) as base supply officer.

All foodstuffs served in the mess hall at the air station were requisitioned through a central dispensing system set up by the Navy's Paymaster General. Nothing could be purchased locally. This not only resulted in substantial cost savings and allowed for strict quality controls but, with guidelines issued for their menus, the bluejackets were assured a variety of nourishing, well-balanced meals planned by a nutritionist. During November of 1917, a typical 7-day bill-of-fare appeared in the national press and is included below to show how well the men were fed:[21]

MONDAY

Breakfast-Fried bacon, fried eggs, toast, rolled oats, milk and sugar, bread, butter, coffee.
Dinner-Veal fricassee with dumplings, mashed potatoes, kidney beans, apple pie, bread, butter, coffee.
Supper-Vegetable soup, crackers, roast ribs of beef, onion gravy, ginger cake, jam, bread, butter, tea.

TUESDAY

Breakfast-Fried bologna, fried potatoes, rolled oats, milk and sugar, bread butter, coffee.
Dinner-Vermicelli soup, crackers, mashed potatoes, kidney beans, apple pie, bread butter, coffee.
Supper-Fried hamburger steak, fried onions, lyonnaise potatoes, coconut cake, fruit jam, bread, butter, tea.

WEDNESDAY

Breakfast-Cereal, milk and sugar, baked beans, tomato catsup, ginger cake, rolls, bread, butter, coffee.
Dinner-Chicken soup, crackers, roast chicken with sage dressing, mashed potatoes, creamed carrots with peas, jelly layer cake, ice cream, bread, butter, coffee.
Supper-Salmon salad, mayonnaise dressing, baked macaroni and cheese, rice custard, bread, butter, tea.

THURSDAY

Breakfast-Broiled beefsteak, onion gravy, mashed potatoes, chilled sliced pineapple, bread, butter, coffee.
Dinner-Breaded veal cutlets, tomato catsup, French fried potatoes, mashed turnips, mashed potatoes, apple pie, bread, butter, coffee.
Supper-Railroad hash, tomato catsup, apple cake, hot rolls, bread, butter, tea.

FRIDAY

Breakfast-Grilled frankfurters, griddle cakes, sirup, fruit jam, bread, butter, coffee.
Dinner-Tomato soup, crackers, creamed codfish on toast, browned potatoes, mince pie, bread, butter, coffee.
Supper-Roast loins of beef, brown gravy, mashed potatoes, chili beans, peach cake, bread, butter, tea.

SATURDAY

Breakfast-Boston baked beans, tomato catsup, coffee cake, bread, butter, coffee.
Dinner-Breaded loin pork chops, mashed potatoes, lima beans, sauerkraut, peach and apricot pie, bread, butter, coffee.
Supper-Veal curry with chicken, boiled rice, bread pudding with sauce, bread, butter, tea.

SUNDAY

Breakfast-Fried corned-beef hash, griddle cakes, sirup, bread, butter, coffee.
Dinner-Roast loins of pork, sage dressing, browned potatoes, stewed lima beans, cottage pudding, lemon sauce, ice cream, bread, butter, coffee.
Supper-Cold sliced meats, potato salad, French dressing, cold beans, jam, bread, butter, tea.

As for problems, the major one the department encountered was in transporting the materials and supplies from the in-town freight depot five miles away. These had to be picked up with an inadequate number of trucks using back roads that many times were in poor condition due to rain, snow or ice. It was most evident in the procuring and handling of the tremendous amounts of coal needed during the abnormally cold winter of 1917 - 1918. As many as eight to ten battleship-gray coal cars would be brought to the railroad siding at a time, all of which had to be unloaded manually into waiting vehicles, only to have them emptied out in the same manner at the air station.[22]

In general, the duties of the supply department at Chatham were similar to those at any other small stateside naval shore station except that, in addition, a great number of aeronautical related items were also involved.

The Chatham railroad depot and freight yard. Here all shipments of supplies, building materials and military equipment were transferred to trucks for the five-mile road trip to the air station. Note the horse-drawn hearse parked to the left in the picture. *Photo form the Author's Collection.*

Medical Department

The medical department, another important non-line support unit, was charged with the responsibility of maintaining good health at the air station, and providing proper care of the sick and the injured. It was headquartered at the dispensary, a single story wooden building, 30 feet by 135 feet with 20 beds, located at a corner of the property not far from the ocean. The base had also been allocated a Ford ambulance by the First Naval District and had been extended the resources of the Chelsea Naval Hospital in Chelsea, Massachusetts as a back-up facility when needed.

Sick call was sounded about 8:00 A.M. each day at which time the medical officer examined those men who presented themselves for treatment; then, he would make the daily rounds of patients confined to the dispensary. After completing these calls he frequently spent time with the pilots inquiring about any physical or mental effects they might be experiencing in the air, while he quietly observed them for signs of fatigue, stress, and mood changes. The science of aviation medicine was still in its infancy. Thus, on occasion, the medical officer himself would go up as a passenger to try to become more knowledgeable in what the men were going through while flying these temperamental blimps and hydroplanes.[23] Other tasks of the department involved conducting periodic inspections of the living quarters, the galley, the food storage compartments, the refrigerators, and the heads for cleanliness, while monitoring the disposal of waste and the testing of the water supply. As a part of the Bureau of Medicine and

The dispensary at Chatham Naval Air Station looking southeast with the rear of the station ambulance shown in the parking area. *Photo courtesy of the Boston National Historical Park, Charlestown, Massachusetts.*

Surgery under the Surgeon General, it ordered all of its own supplies, medicines and equipment. It further maintained all its own records as well as the individual health files of the base personnel.

The Spanish influenza epidemic, which was ravaging the country in the fall of 1918, accounted for only one death at Chatham which was that of Joseph D. Yanacek, Quartermaster 3rd Class, who died on September 19 of pneumonia brought on by this highly contagious disease.[24] That only a single case occurred at the base serves as a tribute to the continuous hard work of the medical staff. The following day William J. Corbett, Chief Electrician (RO), also succumbed from pneumonia, but his was caused by exposure due to partial immersion. He had been forced to remain in the water up to his hips for some time before being disentangled from the wreckage of a flying boat, which crashed against a landing stage the previous week. The others in the plane escaped injury.[25]

It should also be noted that the Senior Medical Officer, because of his age, rank, and relative availability would usually be appointed to preside at each air station court martial. This was true during the tour of duty of Commander Henry B. Fitts (Medical Corps),[26] and for that of his replacement in mid-1919, Lieutenant R. DeB. Clarke (Medical Corps).[27] Although presiding at a court martial was a time consuming assignment, the number held at Chatham was small. One about every three months was the average.

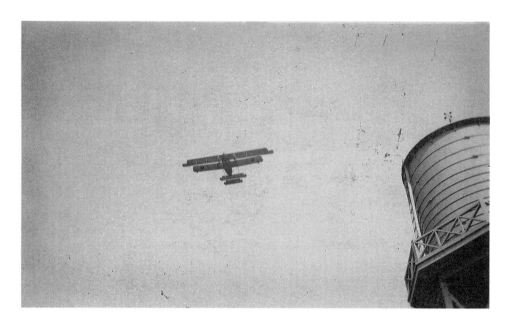

Above: An HS-2L flies gracefully above the air station's 20,000 gallon fresh water tank. **Below:** Some of the Officers at Chatham, reading left to right; Fisher, Hoopes, Woolsey, Flood, Lange, Cassidy, Hines, Bolin, Weston, Hudson, Brennan and Krouse. Jerry the mascot is in the foreground. Gobs are Machinist Mates Welch and Edwards. The plane is HS-2L No. 1850. *Photos from the Author's Collection.*

A wrecked HS-2L floated peacefully on Pleasant Bay after failing to recover from a low altitude slideslip maneuver. *Photo from the Author's Collection.*

The Organizational Chart

All of the departments were working for the common goal of keeping the planes, blimps, and kite balloons in the air, and on as regular a flight schedule as weather would permit. The department heads, in conjunction with the Squadron Commander for planes and the Squadron Commander for blimps, reported to the Executive Officer each morning at officers' call and kept him updated throughout the day of any status changes involving station routine or air operations. The Executive Officer, in turn, reported all information to the Commanding Officer to complete the local chain of command.

Officers' call was also the time when the Executive Officer passed on to those assembled the orders of the day and other information that the Captain wanted disseminated.

Discipline

The personnel at the air station were expected to obey every order and regulation issued by higher authority. It was each man's duty to perform well whatever task he was given to the best of his ability and in a timely manner.

Disobedience, neglect of duty, and poor behavior required that disciplinary action be taken, and in 1918 infractions were handled, depending on their degree of severity, in the following manner:[28]

1. By the Commanding Officer if the infraction was relatively minor, warranting confinement to quarters, restriction to base or periods of extra duty.

2. By a Deck Court if the offense merited a sentence of up to 20 days in confinement or 20 days loss of pay.

3. By a Summary Court Martial when a punishment of up to 30 days in solitary confinement, loss of 3 months pay and a bad conduct discharge was appropriate.

4. By a General Court Martial for the most severe or habitual breaches of discipline or for a criminal act that justified imprisonment at hard labor for 6 months to any number of years, loss of pay for 6 months or more, and a dishonorable discharge.

Chatham's Fiscal Year Disciplinary Report for July 1, 1918 to June 30, 1919 is included to show the number of infractions that occurred, the type they were, and how each was punished at the local base:[29]

"1.   A Summary of General Courts Martial

(a) One (1), two (2) days AWOL., Sentence; one (1) year in Naval Prison, Portsmouth, N.H.

(b) One (1), one (1) day AWOL., Sentence; six (6) months Confinement to Station; six (6) months Loss of Pay.

(c) One (1), one (1) day AWOL., Sentence; six (6) months Confinement to Station; six (6) months Loss of Pay.

Desertions; three (3), from January 30, 1919.

2. Petty Punishments

One (1) A.W.O.L. 36 hrs.; 3 days Solitary Confinement B&W.
Two (2) A.W.O.L. 9 hrs.; 30 days Restriction to Station.
Four (4) A.W.O.L. 48 hrs.; 5 days Solitary Confinement B&W.
One (1) A.W.O.L. 3 hrs.; 15 days Restriction to Station.
Two (2) A.W.O.L. 2 hrs.; 10 hrs. Extra duty.
One (2) A.W.O.L. 12 hrs.; 10 hrs. Extra duty.
Five (5) A.O.L.   57 hrs.; 30 days Restriction.
One (1) A.O.L.   4 hrs.; 10 hrs. Extra duty.
Two (2) A.O.L.   10 hrs.; 10 hrs. Extra duty.

One (1) A.O.L.   5 hrs.; 30 days Restriction.
Two (2) A.O.L.   23 hrs.; 30 days Restriction.
One (1) A.O.L.   12 hrs.; 30 days Restriction.
One (1) A.O.L.   8 hrs.; 14 days Restriction.
Two (2) Absent from Muster; 30 days Restriction.
One (1) Absent from Muster; 10 hrs. Extra duty.
One (1) Absent from Muster; 5 days Solitary Conf. B&W.
One (1) Inattention to duty;   5 days Solitary Conf. B&W.
Two (2) Inattention to duty;   5 hrs. Extra duty.
One (1) Inattention to duty;   10 hrs. Extra duty.
Two (2) Sleeping in; 30 days Restriction to Station.
Six (6) Sleeping in; 15 days Restriction to Station.
One (1) Destroying Government Property; 5 days. S.C.
Seven (7) Destroying Government Property; 10 hrs. Extra duty.
One (1)   Destroying Government Property;   5 hrs. Extra duty.
One (1) Insolence to Superior Officer; 10 hrs. Extra duty.
One (1) Insolence to Superior Officer; 5 hrs. Extra duty.
One (1) Neglect of duty; 10 hrs. Extra duty.
One (1) Neglect of duty;   5 hrs. Extra duty.
One (1) Shirking duty; 5 hrs. Extra duty.
One (1) Disobeying Orders; 30 days Restriction.
Two (2) Disobeying Orders; 10 hrs. Extra duty.
Six (6) Disobeying Orders;   5 hrs. Extra duty.
Two (2) Failing to salute Colors; 10 hrs. Extra duty.
One (1) Failing to salute Superior Officer; 5 hrs. Extra duty."

A glance at the station logs for this period will show that the majority of infractions were committed after January 1, 1919. It was then that the reservists were becoming frustrated with the military way of life in peacetime and were anxiously awaiting their return to civilian status.

Leisure time – on the beach at the Chatham Naval Air Station.
Photo from the Author's Collection.

Above: Two HS-2L's on dollies parked at the top of the seaplane hangar apron. *Photo from the Author's Collection.* **Below:** A hand crank in position to start a Liberty engine on a Curtiss HS-2L flying boat. *Photo courtesy of Robert S. Hardy and the Chatham Historical Society.*

Chapter Six

The Armistice and Celebrations

By the end of September it was becoming apparent that most of the Central Powers were disillusioned with the war, and they began putting forth individual feelers for peace. Bulgaria was the first to seek a separate armistice and consummated one of unconditional surrender on the 29th of September. A month later, on October 30, Turkey signed to the same terms. Then Austria-Hungary, the dual-kingdom and strongest ally of Germany, collapsed politically, and its military leaders, acknowledging defeat, laid down their arms on November 3. Germany was now alone. Her army was in retreat on the western front. It could see no way of stopping the Allied offensive from eventually crossing the Rhine and laying waste to the Fatherland. In the factories, workers were in revolt. At Kiel the fleet refused to obey its orders to sail. Germany had no alternative but to seek peace. On November 9 the Kaiser abdicated and fled to Holland. The next day a Socialist Republic was proclaimed. On November 11, at 11 minutes past 11:00 A.M., the guns on both sides fell silent. The final armistice which had been signed earlier that morning went into effect. The last of the Central Powers had now capitulated, the "war to end all wars" was over, and the free world took comfort in its new found peace.

Peace

The first official communication relating to the cessation of hostilities was relased by the State Department at 2:45 A.M. on Monday, November 11, announcing that the fighting would end at 11:00 o'clock that morning, Paris time. The timing of this communiqué was fortunate in that it allowed Boston newspapers to break the story in their early editions, causing an atmosphere of unparalleled celebration beginning with the work-day commute.[1] When the exuberant workers finally arrived at their work places, whether in the city or in their towns, they found the doors open but business suspended in favor of management-sanctioned victory parties of every description. Schools were closed, transportation went off schedule, and bars were ordered to shut down for safety sake.[2]

In Boston, many people were spilling out into the streets joining a hastily conceived downtown parade made up of soldiers from the harbor forts, sailors from the Bumpkin Island Training Station, and yeomanettes from both the First Naval District Headquarters in the Little Building and the Charlestown Navy Yard.[3] Many others went seeking out churches and synagogues to give quiet thanks to God for the long awaited end to the fighting. In the evening William Cardinal O'Connell, the Archbishop of Boston, intoned the solemn "Te Deum", a centuries-old Latin Hymn of thanksgiving, at a packed Cathedral of the Holy Cross. Earlier in the day Episcopal Bishop William Lawrence preached to an overflow congregation in St. Paul's Cathedral that left throngs stranded outside on the sidewalk. To accommodate these worshipers, the Bishop repeated the service immediately upon the conclusion of the scheduled one.[4]

Unexpected Holiday

Governor Samuel McCall proclaimed the next day a legal holiday encouraging every city and town in the Commonwealth to continue to celebrate the return of peace in an appropriate manner. Schools, businesses, banks, and manufacturing plants would not open, and licensed establishments throughout the state were again requested to refrain from selling liquor. From the mayor's office came word that the mayor would organize a grand scale patriotic parade in the heart of the city on the holiday afternoon. Eagerly assisting Mayor Peters in the intricate planning were both the ranking Army officer in the area, Major General William Crozier, and the Commandant of the First Naval District, Rear Admiral Spencer Wood. To add even more color to the spectacle, General Crozier agreed to serve as Chief Marshall and to lead the march on his favorite mount, "Brownie", followed by his complete staff astride beautifully groomed cavalry horses. Admiral Wood, not to be outdone by the Army in providing parade attractions, instructed the Commanding Officer of the Chatham Naval Air Station to have planes fly over and put on an aerial show above the line of march.

Parade and Flyover

On Tuesday afternoon, November 12, shortly after the parade started at the corner of Arlington and Beacon Streets, a steady but unfamiliar drone was heard in the distance coming from the direction of the harbor. As the sound grew progressively louder there appeared, approaching in formation, eight HS flying boats which began performing squadron evolutions as they passed over Boston Common and the assembly point. The flight was under the leadership of Ensign Alfred W. Hudson (Naval Aviator 490) who acted as flight commander. It had left the air station after the noonday meal, flying the 65-mile distance on various courses at various speeds in order to time its arrival as directed to coincide with the start of the event. As the record crowd of spectators looked skyward and the pilots continued their maneuvers over an expanded area, General Crozier was leading the marchers down Beacon Street past the reviewing stand set up in front of the State House. He led them to School Street, then on to Washington, to Milk, to Federal, to High, to Summer, to Winter, to Tremont, to Boylston Streets and finally to the terminus at Park Square. All along the route the planes performed overhead as an estimated one million onlookers thrilled to what they saw both on the streets and in the air.

The parade was composed of bands and units of servicemen, servicewomen, and civilians numbering nearly 20,000 in total who walked the 1½ hours needed to reach Park Square where it disbanded. The planes circled about until the last segment was underway and then landed on the Charles River in Cambridge for gas and oil before starting the return trip to their base on the Cape.[5] Only six arrived there as planned. One, with engine trouble, was obliged to land in Boston Harbor where it taxied to the Charlestown Navy Yard for assistance. Repairs were effected overnight and the next morning it departed at 10:45 A.M. arriving back at the air station about lunchtime.[6] Another HS-2L, 1917, was forced down with a cracked cylinder off Plymouth but proceeded slowly on the surface into Plymouth harbor and beached near the foot of Nelson Street. It remained on the shore for two days before mechanics from Chatham could replace the damaged part for the final leg of the flight home.[7]

In addition to Ensign Hudson, the other participating pilots included Ensign Isidor Richmond (Naval Aviator 918), Ensign Carlyle D. Weston (Naval Aviator 928), Ensign Herbert Schiff (Naval Aviator 916), Ensign Frederick C. VanDusen (Naval Aviator 937), Ensign William J. Shilling (Naval Aviator 951), Ensign Richard A. Marschat (Naval Aviator 1027) and Boatswain Earl E. Reber (Naval Aviator 2696).

Patrols Continue

Patrols Continue

When Admiral Wood originally contacted Chatham on the previous day the pilots upon hearing of it assumed, with the war over, every plane available would be sent to participate. To the disappointment of many, this was not to happen. The Secretary of the Navy, Josephus Daniels, had instructed all naval commands in Europe as well as ships and shore bases along the east coast to show no relaxing of vigilance once the armistice came. He wanted every German submarine and other warship scheduled to surrender to be accounted for before any variation in existing daily operations could be approved.[8] This meant that search patrols out of Chatham would continue as usual until further notice, thus limiting the number of aircraft in the Boston flyover.

The following day all of the Boston papers ran front page stories on the grandeur of the city's extravaganza, and each article included extensive coverage of the activity aloft. Aircraft were still a relatively new phenomenon to the average American; so, when such phrases as "airplanes add to spectacle", "airplanes a star feature", "several great war planes", and "eight of the latest naval machines" appeared in print, it stimulated peoples' imagination and directed their attention to the progress in naval aviation.

Chatham Celebrates

Chatham Celebrates

The air station was also involved in a second celebration on November 12 which was much smaller in size than Boston's but equal to it in patriotic fervor. The Town of Chatham's victory parade was led by two marshals on horseback with the Orleans Band immediately following. Then, among the other units in the line of march, came a large contingent of sailors from the local base plus Captain Eaton riding in his car. Cheering, flag-waving crowds lined the downtown streets as both on-lookers and participants shared the joy of the war being over.[9]

Supporting Sports Events

Supporting Sports Events

Other positive publicity for the Navy came from their competing in the New England Service Football League. These were teams formed from personnel stationed at the larger military and naval duty stations in the area, and each featured a number of former college standouts who had left school to volunteer or who had enlisted after graduating. The quality of play was such that games attracted a widespread following, and all admissions collected at the gate were turned over to the United War Work Fund. With unbeaten Camp Devens scheduled to play the also unbeaten Naval Radio School at Harvard Stadium on November 16 at 2:00 P.M., Admiral Wood again contacted Chatham for planes to come to add color and excitement but not to interfere with the play on the field. That day 18,000 partisan fans witnessed two Chatham-based HS flying boats conduct a pre-game air show by circling the field at a low altitude, by performing several different flight patterns, and then by departing in formation as the players lined up for the opening kick-off.[10]

Two days later, to further add to the United War Work Fund, the base personnel set up a prize fighting ring inside the Chatham blimp hangar and invited the townsfolk to come and see some colorful exhibitions of Navy boxing. One match was humorously dramatic, another featured the boxers in outlandish costumes, and a third was just plain slap-stick comedy! The grand finale however was legitimate and proved to be old-fashioned pugilism at its best. The

Fund increased by the impressive amount of $312.31 that night from the sale of admission tickets, and a voluntary collection taken up before the main event.[11]

An additional appearance over Harvard Stadium ordered by the Commandant occurred on Thanksgiving Day, November 28, at 10:30 A.M. There the First Naval District Headquarters team was pitted against that of the Naval Radio School in what was to be the final service league game ever played in Cambridge. Again two HS-2L's responded to orders and went through their now somewhat familiar aerobatics. Headquarters beat Radio 20 to 0 to win the local Navy championship, and the return flight was uneventful as the pilots were getting accustomed to the Chatham to Boston/Cambridge to Chatham run.[12] The service football league then shut down for the winter and was never to resurface because of the extensive personnel reductions that took effect over the summer in all branches of the armed forces.

With the end of November came the final submarine patrols out of Cape Cod, freeing up the planes for public relations activities as weather permittted. Politicians in Maine were quick to take advantage of the situation and asked that flying boats be flown up to help promote the sale of War Savings Stamps in their state. These were sold through local post offices, and enabled people with limited income to acquire bonds by making a small purchase on a regular basis until the price of a bond was reached. Each municipality had an annual quota to sell and, as might be expected, attaining it became more difficult now that peace was here.

Off to Maine

In response to the request, two HS-2L's, one piloted by Ensign Adams and the other by Ensign Schiff, left Chatham on Tuesday, December 3, for a 150 mile flight to Portland. Despite occasional pockets of fog and some snow squalls, both arrived in less than three hours which included a short weather-related stop in Portsmouth, New Hampshire. Although there was limited visibility, the planes attracted attention enroute, and ground stations along the coast continually reported each new sighting, keeping the general public advised of the aviators progress northward. Docking took place at Holyoke Wharf, and arrangements had been made to house the men at the local Naval Reserve Station for the duration of the visit.[13]

The next day, December 4, flyovers were to be conducted in both the morning and afternoon to drop patriotic literature, but bad weather caused a postponement. On December 5, upper level gusts were recorded at 65 mph forcing a further delay. Fortunately, by noon the wind had abated; so, at 2:15 P.M. Ensign Adams taxied out into the channel and took off, gaining altitude through a series of tight upward spirals much to the enjoyment of the spectators. He was then joined by the second plane above the Eastern Promenade where the pair performed various maneuvers together over the harbor for 30 minutes. The noise of the engines, amplified by the low altitude, caused many to rush into the streets to gaze, while teachers hurried their pupils to the school windows to witness the historical happenings. Finally, to everyone's delight, the pamphlets of red, white and blue began to flutter down encouraging all to buy War Savings Stamps to help offset the cost of "bringing home the boys".[14] After an hour in the air, the pilots ended their performance and moored their planes, 1856 and 1916, for the night. On the 6th, they were scheduled to "bomb" the ports of Boothbay Harbor and Rockland but a return of stormy conditions once again kept them from flying. It remained inclement for the rest of the week and, with ice beginning to form around the docks, they left for Chatham early on the 19th of December. The 1916 arrived at the air station in the afternoon without incident while engine trouble forced 1856 to land at Provincetown.

Christmas Time

On Christmas Day, Captain and Mrs. Eaton entertained all the officers at an open house where a huge, brightly lit Christmas tree was the center of attention. To make it even more appealing, its branches were laden with gifts and candies for everyone, which resulted in a very enjoyable social occasion.[15]

Three days later reality returned when two of Chatham's aviators, Ensign Shilling and his observer, J. J. Halvorson, had a narrow escape from death in the icy waters of Boston Harbor. The plane they were flying suddenly lost power while descending for a routine landing and sideslipped into the channel near Commonwealth Pier. Neither man was injured, but both were cold and exhausted when picked up by the rescue vessel that went to their assistance.[16]

Planes at Plymouth

Some of the flights to Boston never made it beyond the South Shore such as the one on December 30, 1918, when two HS-2L flying boats, 1457 and 1917, landed unexpectedly in Plymouth harbor about mid-morning. They taxied toward the beach section at the end of Nelson Street and, once reaching shallow water, quickly turned the hulls a full 90°. This maneuver caused the right wings to extend over the sand, and the crews used the lower ones as a gangplank to come ashore without getting wet. The planes were on their way to Boston, but a heavy fog over the city caused them to divert to Plymouth to wait for a weather change or alternative instructions. They stayed about an hour while several hundred people gathered in the mud to examine them, and then orders were received to return to Chatham. Included in the crowd were many school children on their Christmas recess who asked endless questions about the bomb releases, the machine gun fittings, and the radio apparatus.[17] No bombs or machine guns were aboard however as the Navy had already started to adapt to peacetime conditions.

A second incidence of Plymouth being used as a refuge occurred on Tuesday, January 28, 1919. Two HS-2L's were on a routine overwater flight to Boston when they encountered an offshore fog causing them to alter course and follow the shoreline as a safer route. Both passed over Plymouth about 10:30 A.M. and proceeded northward toward Duxbury, apparently experiencing no difficulties. Three-quarters of an hour later, one of them, 1850, re-appeared over Plymouth, landed in the harbor and came ashore at the end of Brewster Street with a broken cam shaft.

After the craft was secured by throwing its anchor into the mud, the observer surprised the gathering crowd by releasing a homing pigeon that circled high in the air, turned, then flew southeast to notify the air station of the new situation. Later, a second pigeon was sent to further advise that a leak had developed where the hull had struck a small rock while being beached. The messengers got through and a repair party arrived by automobile late in the afternoon with the necessary parts and equipment. The mechanics worked as steadily as weather would permit, but it was not until Thursday, January 30, that it took off fully repaired. Once again several hundred people visited the site to watch the departure, as the location of the plane was close to the town's business section.[18] Plymouth, with both a sheltered harbor and a sandy beach, became a natural haven for hydroplanes to seek out if they were experiencing weather or mechanical problems over Massachusetts Bay.

The Gloucester halibut schooner *Natalie Hammond* which came upon the wreckage of the B-20 in February of 1919 while fishing off Georges Bank. The vessel's veteran Captain, Charles Closson, managed to get the envelope on board and proceeded to deliver it to surprised naval officials at the Charlestown Navy Yard. *Photo courtesy of The Mariners' Museum, Newport News, Virginia.*

A Wind-blown Blimp

The lighter-than-air section was having some operational problems also. On January 14, 1919, a B-class blimp, B-20, left the air station at 11:00 A.M. on a special flight to experiment with taking aerial photographs and moving pictures from an airship. About 25 miles from Chatham, out over Cape Cod Bay, it suffered an engine failure caused by a plugged gas line and went out of control in an east-by-north direction with the wind at 25 knots. An hour later it had drifted close to the Coast Guard station at Orleans, so the crew quickly lowered their altitude and tried to make a landing by throwing out the anchor to catch onto something firm. Instead of grappling some solid object, which would have arrested the flight, the anchor snared a cable and tore away the communications systems at the Coast Guard facility. When it became apparent the blimp was not going to stop, the four men in the gondola then jumped into the sea from a height of 90 feet off Nauset Beach and swam to safety. The crew included Lieutenant (jg) Walter Griffin, pilot; Ensign Karl Lange, assistant pilot; Ensign Sidney Hickok, photographer; and Machinist Mate Wallace N. Edwards, engineer. The blimp, now unmanned, gained altitude and continued on out to sea at the will of the winds. Once the four had come ashore Griffin complained of soreness in his back. Eager that he receive prompt medical attention, the Coast Guardsmen took them all in a horse-drawn wagon to East Orleans to meet the ambulance from the air station.[19]

Wreckage Found

When word of the mishap was received at First Naval District Headquarters by the Admiral, he ordered that an immediate surface search be conducted from Cape Cod to Machias, Maine in spite of the stormy winter weather. The blimp was finally sighted in a deflated condition on the ocean surface 118 miles southeast of Graves Light. The *USS Aztec (SP-590)* was dispatched from Boston to recover the wreckage, but such heavy gales were encountered that little headway could be made and recovery was deemed impossible at that time. Also, as it was estimated, with the high winds, that the deflated airship could drift up to 500 miles from where it had been reported, the *Aztec* was recalled and the recovery attempt was abandoned.[20] Several weeks later, in mid-February, the lost wreckage was found by the Gloucester halibut schooner *Natalie Hammond* at the southeastern end of Georges Bank in the Great South Channel, 70 miles from Chatham. When the schooner brought it to Boston and turned it over to naval authorities, the envelope was discovered to be in surprisingly good condition considering what it had been through.[21] Never-the-less, a closer examination back at the air station revealed that it was actually beyond the point of refurbishment. The car was never located.

The Goodyear B-20, the last in that class to be built, had been transferred to Chatham from Montauk on November 28, 1918. It was designated as a replacement for the older B-12 which, suffering from continuous usage and innumerable repairs, had been ordered back to the warehouse in Akron for storage. Now, with B-12 shipped to the Midwest in December and with its replacement lost at sea, the Navy found itself without a blimp on Cape Cod for the first time in several months. To rectify this, it instructed the Goodyear Company to send the recently completed B-18 and B-19 to Chatham, one to fill the vacancy and the other as an addition. Both were shipped in January and provided reliable service until reassigned elsewhere, the B-18 in late 1919, and the B-19 in 1920. The B-18, B-19 and B-20 were part of a supplemental contract awarded to Goodyear to build four additional B-class blimps.[22] Each had a modified gondola with a Curtiss OXX-8 100 hp engine at the rear acting as a pusher instead of having a tractor-type as the first sixteen in its class. The gondolas for the above were numbered A-5465, A-5467 and A-5257 respectively.

Wilson Hailed in Boston

On the diplomatic front, President Wilson, who abhorred the use of arms in international disputes and had earlier proposed that a conciliatory Fourteen Point Peace Plan be part of a post-war settlement, left via the troopship *USS George Washington* on December 4, 1918 for the Paris Peace Conference. He wanted the other Allied leaders not to hold out for excessive monetary payments and major territorial concessions from the conquered nations, but to adopt his idealistic program of universal forgiveness and the creation of a world body to maintain the peace. By February 14 phase one of the conference was over. His League of Nations concept had been unanimously agreed upon, but a decision on surrender terms could not be reached; so further discussion was scheduled for the next meeting in March. An encouraged President sailed that day from Brest bound for Boston satisfied in what he had so far negotiated for the world of the future.

On the night of February 24, 1919 the *USS George Washington* arrived at the approaches to Boston Harbor and proceeded up the channel to anchor just off Deer Island. About 11:00 A.M. the following day Wilson appeared on the transport's deck and boarded the *USS Ossipee*, a former Coast Guard cutter now in naval service, for the short voyage to Commonwealth Pier. At that moment he was greeted by every ships' whistle in the area and by nine low-flying hydroplanes that had departed from Chatham to take part in the reception for the returning Commander-in-Chief. Included in the flight were five from Rockaway which had flown up to Cape Cod the day before to be components of the squadron assigned to render honors to the President. A sixth one from Rockaway, 1685, made the trip up to the Cape as well, but was forced to beach at Orleans with engine failure just after take-off that morning.[23] The Cape May Naval Air Station was also scheduled to be represented. However, its two HS-2L's ran low on fuel over Rhode Island and had to land at Providence on the Seekonk River, preventing their participation.[24] A blimp from Montauk likewise missed the event due to high winds over Long Island Sound. This nine plane formation, on display for the first time, was probably the largest concentration of naval air power that New England had ever seen in the fifteen year history of manned flight. It was a great day for the Nation, for Wilson, for the Navy, and for Chatham.

The planes continued to fly overhead in extended welcome until the President disembarked, then they departed the Boston area to return to the air station. Only three arrived as scheduled about 12:30 P.M. With the sustained winds now at 40 mph, four chose to seek temporary shelter at Marblehead while one did likewise at Plymouth and the other at Marine Park in Boston. All eventually reached their starting point.[25]

The four Chatham planes were flown by Lieutenant Commander Harold T. Bartlett (Naval Aviator 21) up from the Office of Naval Operations (OpNav) in Washington with Lieutenant Edward P. Brennan the Squadron Commander at Chatham as assistant pilot; Lieutenant (jg) Alfred W. Hudson with Ensign Samuel H. Krouse (Naval Aviator 960) as assistant; Ensign John C. Flood with Ensign Marschat as assistant; and Ensign Carlyle D. Weston with Ensign Alfred M. Pride (Naval Aviator 1119) as assistant. Commander Louis H. Maxfield (Naval Aviator 17) from the Bureau of Navigation (BuNav) in Washington was in overall command and had arranged for two moving picture photographers to go aloft to record

An aerial view of Boston Harbor in 1918. Many a pilot from Chatham landed here either on a routine flight to First Naval District Headquarters, or when his plane experienced mechanical problems over Massachusetts Bay. *Photo courtesy of Robert Stanley, Portsmouth, New Hampshire.*

the arrival from the air.[26] Once back at the base, the pilots received congratulations in a message from Admiral Wood for the skill they displayed in overcoming strong and treacherous winds over Massachusetts Bay to carry out their mission of welcome.

Three days after the President had departed, an HS-flying boat enroute to Boston developed engine trouble, but succeeded in getting to the outer harbor and landed among the many islands. It was on a round-trip courier flight from Chatham to the First Naval District Headquarters carrying a dispatch pouch from one base to the other.[27] The newer pilots looked forward to these assignments and the challenges of landing in a busy harbor; indeed, the experienced ones also preferred such missions rather than to just take a plane up and fly it in circles to get air time. On this specific flight the downed aircraft was spotted from East Boston, and the navy yard at Charlestown sent a launch to retrieve it. After minor repairs, it returned to the Cape later in the day.

Yankee Division Returns

On April 4, 1919 three planes from Chatham flew once again in formation to Boston to greet this time the transport *USS Mount Vernon* as it approached the Massachusetts coast on its voyage from France. Aboard were the first 5,800 excited and homesick officers and men of New England's own 26th Division on their way to the separation center at Camp Devens, 30 miles west of the city. The initial shipboard sighting of the lead plane is best described in the actual words of a returning veteran of the 101st Regiment of Engineers standing on the deck of the troopship:

"The morning of April 4th found everyone on deck at an early hour, for it was known that the boat would dock that day. The sea was glassy calm, but during the night a dense fog had shut down all around, and land could not be seen. Before long it was realized that the boat was hardly making headway, and promptly all kinds of rumors were passed around: the engines were out of commission; the ship had run out of coal; it was waiting for an escort into the harbor; orders had been received sending the boat to New York instead of Boston. More waiting; round and round a buoy the ship slowly circled. Perhaps the fog lay heavily in and around the harbor and the boat could not dock that day. All sorts of horrible possibilities were suggested, when suddenly out of the fog, roaring the first welcome home, came a U S Navy hydroplane. What a shout went up! Then the men watched as it circled overhead and waved to the pilot in the cockpit until it headed off toward the harbor whence it had come. Almost at once the ship started off into the outer harbor. Dimly through the fog loomed Minot's Light and vague lines of the city took shape as the *Mount Vernon* passed on close to the harbor forts into the inner bay."[28]

The remaining elements of the 26th Division managed to arrive on several different ships docking individually over the next two weeks. Eventually all of the 20,000 plus members were once again together as a military unit on American soil. On April 25 fourteen lengthy trains returned the division to Boston for its final parade. There, with pride and joy, the soldiers marched before hundreds of thousands of flag-waving home folks lining the streets to cheer and to welcome back these local men of the American Expeditionary Force (AEF).[29]

As part of the planned festivities, four HS-2L's left Chatham at 11:15 that morning to participate with flying demonstrations along the parade route. This meant circling Boston Common, which was the troop assembly area, and accompanying the line of march around the Common and the Public Garden to Commonwealth Avenue into the Back Bay. The return was via Massachusetts Avenue and Columbus Avenue to the dispersal point at Park Square.[30] It was a lengthy parade covering the heart of the city, but no one tired of seeing the 26th Division marching in full battle dress with components of naval aviation flying above as an honor guard.

Lost at Sea

Only three planes however, the 1850, 1916 and 1918, returned to the air station after the festivities. One of the returning pilots saw HS-2L 1856, with its crew of three, forced down in rough water about eight miles northeast of Plymouth. At 8:25 A.M. the following morning a homing pigeon arrived at the station loft with the message "2:20 P.M. We are going to taxi toward Provincetown, signed B. Tornes 'observer' ". Despite continuous searches over the next three days by both surface vessels and aircraft the pilot Lieutenant (jg) John S. Buchanan (Naval Aviator 276), the assistant pilot, Ensign John C. Howard (Naval Aviator 1949) and the observer, Bernard Tornes, Electrician 1st Class, were never seen again.[31]

The Boston Post reported in its May 1 edition that one of Buchanan's last known acts was to wave to his parents as he encircled their house at 381 Huntington Avenue while over the Boston area. The same article went on to say that a camera, a pair of goggles and a leather flying coat had been found by a fishing boat off Provincetown, all probably belonging to Ensign Howard.

The 26th Division marching down Tremont Street in Boston in its final parade on April 25, 1919. Four planes from Chatham circled above the entire route in a continuing aerial tribute. This photograph was taken from the Little Building, the headquarters of the First Naval District, at the corner of Tremont and Boylston Streets. *Photo courtesy of Robert Stanley, Portsmouth, New Hampshire.*

Later, scattered debris from the 1856 drifted ashore at Race Point and wreckage was sighted by the destroyer *USS McDermut (DD-262)* on May 10 at forty-three miles, 90°T from Peaked Hill Bar but no bodies were recovered.

More Training

While the 26th Division was in the process of being brought home for discharge, post-war training at Chatham continued but on a limited basis, using for principal instructors those pilots who had flown HS-2L's overseas. These men, with their experience in England, Ireland, and France were passing on to others who were interested the finer points of flying learned under combat area conditions.

From time to time some of these flights went awry as evidenced by one on April 8. On this occasion a surfman on beach patrol reported at 10:30 A.M. that a flying boat was down 2 miles northeast of the Chatham Life Saving Station and was drifting seaward. On board the disabled craft were Ensign William P. Smith (Naval Aviator 644), the pilot; Ensign Philip L. Haynes (Naval Aviator 2608), the assistant pilot; and an unidentified enlisted man who served as mechanic/observer. Smith, a former instructor at Moutchic Naval Air Station in France, had been on a training flight familiarizing Haynes with the features of an HS-2L when the engine failed.

The lifesavers rowed out and secured the plane to their boat, then anchored in deep water to await assistance. At 12:15 P.M., while still at anchor, a message was wigwagged from the beach telling them to bring Haynes ashore to call the air station. He was rowed in as instructed and the conversation that ensued determined the engine could not be fixed at an anchorage. The lifesavers then returned Haynes to the plane and all continued to wait. At 2:00 o'clock the Sea Sled arrived, took the 3 airmen on board and towed the aircraft slowly back to the base.[32] These training flights in the tired HS-2L's were becoming known for teaching the trainees more about frustration and patience than about how to control a flying boat on an offshore patrol!

A District Eliminated

Also during this period, the Second Naval District, which extended from Buzzards Bay to New London, Connecticut and had its flag at Newport, was dissolved for budget reasons. Its former operating area was split up between the First and the Third Naval Districts with Point Judith, Rhode Island serving as the dividing line. The section added to the First Naval District included the waters of southern Massachusetts and Narragansett Bay as well as the port cities of New Bedford, Fall River, Providence and Newport. Chatham, the air arm of the First Naval District, thus replaced Montauk as the station responsible for all flight operations in the newly acquired region.[33]

Admiral Sims

Shortly after this took place there was a hero's welcome in New York City for Admiral William S. Sims, returning home after completing his tour of duty as Commander of all United States Naval Forces Operating in European Waters. When the country entered the war he had been relieved as President of the Naval War College at Newport and appointed to this newly created command in London to work with the First Sea Lord of the Admiralty, Admiral Jellicoe, as well as his counterparts from both France and Italy. Sims was a good choice as his tenacity and non-conformity were instrumental in bringing about the convoy system, which went a long way toward nullifying the U-boat threat in the Atlantic. He also was our country's official representative at Scapa Flow when the German High Seas Fleet surrendered in accordance with the terms of the armistice.

Leaving New York on April 11, after his highly publicized return, the Admiral reported, as ordered, to Newport to once again assume the Presidency of the War College. Upon his arrival he was greeted with an elaborate welcoming that included air cover from Chatham patriciping over Rhode Island for the first time. The air station's role in the Sims reception was scheduled to include two HS-2L's flying above the destroyer *USS Sampson (DD-63)* as it approached Narragansett Bay and continued on up to Newport's inner harbor to disembark the Admiral. However, only one plane, the 1854, piloted by Ensign Flood, carried out the assigned escort as the other, flown by Ensign Pride, experienced an engine problem over Woods Hole and was forced to return.

Flood, with his crew of Chief Machinist Mate E. R. Jason and Radioman M. V. Horgan, flew low over the destroyer as it came up the bay to its designated anchorage. Later, as the official party was being taken ashore, Flood returned in the 1854 and buzzed the Admiral's launch so Sims could get an even better view of an HS-2L in flight. The aviators then landed for the night at the nearby Naval Torpedo Station and departed at noon the following day, circling the city several times before heading down the channel back to Chatham.[34]

Stuck in the Mud

Blimps had their trouble also. The next day, in a non-related mission, the B-18 developed an engine problem while on a routine training flight and came down on the mud flats 1½ miles southwest of the Orleans Life Saving Station. Those aboard were the pilot, Lieutenant (jg) Karl Lange, with a crew composed of Chief Machinist Mate Williams and Chief Quartermaster Fields. Fortunately the three were able to restart the engine in a short period of time but could not get the blimp to lift off as the two large cylindrical rubber landing pads had become embedded in the mud. With the help of the nearby lifesavers, these were eventually dug out, and Lange flew B-18 back to the air station with no further misfortune. Because of the efficiency of all concerned, the whole flight interruption was only three hours, and no assistance from Chatham was needed.[35]

Mooring Buoys

April then came to a close on another pleasant note when a request for twelve 44" x 48" drum floats, to be used as mooring buoys for the flying boats, was approved. Here-to-fore, when the planes were idle but not in the hangers or on the concrete parking areas, they were either beached or anchored about 20 yards off shore. Both of these alternatives had disadvantages as hulls could be damaged while being pulled across the sand, and collisions could occur if the anchors dragged. But these new buoys, designed originally to hold up submarine nets, eliminated such potential hazards. In addition, the center ringbolt at the top of each one allowed for faster get-aways in times of emergency.[36]

Victory Loan Flights

In the funding area, one of the methods used to finance the recent war was conducting four separate Liberty Loan drives which offered various small-denomination, interest-bearing government bonds to the American public as an attractive and patriotic investment. A fifth such effort, called the Victory Loan, was initiated after the armistice with a close-off date of May 10, 1919. The drive was lagging behind expectations; so, the last ten days of the campaign became critical to its success. As a solution, several noteworthy and attention-getting events were scheduled around the country during that critical period to make sure the goals were reached.

Boston set May 1 as the date for its gala bond selling rally which would feature a former U-boat moored at the Esplanade in the Charles River Basin, fifteen pieces of heavy artillery on the Common, and the first blimp ever to be seen over the city. The submarine would be open to visitors, the cannons would fire black powder, and the airship would "bomb" the crowd with leaflets - all trying to stimulate additional bond sales.

The B-18 left for Boston that morning arriving at the festivities via Plymouth and Quincy. In flying over Plymouth about 10:00 A.M. it passed close above the downtown section, dropping literature which it had planned to drop on April 28 when that flight was canceled because of fog. The leaflets on the way down were unfortunately caught in a sudden breeze and landed in the harbor out of reach of all except those watching from boats offshore.[37]

Its subsequent participation over Boston was apparently an outstanding success as evidenced by the following article quoted from the local press of May 2:

``The appearance of the big, cigar-shaped dirigible caused a tremendous sensation in the downtown section as it flew over the Common. After circling about for a time distributing hundreds of ``Gift from Heaven'' circulars, the aerial visitor flew off in the direction of Lynn, returning about noon and flying over the Back Bay and Brookline, to the intense excitement of all in the region who heard the whirr of its motor or caught a glimpse of the huge aircraft. So low did the dirigible fly in passing over Beacon Street in Brookline that dogs became excited by its presence and jumped around barking furiously. About 12:30 P.M. the dirigible, after circling several times over the down-town section, flew off again in the direction of Chatham.''[38]

In between its two separate Boston appearances that day, the blimp had flown off to make leaflet drops on Lynn, Marblehead, Salem, and Gloucester, in that order, before returning to Boston Common via Rockport, Essex, Ipswich, and Beverly. On its way to Lynn it spotted a one-story wooden building on fire and, by making peculiar circular maneuvers, attracted the community's attention to smoke issuing from the roof of what was a rag shop on West 3rd Street, Chelsea, near the Chelsea/Everett line. Everett firebox No. 14 was sounded by those watching below, and Everett fire trucks responded to find the Chelsea ones just arriving at the scene also.[39]

Another incident which happened later that morning showed that the well-intentioned public still had a lot to learn about lighter-than-air flight. The Gloucester Liberty Loan Committee wanted to make the visit memorable for the crew of the blimp, so two Boy Scouts were positioned on the roof of the YMCA building to extend the city's official welcome by wigwag. The message that was to be sent read as follows:

``Gloucester greet you. The bond buyers
are looking up. Everyone is buying!''[40]

The idea was unique; yet transmitting a message of this length by the method chosen proved impossible to do in the brief period that the craft was overhead. The Boy Scouts were not disheartened in the least as they and their mentors had the best viewing spot in the Cape Ann area.

The presence of the airship caused so much favorable comment on its Boston trip, that the New England Liberty Loan Committee made arrangements with the First Naval District to have one fly over the city every day the following week, sometime between noon and 5:00 P.M. if weather permitted.

But Boston and vicinity was not the only area to have lighter-than-air assistance in selling bonds for this drive. New Bedford had a similar such flight targeted for April 26 which unfortunately had to be cancelled because of high winds. The operations office at Chatham knew the people were disappointed so, three days later, April 29, the other B-class blimp, the B-19, was sent there for a simple flyover to keep interest high until the actual bond drive flight could be rescheduled. About 9:00 A.M. the huge craft appeared as ordered, crossed the city east to west and traveled at a good rate of speed in spite of moderate head winds. As it swept across, it began to descend. This caused a number of the spectators to hurry towards the open spaces of Buttonwood Park in hopes of seeing it land. The pilot had no such intention of landing as he was just providing the best view possible for all those gazing in awe at the unfamiliar sight in the sky. Once beyond the Park, he regained his altitude and continued along in a westerly direction to create more excitement at the next city along the coast.[41]

Later that morning the giant visitor arrived over Fall River, coming in low from the southeast and proceeding toward the downtown section, where it hovered for the benefit of the many watching from the streets. Fall River was scheduled to have its bond drive flight and ground show on May 1; so this performance was also just to keep the anticipation level rising for the upcoming main event. Soon the blimp regained altitude and circled the city for several minutes before departing over the waterfront in the general direction of Providence. The Fall River Daily Globe of April 29 described the city's reaction to its first ever sighting of an airship in flight with the following front page article:

> "The dirigible seemed to operate with ease and, as it was the first to fly over the city, it created a great deal of interest. Shops were deserted while the craft was passing overhead and it was the first opportunity the local public has had to see a real military balloon under full sail."

Shortly before noon it could be seen approaching Providence where it flew low over the central part of the city to allow those watching to view it in some detail. As again it was just on a warm-up flight, it soon turned and retraced its route over the business district. It then continued down Narragansett Bay to NAS Montauk where it landed at 1:00 P.M. that afternoon and remained overnight.[42] The people would have to wait until May 2 for the stunts and excitement associated with the bond drive as that was the date Providence had designated to officially promote their sale.

On May 1, the B-19 flew from its stay at NAS Montauk back to Fall River to participate in their Victory Loan activities. Arriving at 2:00 P.M. it circled over the bay and the southern portion of the city creating great interest and anticipation. A rumor had started that a man would parachute from the gondola into the harbor, and the crowds were especially heavy along the waterfront. No jump ever occurred but leaflets were dropped all over the downtown section causing a souvenir scramble among the adults as well as the children. After a final circling of the area, the craft flew out to sea.[43] The rescheduled flight over Providence on May 2 never took place because of weather.

Chatham was able, after all, to supply the coverage for the rescheduled New Bedford event with a blimp going there on Sunday May 4 and dropping not only the usual leaflets, but some which contained a novel new feature. Included in those that floated down were five personally signed by the publicity chairman of the New England Bond Committee, John K. Allen. Any person finding one of these could redeem it at the Federal Reserve Bank of Boston for a German helmet taken from the battlefields of France.[44] This time the weather cooperated and the circulars fell on a large crowd of sky watchers, but not a single one with a signature was ever turned in.

Over Rhode Island

Celebrations were popular. Taking the cue from Boston's gala review of the 26th Division, Rhode Island decided to hold a tribute of its own in Providence for all the Great War veterans from that state. The date was set for May 5 and an elaborate parade, reviewed by Admiral Sims and General Edwards, began at Exchange Place at 1:30 P.M. and wound its way through the streets of the downtown area. All during the march, two planes from Chatham accompanied the men, women, bands, and floats that followed the route to Market Square where the last participants dispersed about 3:00 o'clock. An hour later the spectators, now at Melrose Park watching a baseball game between the two services, saw the planes re-appear and shower "Welcome Home" cards on everyone before returning to their base.[45] Once completing these events of early May, Chatham's assistance at bond drives and its providing of aerial salutes was nearly at an end.

When an HS-2L was involved in an aerial photography mission, a graflex camera holder was rigged on the starboard side of the forward cockpit as seen in the above photograph. *Photo courtesy of the National Archives, Washington, D.C.*

Chapter Seven

Post War Activity

Now that the war had been over several months, the career officers in naval aviation began to seek out high-profile peacetime challenges, and at the top of list came transAtlantic flight. The excitement for this was initially created in 1913 when the London Daily Mail offered a 10,000 Pound prize to the first aviator to fly between North America and Great Britain or Ireland in either direction. But what had seemed totally unrealistic in the early 1900's now had a reasonable chance for success given the improved state of technology; thus, several contestants on both sides of the ocean commenced preparations for the attempt. Although the Navy would not be eligible for prize money, it wanted the honor of being in the record books as the first to cross and, with its big new flying boats, it had as good a chance as any to accomplish this feat. Rockaway Naval Air Station, on lower Long Island, was selected as the staging area because of its proximity to the Garden City Curtiss plant, where the war-initiated NC development and construction contract was being completed.

NC-4 at Chatham

Initially all four planes were scheduled to participate, but NC-2 was withdrawn in early April to be available as a quick source of replacement parts should the others be in need. The first order of business for the remaining three was to get to the selected departure point of Trepassey, a small fishing village at the eastern tip of Newfoundland. On Thursday, May 8, 1919, at 10:00 A.M. the NC-1, NC-3 and the NC-4 took off from Rockaway bound for a fuel stop at Halifax on the first leg of the flight plan, but only the NC-1 and the NC-3 arrived there as scheduled. The NC-4 had experienced problems with two of its four engines and was forced to land at sea about eighty miles off Cape Cod.

The Nancy Four, as it was nicknamed by the press, was a very large plane for its day with an upper wing span of 126 feet, a length of 68 feet and height of 24 feet. The 400 hp Liberty engines, three of which were tractor-type and one a pusher, gave it a maximum speed of 84 knots. Fully loaded, with its crew of six, it weighed 28,000 lbs. The crew on this flight consisted of Lieutenant Commander Albert C. Read (Naval Aviator 24) commanding officer and navigator; Lieutenant Elmer Stone, U.S. Coast Guard (Naval Aviator 38) pilot; Lieutenant Walter Hinton, (Naval Aviator 135) co-pilot; Ensign Herbert C. Rodd, radio officer; Lieutenant James L. Breese, engineering officer and Chief Machinist Mate Eugene S. Rhoads, engineer.[1]

Read, being an experienced navigator, had little trouble plotting a course for Chatham, and the plane appeared off the air station in the early morning of May 9, after taxiing for fourteen hours on its two remaining engines. When it was spotted from the shore the duty boat crew, with Chief Machinist Mate Charles F. Devine in charge, manned the Sea Sled and proceeded to tow the crippled craft to the station's boat dock.[2] There Lieutenant Eaton offered Read the full cooperation of the base and its personnel to do whatever was necessary to get the plane airborne again for Nova Scotia.

Chief Machinist Mate Grover C. Farris, an experienced aviation mechanic stationed at Chatham, was placed in charge of the repair crew that was detailed to assist engineer Breese and mechanic Rhoads.[3] Called in to lend his skill was George Goodspeed, a local resident employed by Bearse's Garage, whose knowledge of engines was unsurpassed in the area.[4]

Above: The NC-4 at the boat house dock for engine repairs in May of 1919. *Photo courtesy of Robert S. Hardy and the Chatham Historical Society.* **Below:** The NC-4 at Chatham on May 13, 1919 waiting to depart for Halifax, Nova Scotia. *Photo from the Author's Collection.*

Above: The first plane to cross the Atlantic Ocean was the Naval flying boat NC-4. She made her successful flight in May of 1919. *Photo courtesy of the National Archives, Washington, D.C.* **Below:** The NC-4 was restored by the Smithsonian Institution. She is on display at the Naval Air Museum in Pensacola, Florida and is open free to the public. *Photo by William P. Quinn, Orleans, Massachusetts.*

Once the faulty units were disassembled, both coincidentally on the same center nacelle, it was determined the rear pusher-type could be refurbished with a complete overhaul while the forward tractor-type was beyond repair and required replacement. Both jobs were completed in four days time despite bad weather, but the repair party was forced to install a less powerful engine as no high-compression models were available in Massachusetts. It would suffice, however, to get the plane to Trepassey where a spare 400 hp Liberty was aboard the naval vessel recently positioned there to aid the mission in any way necessary. During the stopover on the Cape, Lieutenant Commander Read made the most out of the delay by going off the base to shop and to renew old acquaintances in the town. He was no stranger to Chatham having lived up by Mill Pond with his family in younger days while his father served as the local Baptist minister.[5]

With everything fixed, the NC-4 was ready to continue its journey northward but one of the electric starter motors malfunctioned just before take-off and only Rockaway had extras specifically designed for the Nancys. The staging area was contacted by radio and new starters were delivered by a fast twin-engine F-5L flying boat whose pilot had volunteered to make a risky night landing between the unfamiliar sand bars at Chatham.[6]

The F-5L which flew up from Rockaway with the replacement electric starters the NC-4 needed to continue the attempt at making an Atlantic crossing. *Photo from the Author's Collection.*

After these further repairs tested satisfactorily, Read and his crew finally took off for Halifax on May 14 at 9:05 A.M. escorted across Massachusetts Bay by HS-2L's 1850 and 1916. Fortunately he caught up with the other NC's at Trepassey. All three then made the transAtlantic departure two days later but only NC-4 reached Europe allowing the Chatham Naval Air Station to have played a significant part assisting the plane and the men that made the historic flight.

Flying the Baseball Team

An interesting sidelight here is that the NC-4 repairs forced the air station to postpone an inter-service baseball game with Fort Rodman set for Sunday, the 11th of May. There was no alternative but to reschedule it, as several mechanics fixing the big flying boat were also members of the team. The new date agreed upon was May 18. That weekend, to the surprise of all, the Chatham nine flew to the New Bedford harbor fort in several planes making it, in all probability, the first time ever that an entire team traveled by air to play a baseball game.[7] They had apparently established a new first with their 60-mile overwater flight, but there was less to boast about on the field as they lost to the Army 12 to 6.

General Edwards

Also during that week of May 11 a distinguished Army officer, Major General Clarence R. Edwards, made an informal visit to the base while he and his wife were vacationing on the Cape.[8] General Edwards, who had organized the 26th Division in 1917 and then led it through some of the hardest fighting in France, had won the admiration of those who served with him in the trenches. The personnel at Chatham considered it a privilege to welcome such a man and felt honored that he had come to see the operations of a naval air station during his leisure time.

Fatal Crash

The euphoria that was enjoyed by successfully repairing the huge NC-4 quickly changed to a mood of sadness on the morning of May 19. Word circulated that Lieutenant (jg) Charles L. Ostridge (Naval Aviator 231), out on a training flight in HS-2L 1916, had gone into a tailspin at low altitude and then into the sea about 11:00 A.M. one mile from the Orleans Coast Guard Station. In spite of a search which lasted until May 30, Memorial Day, his body was never recovered.

The wreckage of the HS-2L 1916 after being pulled onto the beach near the Orleans Coast Guard Station. The pilot, Lieutenant Ostridge and the observer, Quartermaster 1st class Hartenstein were both killed while Ensign Welch, the assistant pilot, was seriously injured. *Photo courtesy of Robert S. Hardy and the Chatham Historical Society.*

A close-up view of the wreckage of HS-2L 1916 showing the yoke with its dual steering control mechanism. *Photo courtesy of Robert S. Hardy and the Chatham Historical Society.*

On that final day two HS-2L's concluded the effort by dropping flowers on Cape Cod Bay in memory of their missing comrade. Ironically, he had arrived at Chatham only three weeks earlier having previously served at patrol bases in Ireland and at Hampton Roads, Virginia.

Also killed was his mechanic, Herbert Hartenstein, Quartermaster 1st Class, whose remains were located and buried with full military honors in Reading, Pennsylvania. The assistant pilot, Ensign Everett P. Welch (Naval Aviator 997), another recent returnee who had won the *Croix de Guerre* for making a daring sea rescue in the Bay of Biscay, survived but was in serious condition when taken to the base dispensary. He was transferred to Chelsea Naval Hospital where he recovered and continued his aviation career at the Cape May Naval Air Station. The badly wrecked plane drifted ashore the next day two miles south of the Coast Guard Station where, after an investigation, the Liberty engine was salvaged but the rest of the craft was soaked with mineral oil and burned on the beach.[9]

The C-5 Adventure

But the advantage of attempting a high-profiled transAtlantic flight was not limited to those naval officers who flew planes. Back when the NC-flying boats were just being tested at Rockaway, a group of aviators attached to the lighter-than-air detachment at Cape May were quietly making plans of their own. They had experienced a great amount of satisfaction with the performance of the recently developed C-class blimp and felt, after certain modifications, one of these could make the flight across using a Newfoundland-to-Ireland route. The concept was forwarded to the Chief of Naval Operations who approved it, and No. 5 was designated as the one that would make the attempt.

A B-class blimp preparing to enter its hangar. The hangar doors had been slid open and can be seen standing erect on either side of the empty bay. *Photo courtesy of Robert S. Hardy and the Chatham Historical Society.*

The C-5, made by Goodyear, had an envelope of rubberized cotton fabric 192 feet in length with a 43 foot diameter and contained 180,000 cubic feet of hydrogen. The two 120 hp Union engines allowed the C-class blimp an endurance aloft of 47 hours or 2,150 statute miles at a cruising speed of 45 miles per hour. The crew for this special flight numbered six and consisted of Lieutenant Commander Emory W. Coil (Naval Aviator 96) commanding officer and pilot; Lieutenant John B. Lawrence (Naval Aviator 580) assistant pilot; Lieutenant (jg) David P. Campbell (Naval Aviator 1543) coxswain; Ensign Marcus H. Easterly, radio operator plus Chief Machinist Mates T. L. Moorman and H. S. Blackburn, as flight engineers.[10] They flew it safely to Montauk on May 8 for a final fuel top-off and for some minor servicing prior to departure for St. John's, Newfoundland. At 7:00 A.M. on May 14 the C-5 was taken out of her hangar by 300 line-handling sailors and walked to the landing field after a special tuning-up detail worked all night further testing the engines and equipment.[11]

At 8:00 A.M the regular crew in the modified blimp took to the air at Montauk on their 1,200 mile flight to Newfoundland, flying a course which would take them directly over Chatham and Halifax enroute to St. John's. The Chatham Naval Air Station was put on alert to provide emergency assistance if necessary during this part of the flight, but none was needed. The C-5 passed over the air station at 10:10 A.M. at an altitude of 1,000 feet in perfect flying weather.[12] As this was just about one hour after the repaired NC-4 had taken off from Chatham on its way to Halifax, it became apparent that there was now a competition within the Navy itself for the honor of being the first across.

The rest of the C-5's trip was considered routine though winds picked up and were getting tricky at the time of the landing the following morning. At 11:15 A.M. on the 15th, Coil and his men turned the airship over to the navy ground crew sent there on the cruiser *USS Chicago (CA-14)* for that purpose, and the aviators sought some well deserved rest. Coil was

FLY PAPER

Vol. 1.   No. 8.   U. S. NAVAL AIR STATION, CHATHAM, MASS.   Price Five Cents

CHRISTMAS NUMBER A WINNER

Now that the words Fly Paper are on the tip of most everyone's tongue, from Chatham to Frisco, the time has come when the staff can safely undertake to send out a real "Special Number"; and just to show the public that they can do it, out it comes Christmas Eve.

A word of advice to the people who are interested in this paper—don't get left; order now from any of the following dealers: F. J. Quilty, Chatham; Cobb's Drug Store, Chatham; Todd's Grocery, Harwich Centre; Megathelin's, Harwich Port; and at the Station Canteen.

For the first time in the history of this paper, a colored cover will appear, with the most attractive cartoon in colors that you ever saw, then the entire printing will be in special ink, and contain many useful hints for the coming year.

The price of this issue will be 10 cents, and by sending your name and address to the editor, you will receive this number, Christmas Eve. These instructions are for those who are not in reach of the above dealers, and who wish to receive a copy.

ATTENTION, CHATHAM!

Is food cheap or expensive in the city you live in? Government figures show that for a family of five with a $1300 income, Lawrence, Mass., is the most expensive city, food there costing $602 per year. Fall River, Mass., is next, at $599, and New York is third, at $597. The twin cities of Minnesota—Minneapolis and St. Paul —are lowest with $481.

Seems as though the Government has overlooked Chatham, Mass.; but cheer up, they'll get here yet.

HAPPENINGS DURING THE PAST WEEK

Lieut. Lange played football at Ipswich.

Doc. Clarke went to work. Started "jabbing" everybody.

Farris has returned to the ship. None the worse for his trip.

Water system went on the rocks. (Weekly happening).

Ensign Medusky promoted to Rear Admiral. In his own mind.

Dutch Neidlinger promoted to Squadron Commander. (Don't ask what of).

McEvoy reported back from 30 days' leave. Yes, he looks alright.

Lieut. Sheehan, acting Executive Officer, Engineering Officer, and, oh, that's enough, I guess.

Ensign Griffin was the busiest man on the station.

K. OF C. NOTES

Moving pictures will be shown at this building every Sunday, Monday and Thursday evenings in the future, and free articles will be distributed after the pictures each night.

During the past week, Wallace Reid appeared in his new release, "Men, Women and Money," which took the audience by storm. This picture has been the big attraction at many of the large cities, and proved to be likewise at this station.

December player-piano rolls have just arrived, which include all of the new dance and song numbers.

Catholic church party will leave this station next Sunday morning at ten o'clock. Those wishing to attend service will give their names to the secretaries not later than Saturday noon.

The front page of FLY PAPER, the newspaper of the Chatham Naval Air Station, which was published bi-weekly from July of 1919 to the end of the year, and then monthly until May of 1920 when the base was placed in a non-operating status. *Courtesy of Robert S. Hardy and the Chatham Historical Society.*

awakened shortly to learn that the winds had steadily increased, that the C-5 had blown from its mooring in a 60 mile per hour gust, and that it was now on its way out to sea unmanned.[13] Later that day the Liverpool-bound British freighter *War Nigor* radioed she had spotted a deflated gas bag floating on the surface 85 miles east of St. John's.[14] The next morning the *USS Edwards (DD-265)* arrived in the area but failed to locate any wreckage. A dismayed Coil immediately contacted Washington by radio to report the loss of the blimp and then requested that the C-3 be modified as soon as possible to serve as a replacement. He also suggested that the departure point for Ireland be changed to Chatham where there were hangar facilities available with full airship support services.[15] This request was never acted upon as the eyes of the Navy were now focused on the NC-4 which was steadily making her way to England in quest of the record.

FLY PAPER

At about this same time the enlisted men, with full support from their officers, commenced the publishing of a station newspaper under the attention-getting name of "FLY PAPER".[16] Each edition carried news of the base, happenings in the nearby communities, a short story, some humorous articles, and several small display ads solicited from local merchants. The initial officer staff consisted of Howard E. Gamble (Secretary of the Knights of Columbus activities) editor-in-chief; Ensign Leon A. Griffin (Communications Officer) assistant editor; Lieutenant (jg) J. O. Strickland (Executive Officer) business manager; and Ensign John C. Flood advertising manager.[17] The names would change with some frequency as personnel transfers were becoming a common occurrence. The paper was printed every two weeks by Goss Print of Harwich, owners of the Harwich Independent, and could be purchased for 5¢ a copy at the station canteen as well as at the following off-base locations: J. F. Quilty's Soda and Gift Shop (Chatham); Smith's Drug Store (Chatham); The Chatham Community Club; Todd's Grocery Store (Harwich Center); and Megathlin's Store (Harwichport).[18] All proceeds from the sale of the papers, as well as the revenue from the advertising, went toward the enlisted men's welfare fund.

Reserves Want Out

Chatham for some months now had been a naval station without a purpose. Created in war to protect Nantucket Sound and the approaches to Boston Harbor, its purpose was fulfilled as the fighting had ceased and the U-boats had come under Allied control. Since its inception, it had been manned in both the officer and enlisted ranks by a small complement of career personnel, sharing the responsibilities with a large number of reservists on active duty. The typical enlisted reservist, driven by patriotism, had signed up for the required four year period to do his part to bring about the defeat of the Central Powers. He was officially classified as a member of the United States Naval Reserve Force (USNRF),[19] was conscientious in performing his duties and quickly adapted to Navy life much to the surprise of the old-timers. He was the answer to a critical manpower shortage at the start of and during the war. Now the war was over and the enlisted reservist had done his job. He wanted to return to civilian life in spite of the time left in his commitment. He was a temporary sailor who did not feel needed at an air station that had no mission. It was all the more puzzling to him because BuNav Circular Letter No. 212-18, dated November 21, 1918 allowed Class 5 reservists (those attached to the Naval Reserve Flying Corps) as well as certain other categories to be released from active duty upon written

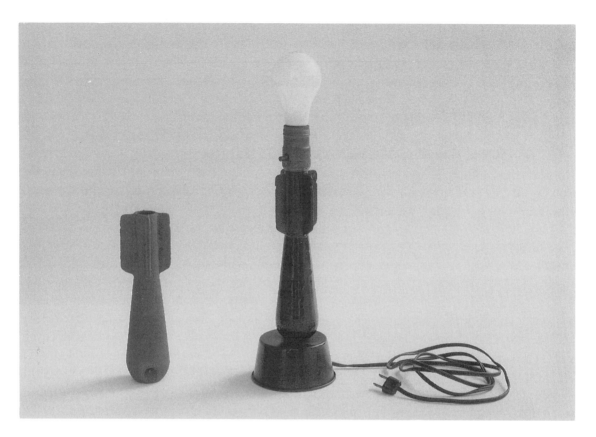

Above: Some of the ``trench art'' created by the men at the Chatham Naval Air Station. A two-pound practice bomb in its original state is on the left while one that has been converted into a table lamp is on the right. **Below:** A souvenir letter opener made from a 30-caliber rifle bullet. One side of the blade is engraved with the outline of an R-9 seaplane while the other contains the words ``U.S. Naval Aviation, Chatham, Mass 1918.'' *Photos from the Author's Collection.*

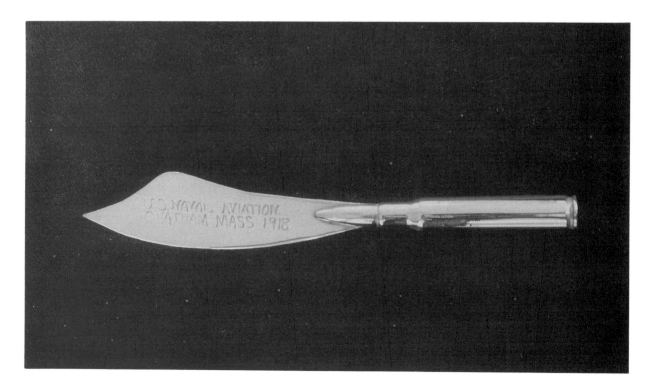

request if they were not considered indispensable.[20] Many had applied but had not received a response because of bureaucratic delays.

As the wait continued, some of the more ambitious took up the popular military pastime of creating pieces of "trench art" - useful household objects fabricated from old military equipment and spent ammunition casings - that were much sought after as souvenirs, and as gifts for loved ones. Items that were known to have been made at Chatham included letter openers from 30-caliber rifle bullets, and table lamps from small two-pound practice bombs.

To add to the frustration at Chatham, the officers mess had been closed in early March following a cost-cutting directive from Washington that shut down those at all the smaller naval stations.[21] This caused several in the commissioned ranks to move to various in-town locations while a dozen others leased the former officers club on the bluff overlooking the base. With their living quarters outside the gate and with little opportunity to fly because several planes were now laid up for economy reasons, reserve pilots had but slight interest in the Navy beyond their hours of duty.

Many that had been in Europe had flown only British, French or Italian planes and had never even seen an HS-flying boat let alone operate one.[22] The majority, once they were back, lacked enthusiasm for further training, and those who did show interest had difficulty scheduling one of the few HS-2L's available. Most officers were anxious for immediate release, but a few did want to stay in the Navy temporarily, just to draw pay until the colleges re-opened in the fall.[23]

A further contribution to feeling disgruntled was the matter of overcrowding at both the officer and enlisted man levels. Once peace arrived, there was pressure on naval authorities to bring home the overseas personnel, especially in aviation which had a high percentage of reservists. Being acutely aware of this, the Secretary of the Navy issued instructions that these men were to be returned as quickly as practical, and that they were to be assigned to the naval air station nearest to their home while awaiting separation.[24]

This meant that the many from Maine, New Hampshire, Vermont, Massachusetts and Rhode Island would come to Chatham which was already over capacity. The overcrowding was due to the fact that the newly built large barracks building could not be occupied for lack of an operational filter bed in the sewer system. Berthing was so strained that at one point in February, 30 officers and 54 enlisted men were quartered at the former Marconi Radio Station, but this proved to be only a short term remedy as the Navy returned the site to the owners on March 31.[25] A further problem occurred in feeding all these newcomers, for naval authorities had now ordered construction of the new mess hall stopped because of a general appropriations cut-back.

These conditions extended into spring and on Monday, May 5, the base was inspected by Captain John J. Hyland of the First Naval District, along with three officers from the Office of Naval Operations; Commander John S. Higgins, Lieutenant Robert H. Lake, and Lieutenant (jg) LeRoy Flint, none of whom were aviators.[26] They found that there were no air operations, that eight planes had been disassembled for the winter and were still in lay-up, that all the officers and some of the men were living off the base, and that Chatham was filled with pilots who could not be utilized. In addition, many of the enlisted men had not been assigned to any specific tasks as there was little happening on the average workday.

New Commanding Officer

Shortly after all the special events of May, a change of command occurred in early June that saw Eaton, now a Lieutenant Commander, replaced for medical reasons by one of the pioneers of naval aviation, Lieutenant Commander Nathan B. Chase (Naval Aviator 37). Chase at one time was in charge of the Bay Shore Naval Air Station on Long Island, the main training facility for reserve flying officers.[27] An Annapolis graduate with a proven leadership ability, he was the right choice for Chatham where a morale and discipline situation was noticeably developing because of post-war demobilization and disorganization. It was a condition that existed throughout the Navy and would be difficult to alter at the local level.

Morale Improves

The solutions to Chatham's problems came out of Washington in the form of two directives which arrived in the latter part of June. The one with the stronger impact mandated that all remaining Class 5 reserve personnel throughout the Navy be released from active duty by July 30, 1919. Each was to be returned to civilian life and placed in either a volunteer reserve or inactive status for the remainder of his enlistment.[28] This instruction effected almost everyone at the air station leaving only 16 officers and 25 enlisted men to operate the entire base. The second directive came at approximately the same time announcing that Chatham was to become a major aviation recruiting center for several weeks and had been picked as the location where all future flight mechanics from the First Naval District would receive their introductory technical training.[29]

The Army and Navy Club of Chatham, the former estate of Mrs. H.E. Jepson. During the war it was owned and operated by local residents to provide a ``home away from home'' for those off-duty servicemen stationed on Cape Cod. *Photo from the Author's Collection.*

The Army and Navy Club

To close out the busy month, the final report of the popular Army and Navy Club of Chatham was noted with proper recognition. It was founded, sponsored, and staffed, by dedicated local citizens to provide a quiet home away from home for servicemen and to give them a comfortable place to relax when off duty. Members from any branch of the armed forces were invited, but the personnel of the air station were the ones most able to benefit from its location and to use the facilities. In October of 1918 the club took a major step forward and obtained a permanent home by purchasing a large estate on Cross Street. It had been owned by Mrs. H. E. Jepson and included extensive well-groomed grounds overlooking the so-called Oyster Pond.[30] It was perfectly suited for the use the new buyers intended, offering writing rooms, rest rooms, and hot baths from 10:00 A.M. to 10:00 P.M. each day, with an evening meal served from 6:00 P.M. to 9:00 P.M.. The club's year-end newsletter indicated over 2000 people signed the guest book in December alone. Over 1400 dinners were served that same month, 130 of them being on Christmas Day when the traditional roast turkey with all the fixings was featured. A month earlier, Thanksgiving had been an equal success with the same meal.[31] Funding came from business subscriptions at $5.00 or more a month, and from other private sources that wanted to show their gratitude to those serving their country.[32] The entire operation was a credit to the community of Chatham.

Appreciation

The servicemen were appreciative of this generosity and, when the opportunity arose, were known to give of themselves in return. One notable occasion happened the night the Chatham Red Cross scheduled a fund raising benefit featuring local entertainment. Listed on the evening's program, along with Joseph C. Lincoln reciting Cape Cod ballads and the auctioning off of a French military poster, was a twenty-sailor chorus from the air station singing a medley of wartime songs. The press reported the songfest was a marked success with the audience enthusiastically joining in, and that the Red Cross treasury had increased by $500 when the final tally was made.[33] Other instances of community involvement included the station's orchestra playing in concerts at the Congregational Church, and the sailors sharing parts with civilians in the locally produced minstrel shows held at the Orpheum Theater.

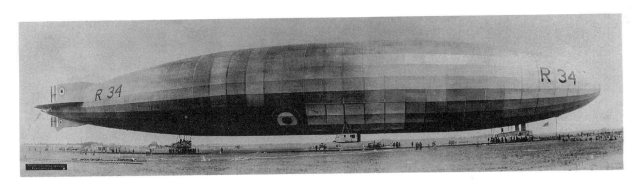

The British dirigible R-34 made the first non-stop transAtlantic flight in July of 1919. Shown here at Mineola, New York, it passed directly over Chatham where the personnel of the Naval Air Station were ready to receive it in case of emergency. *Photo from the Author's Collection.*

The R-34

The United States Navy had not been alone in making preparations to fly the Atlantic using a lighter-than-aircraft. The British were working on similiar plans, but their entry was a huge rigid model with which we had no experience. His Majesty's Airship R-34, as it was designated, was 643 feet long with a diameter of 79 feet and a height of 92 feet. It had a capacity of 1,950,000 cubic feet of hydrogen, and its five 250 hp engines provided a cruising speed of 45 mph. The R-34 was actually an adaptation of the German Zeppelin L-33 captured almost intact in southeastern England, when forced down by a patrol plane during the war.

The objective was to fly from Scotland to Mineola, Long Island and return, thereby setting three records; the first to fly east-to-west, the first to fly east-to-west non-stop, and the first to fly round-trip. The airship departed East Fortune, Scotland July 2, 1919 on a flight plan that would take it across the Atlantic to Newfoundland, then Southwest to Halifax, and over the Chatham and Montauk Naval Air Stations to the Army Air Corps landing field in Mineola. Senior officer on the flight was Brigadier-General Edward Maitland, but the captain of the airship and commanding officer of the crew of thirty was a distinguished wartime blimp pilot, Major George W. Scott. To further support the effort, two British flying officers, Lieutenant Colonel Lucas and Major Fuller, were sent in advance from Great Britain to Long Island with eight experienced airmen to instruct the Americans in the proper techniques of landing such a large craft.[34]

The flight was proceeding in a routine manner, until heavy winds were encountered off the coast of Greenland requiring an increase in the rpm's to maintain course and headway. As the unexpected winds continued, the fuel supply became a concern to the extent that, over Nova Scotia, Major Scott radioed the American authorities the R-34 would now need to land at Montauk. As the airship met further strong headwinds over the Bay of Fundy and along the coast of Maine, he again radioed, this time requesting a vessel be positioned off Cape Cod as a precautionary measure. The Navy's response was to dispatch two destroyers to the Cape area immediately and place Chatham on full alert for a possible emergency landing.[35] Major Fuller, who was in New York awaiting any new developments, drove to Cape Cod prepared to oversee the line handlers at Chatham who were not familiar with mooring a rigid airship of Zeppelin size.[36] The anticipated time for such a landing, if needed, was around dawn on Sunday morning, July 6.

Chatham is Ready

When Chatham received the alert call on Saturday, the duty section was mustered and, although sufficient in size to keep the base in normal peacetime operation, it fell far short of the number of hands needed to line-handle the giant airship that was approaching. In addition, the preceeding day was the Fourth of July, the first celebrated since the war ended, and an unusual number in the off-duty sections had taken advantage of the long weekend to leave the air station.

This part of Cape Cod was a wonderful place to be stationed during the summertime when the world was at peace, and the officers and men knew how to make the most of what it had to offer! There were several inns in Chatham, Orleans, Harwich, and Hyannis for food and drink; dances every night at pavilions in downtown Chatham and at Mill Hill in West Yarmouth; movie theaters with the latest films; tennis courts at the Chatham Community Center; general relaxation at the Army and Navy Club of Chatham; sandy beaches in abundance; and house parties that local residents would organize for the personnel of the station.

The duty officer needed these men back at the base as soon as possible and ordered the shore patrol into the towns to round them up. Liberty was canceled and they were to return to be quickly trained in how to assist with the impending emergency. The area to be searched was extensive, the number of locations many, the time short, and the trucks few; so, outside help was called upon to assist. Local resident Wallace Dexter, who drove the jitney bus for the Chatham

Above: The parking lot in front of the Officers Club as it appeared on a summer's afternoon. *Photo courtesy of Robert S. Hardy and the Chatham Historical Society, Chatham, Massachusetts.* **Below:** Sailors on liberty in downtown Chatham in front of J.F. Quilty's Soda and Gift Shop. Second from left is Dennis W. Buckley, Yeoman 2nd class, father of the author. *Photo from the Author's Collection.*

Bars Inn, was pressed into service along with the vehicle, and he made two trips in the fog-shrouded night delivering more potential line-handlers, the last few stragglers being brought to the base about 2:00 A.M. Sunday morning.[37] The morning wore on and the air station was ready, but a slackening of the winds allowed the R-34 enough additional fuel to pass overhead and continue on to Mineola without stopping at Montauk either. Eventually, all three records which were sought were achieved as the airship arrived back in the British Isles on July 13, 1919 to complete the round-trip attempt. Back at Chatham, the emergency never happened so the interrupted liberty was reinstated, and the base returned to normal operation.

Presentation at Gloucester

Chatham was not the only place in Massachusetts celebrating the long Fourth of July weekend in a somewhat unusual manner. The city of Gloucester was holding a holiday parade which featured the hull of the famed HS-1L 1695, flown by Eric Lingard. It was the first aircraft ever to defend American shores from direct enemy attack

Lingard was a native son and the people were using the parade as a way of honoring his memory, while at the same time, displaying the historical relic they had obtained to place atop a permanent monument yet to be built in Stage Fort Park. The city had petitioned the Navy Department for the hull of the plane once the war was over, and this had recently been approved by Secretary of the Navy Daniels. It was just the wooden hull that was requested as the fabric-covered wings, rudder and tail assembly could not feasibly be included in any outdoor memorial.[38]

Delivery was made by the submarine chaser *SC-268*, which towed the stripped down flying boat from Chatham and turned it over to the city with appropriate ceremonies on July 3, 1919.[39] Included in the program was the re-reading of a letter Franklin D. Roosevelt, Assistant Secretary of the Navy, had written to Lingard's next of kin, his sister Olga, saying in part that Eric had "lived up to the best traditions of the Navy and I cannot speak too highly of his gallant work." When the presentation was completed, Ensign A. M. Pride, who had piloted HS-2L 2238 to Gloucester as a part of the special weekend events, put on an air show starting at 3:00 P.M. For one hour he thrilled the spectators with his turns, banks, and low altitude flying which the Gloucester Daily Times described as "spectacular".[40] The next day the hull of 1695 was taken out of the water, placed on a flatbed truck, and driven in the local Fourth of July parade as the feature attraction, while 2238 and a new arrival from Chatham, 2241, flew in tribute overhead.[41] Ironically, the monument was never erected, and the whereabouts of the hull is unknown.

Lieutenant Baylies

When the two planes were at Gloucester, two others were over New Bedford paying homage to another fallen airman. An elaborate celebration was being held there also, and one of the events was to honor Lieutenant Frank L. Baylies, its most noted war veteran. Baylies was a local boy who volunteered to fly for France and was assigned to Escadrille Spa. 3, a French fighter squadron. Before he was killed on June 17, 1918 in combat over Germany, he had received credit for downing twelve of the enemy, with eight more probables, making him one of the leading aces of the Allies.[42]

Above: The hull of the HS-1L 1695, Ensign Eric Lingard's plane in Gloucester Harbor on July 3, 1919 after being towed there from Chatham. The next day, as instructed by the Secretary of the Navy, it was presented to the City as a war memorial. **Below:** Upon receiving the hull of HS-1L 1695, the City placed it on a truck and made it the featured attraction in the annual Fourth of July parade. *Photos courtesy of the Cape Ann Historical Society.*

New Bedford had selected noontime to hold the dedication ceremony naming the intersection of Acushnet Avenue, Belleville Road and North Front Street "Baylies Square", as a permanent tribute to their international aviator. The holiday planning committee, feeling that planes should be included, had earlier invited the naval air station to participate; so, exactly at twelve o'clock, as had been planned, two flying boats appeared over the city. Then one of them turned and came flying in low over the dedication spot showering roses on both the dignitaries and the crowd gathered for the occasion. The other stayed well above and commenced circling off to one side "as though guarding the skies against any aerial intrusion on the proceedings below". Mayor Ashley waited until the two planes had once again formed up and flown off in the direction of Cape Cod before beginning to speak, as everyone's attention was in the air while they were visible.[43]

The Chatham Naval Air Station after a light snowfall. *Photo from the Author's Collection.*

Above: Part of the ground crew that maintained the planes at the Chatham Naval Air Station. **Below:** The motor testing shed showing two sailors examining an engine which is mounted on the test block. *Photos courtesy of Robert S. Hardy and the Chatham Historical Society.*

Above: A B-class blimp assisted in the early phase of the 1919 summer recruiting effort which was focused on the near-by cities and towns. Sign above the gondola reads ``Wanted Blimpers – Join the U.S. Navy.'' *Photo courtesy of Robert S. Hardy and the Chatham Historical Society.* **Below:** A rare panoramic aerial view of the Chatham Naval Air Station showing a tethered kite balloon aloft over the landing field on observation duty. *Photo from the Author's Collection.*

Chapter Eight

Recruiting Around New England

Once the decision was announced about the recruiting function, additional career men were transferred in. The recruiting campaign opened with Lieutenant W. G. Green, from the Bureau of Navigation in Washington, and twelve others planning a six week program to cover many cities of New England.[1] Three flying boats, flown by Lieutenant Frank L. Burk (Naval Aviator 481), Ensign Pride, and Lieutenant (jg) Hudson were to be the featured attraction. These men were good choices for the assignment. Each had trained and qualified at least fifty other pilots, and the three averaged more than 800 hours of flight time. Other flight crew members included Chief Machinist Mates Harry Rogers, Charles Milford, Percy Ford, and Grover Farris in addition to Chief Quartermasters Allen Donnelly and William Donnelly. In case of need, Warrant Gunner William L. Shields (Naval Aviator 2695) was designated as an alternate or stand-by pilot.[2]

Green was in charge of the enlistment aspect while Burk, as flight commander, had responsibility for the aircraft and all matters related to flying. The First Naval District had offered the two lieutenants the *USS Edwards (DD-265)* as a mother ship, to accompany them to those ports some distance from the air station where the planes planned to remain overnight.[3] It would carry spare parts, a back-up fuel supply, and extra recruiting materials, while providing the necessary sleeping quarters and meals for the officers and men of the air group. The *Edwards* seemed the perfect solution but, once the itinerary was finalized, a review of the hydrographic charts determined that several harbors on the schedule were either too confined or too shallow to accommodate a destroyer. To overcome this the District added a 110' submarine chaser, the *SC-315*, as a second support vessel to assist at those places where the depth of the water or the lack of turning space was thought to be an issue.

Recruiting Plan

The recruiting plan that evolved was ambitious, covering initially many of the smaller Massachusetts coastal cities as well as some selected seaside towns. Then it would branch out with the planes making flights and stop-overs, hopefully, up three of the largest rivers of New England: the Connecticut, the Merrimack, and the Penobscot, one at a time and in that order. The actual visits would be preceded by the arrival of the advance team riding in two of the air station's automobiles, with Chief Machinist Mate Edward R. "Dynamite" Faxon, an enthusiastic fourteen year veteran, in charge of the detachment and at the wheel of "Lizzie", the lead vehicle. He was to be accompanied by John Adair, Electrician 2nd Class, who would handle any electrical problems that might develop, and by Russell E. Holcombe, Quartermaster 1st Class, who would tend to the pigeons that each plane was to carry.[4]

The Start

To get it all started, a B-class blimp left Chatham on July 24, at 10:15 A.M. on a direct course for Boston but was forced to go inland via Plymouth because of fog in the bay. Proceeding up the coast, it was spotted at noon following the ship channel into Boston Harbor at a relatively low speed and altitude. As it approached the navy yard the pilot turned and flew over the State House, the Common, and the Public Gardens, while the crew began releasing thousands of recruiting circulars that landed throughout the city.

Yeoman 2nd Class Dennis W. Buckley shown in the flying togs worn by enlisted men who were in the forward gunner/observer cockpit. Buckley had just completed a ``hop'' in HS-2L No. 1850 piloted that day by Ensign John C. Flood. *Photo from the Author's Collection.*

At one point the blimp descended to tree-top level causing many to believe it was going to land, but others feared it was having engine problems and was about to crash.[5] These fears were attributed to a sensational news story running in all the papers about an aviation tragedy in downtown Chicago. There, three days earlier, a blimp, owned by the Goodyear Company, caught fire above the Illinois Trust and Saving Bank and went completely out of control. The plunging car fell through the building's skylight pulling the flaming envelope into the counting room, where twelve people were killed and twenty-three others were injured.[6] At Boston however, the low altitude over the Common was just to gain attention for the recruiting effort, as the blimp soon rose above Beacon Hill then swung in a great arc to head back to Chatham via Castle Island and the bay route.

In the Cape Cod Area

The first seaplane phase commenced on Monday, July 28th, and featured locations close to Cape Cod starting with New Bedford, then to Woods Hole/Falmouth, Oak Bluffs, Hyannis and Plymouth before returning to Chatham late Thursday afternoon July 31st.

The New Bedford appearance started off in almost textbook fashion with the weather being perfect, the aircraft performing flawlessly, and the spectators lining the shoreline. The three planes landed in the morning on the calm waters of Clarks Cove, taxied to the foot of County Street, and anchored out just far enough to avoid being left high and dry when the tide receded. Once on the beach the aviators posed for pictures and responded to questions all day long, including one asked by Mayor Ashley who came to extend the hospitality of the city and his best wishes to the group.[7]

About 30 minutes later the three took off to attract still more attention with repeated formation fly-overs, though one of the planes developed engine trouble as it was leaving the water and had to return. The other two continued with the mission and dropped recruiting literature supposedly on downtown New Bedford, but they were flying so fast most of the circulars ended up in either the Acushnet River or in neighboring Fairhaven.

The three pilots involved in this first recruiting effort were Lieutenant Burk, Ensign Pride, and Warrant Gunner Shields. The circulars, or leaflets, that they dropped and would be dropping on cities throughout the entire enlistment campaign read as follows:

> "Now is the time to get in on the ground floor of naval aviation and become an expert mechanic; big opportunities for reserves on inactive duty and ex-service men that have had no previous experience; good pay, good food, fine quarters, and plenty of recreation. For further information apply to the recruiting officer at the U. S. Naval Air Station, Chatham. Uncle Sam is the best boss in the world."[8]

That night both Green and Burk were overnight guests of the fire chief at the central fire station, while the rest of the detachment checked into the nearby Parker House. None had to stay with the planes as an around-the-clock watch was provided by the local police to allow the naval personnel to relax and enjoy the evening.

At 1:00 P.M. the next afternoon the aviators took off from their anchorage, flew over the Times Building, then circled the city before heading on to Falmouth about 20 minutes away. They departed with the satisfaction of signing up twelve men for induction physicals and with the knowledge that a good impression had been made on many, especially on the two young boys who were invited to sit in the cockpit of HS-1L 1189 while it was at anchor.[9] When over Falmouth they dropped leaflets into the wind, but the planes did not land as a bad weather forecast forced their return to Chatham.

The editorial in the July 30 New Bedford Times provides an excellent commentary on the two day event:

> ``The recent visit of three navy seaplanes to this city, held considerable interest for young and old. They provided, in fact, about the best opportunity the "stay-at-homes" in this city have had for viewing seaplanes at close quarters. The sight was nothing new for the men who have been in the army and navy, nor for those who have had the opportunity to travel to any extent since the beginning of the war. But for the majority of citizens, who have not been able to get away from the grind now these many months, it was a distinctly novel treat. The object of the visit was to recruit volunteers for the naval air service, and in that they were fairly successful, signing up 12 men. As a matter of fact, however, the visit would not have been in vain if not a single recruit had been secured, for the educational value of the visit was great, and there are more people talking intimately of airplanes and seaplanes in New Bedford today than ever there have been before. And awakened interest means greater sympathy and support for the government's present and future air policy."

However, not all of the planned visits involving these fragile aircraft went smoothly as mechanical failure, inclement weather, or communication problems would on occasion cause unexpected alterations to their daily operating plans. The stop at Plymouth on July 31 showed how frustrations could develop when the timetable, which had to be released in advance to be effective, could not be followed. The Old Colony Memorial reported on this in their August 1 edition:

> "Announcements written in blue pencil on the reverse side of some printed cards were tacked up about town yesterday morning and announced that three seaplanes would arrive during the forenoon in the interests of a recruiting drive for the U. S. Navy. An outlook was kept on the waterfront by interested ones and up to noon the familiar buzz of the motors was not heard. The man in charge of the advertising end of the scheme told some later that the planes would be here at 1:00 P.M. and the watchers remained on post. It was about 2:30 P.M. that the whizzing of exhausts was heard and two planes showed up over the town circling about and eventually taking to the water as easily as a gull alights, off the foot of Brewster Street, where a comparatively large gathering looked them over."

Confusion also accompanied the visit to Hyannis where the planes landed at Hyannis Park rather than at the foot of Ocean Street as had been announced and remained for only about 20 minutes, while at Falmouth we know they didn't land at all, and the leaflets that were dropped fell into the harbor.[10] It was becoming apparent that improvements had to be made in both the planning and the carrying out of the program at each stop, and that an enthusiastic press was needed to make the effort fully effective.

Upon their return to the air station on July 31, a critique was held of the first four days and from that session came, among other changes, agreement to add additional flying activity during the visits to make them more exciting for the public. On their first few stops the planes had simply landed and taxied to a sheltered cove or beach, where they remained on exhibition while the recruiters mingled with the crowd stimulating interest. Henceforth, the advance party would extend an invitation to each mayor to take a flight over his city and, if he accepted, the local newspaper would be notified before he went up so reporters could be present. What a mayor did was always news, but a mayor in a naval flying suit complete with goggles was rather unique, and in all probability, would get special coverage. It was felt everyone should benefit: the mayor with his attention-getting publicity, naval aviation with more extensive press write-ups, and the paper by selling more copies.

In addition to the mayor, all those men signing up at each stop would be given a 30-minute flight. Homing pigeons would be released as well, not only to interest the crowd but to carry a message back to Chatham of the day's results. Lieutenant Green would no longer accompany the team, but would remain behind to receive the recruits as they reported for indoctrination. Further, Chief Pharmacist Mate Eugene H. Winston would be added to the advance party to give induction physicals on the spot, eliminating in the future the time-consuming trip to Boston for the enlistee. It was also decided to create attractive recruiting posters for Chief Faxon and his men to post in all government offices and municipal buildings upon their arrival at each new location.

The Practice Squadron

The next day, Friday August 1, the advance party led by Chief Faxon driving "Lizzie" left the base early in the morning for Salem, with the planes due to be there about 2:00 P.M. The men arrived in ample time to set up a recruiting display at the post office, to meet the mayor, and then to convince him to see Salem from a cockpit.[11] Meanwhile, the aircraft, which had been instructed by the First Naval District to temporarily depart from their recruiting effort, went that morning to Provincetown to greet the ships assigned to the summer cruise of the Naval Academy. The "Practice Squadron", as it was called, consisted of the flagship USS Wisconsin accompanied by the USS Maine, the USS Alabama, the USS Illinois, the USS Kentucky, and the USS Kearsarge. They recently had been operating in New England waters and were making Provincetown one of their ports-of-call for the first time in several years. The planes, adhering to orders, repeatedly flew over the ships as they steamed in to anchor, while the 1200 midshipmen on board eagerly watched the turns, spirals, and formations being executed above. Flying with them for this special event and attracting attention in its own way was one of the B-class blimps from the air station which came in low and seemed to hover just above the housetops of the village. The welcome for these officers-to-be was also their introduction to the excitement of naval aviation performing at its best.

In addition to the sailors, the townsfolk were thrilled with the aerial display, and the shore was lined with people from all walks of life including members of the famous art colony and the local fishermen who were at that time on strike. Even the daily steamer from Boston blew its whistle as it approached the harbor after the naval vessels were securely at anchor.[12] The planes then left for Salem in fog, came out of it off the Brant Rock section of Marshfield, enjoyed a routine trip the rest of the way, and reached there as planned at 2:00 P.M.

On the North Shore

After flying over the city and performing some basic maneuvers, the pilots landed just off the pier at Salem Willows where Mayor Sullivan, dressed in a flying suit, was conveyed by boat to HS-2L 2238. All three planes took off, formed up at an altitude of 2600 feet and passed over the area several times with the other two serving as honor guard escorts. Ensign Pride, the pilot of 2238, then flew the mayor over Marblehead and Beverly before landing at the Jubilee Yacht Club in Beverly harbor where they anchored for the night. Mayor Sullivan motored back home upon debarking.[13]

At noon on Saturday Beverly's Mayor McPherson, who had also agreed to a flight, was taken above Beverly, Salem and Danvers by Ensign Pride, this time at the controls of HS-1L 1189.[14] Pride was not only an experienced pilot, but he had been to these cities before and had a good knowledge of the North Shore landscape. He could easily identify for each passenger, sitting in the assistant pilot's seat, the many buildings and other places of interest which made it an even more memorable experience.

At the conclusion of Mayor McPherson's half hour adventure, the aviators concentrated on recruiting, flying around both cities, then heading to the Lynn-Swampscott area with Lieutenant Burk in the lead. Burk was a native of Swampscott so automobiles were lined up on the roads for miles and people by the thousands had flocked to the water's edge to watch for the local man to appear. The planes landed in the Blaney Beach section of the harbor and the pilots, upon coming ashore, talked at length about naval aviation, answered questions asked by the

Above: A rare elongated postcard photo showing the arrival of the Chatham-based flying boats at the Blaney Beach section of Swampscott, Massachusetts on Saturday, August 2, 1919. *Photo from the Author's Collection.* **Below:** The planes on their recruiting mission to Swampscott attracted large crowds as the flight leader, Lieutenant Frank L. Burk, was a native of that town. *Photo courtesy of the Swampscott Historical Commission.*

curious, and handed out literature. Later, Pride and Warrant Gunner Shields, who flew HS-2L 1915 this trip, returned to Beverly while Burk remained behind to attend a reception in his honor at the Swampscott Club.[15] After spending the night at home with his parents, he took off Sunday morning to join the others but first gave an exciting solo performance at low altitude for the ones who had turned out early to wave good-by. Once together again at the Jubilee Boat House, the three planes left for Chatham arriving at mid-afternoon on August 3 to quite a reception, as Sunday visiting hours for family and friends were being held as usual at the air station at the time of arrival.[16]

Soon after their return they learned that blimps would no longer participate, even on a limited basis. With the reduced number of lighter-than-air men and line handlers available, orders had been received to deflate both B-18 and B-19 for local storage. Their envelopes were to be packed away in cases, while their motors were to be coated with grease until further notice.

As for the results of the recruiting effort, by the end of the first week seven men had already reported and had commenced their enlistments. These included three from Salem, two of the twelve from New Bedford and one each from Worcester and Washington, D.C. who just happened to be in the area and liked what they heard being offered.

In Connecticut

Monday morning, August 4, the various components of the recruiting team left for New London, Connecticut to commence phase two of their operation. The three planes, this time piloted by Ensign Pride, Gunner Shields and Lieutenant (jg) Hudson, landed near the mouth of the Thames River and came to rest in New London harbor at the Naval Experimental Station adjacent to Fort Trumbull. The two support ships, accompanying the group for the first time, dropped anchor shortly afterwards while the advance party was already scouting out enlistment prospects in the downtown section. Lieutenant Burk arrived by train later in the day and replaced Gunner Shields as the assigned pilot for the remainder of the trip.[17]

The following morning a lingering fog prevented any flying but, by noon, all three were able to get airborne and perform, not only over the city, but over Norwich as well. In between stunts they dropped many recruiting leaflets on both municipalities which were eagerly scrambled for as souvenirs by people of all ages. The next day the flight went down the coast to Saybrook, then turned inland and followed the Connecticut River to Middletown where the planes landed at the Middletown Yacht Club in mid-afternoon, just as the weather was becoming unsettled. Thursday at 10:00 A.M. was the time for Mayor McDowell of Middletown to go aloft and Lieutenant (jg) Hudson, piloting 2241, took His Honor for an extended overview of the river. First, they flew up as far as Cromwell, then reversed course and went south to East Haddam before returning to the yacht club 25 minutes later.[18] After enlisting ten recruits, the aircraft left for the state capital in the early afternoon arriving at the Hartford Yacht Club about 3:00 P.M. No further activity occurred as weather conditions were now deteriorating.

Friday, the planes went up and circled the city dropping more literature, then commenced doing aerobatics and various types of formation flying to attract even more attention. At 2:00 P.M. Hartford's live wire executive, Mayor Richard J. Kinsella, having agreed to go up in 1189 with Ensign Pride, appeared at the dock carrying a small American flag, a signal buoy and an insurance policy. Being mayor of the city known as the Insurance Capitol, he had purchased a $5,000 aviation accident policy of one day's duration from the Travelers Insurance Company for $5.00 to help publicize this new type of coverage just being developed. It protected him against "loss of life, limb, sight and time" caused by any flying mishap and was only the fifth such policy issued by that company.

The small flag was for waving to the people below, but at a certain point he was going to attach it to the signal buoy and drop the whole device from his cockpit, sending a message to the citizens of Hartford. The message on the buoy contained greetings to his constituents and a prophecy that Ireland would soon become an independent country, free of the Crown. It read as follows:[19]

> August 8, 1919.
>
> To the People of Hartford:--
>
> I am sending this message from the clouds in care of the greatest flag in the world, representing the greatest country in the world.
>
> I can see Ireland in the distance, a free people governed by a free republican form of government.
>
> Yours truly,
>
> (Signed) Richard J. Kinsella
> Mayor of Hartford, Conn.

The actual start of the mayor's flight was delayed somewhat when high winds began to blow across the river causing 1189 to drag its anchor and to strike a barge at the opposite shore slightly damaging the plane's rudder. However, temporary repairs were completed quickly, and soon they were off the water. They flew north as far as Wilson's Station, then over East Hartford, turned south along Wethersfield Avenue to Colt Park, and finally circled high above the capitol building before returning. Mayor Kinsella had intended to drop his message near the center of the city, but in throwing it, the box caught in a wing brace. He reached over the side of the plane and retrieved it, then made a second attempt which cleared the plane and, though it was never reported as being found, probably landed in the vicinity of Colt Park.[20]

The HS-2L 2238 seen burning after it crashed into the Connecticut River in Holyoke while on a recruiting flight, August 9, 1919. *Photo courtesy of the Holyoke Public Library.*

Above: An official U.S. Navy photograph dated 1918 showing Liberty aircraft engines being assembled at the Packard Motor Company factory in Detroit. *Photo from the Author's Collection.* **Below:** The Liberty engine of the HS-2L 2238 on the top deck of a river ferry after being recovered from a river depth of fourteen feet on August 10, 1919 opposite the Holyoke Ice House. *Photo courtesy of the Holyoke Public Library.*

The trip ended without incident, and the mayor had been up for about half an hour. In the afternoon all three flying boats again "bombed" the city with leaflets and did more formation flying before heading off to a nearby Army installation, where they threw Navy enlistment circulars to the soldiers as a joke. The aviators, who had signed up another ten men, left Hartford Saturday morning for a flight further up the river into Massachusetts, as they were scheduled to be the featured attraction at the Holyoke Canoe Club's annual Water Carnival.

Western Massachusetts

The three planes made their landings at Holyoke about 12:30 P.M. in the vicinity of Prospect Park, while thousands of people watched from both sides of the river as well as from motorboats, rowboats and canoes. Once the planes began to anchor at the "island", just above the South Hadley Falls dam, several hundred spectators rushed down off the bluff and across the railroad tracks for a better view, forcing the trains to proceed at a mere crawl.

Later, at showtime, only 1189 and 2238 were operable; so Lieutenant Burk and Ensign Pride flew without 2241 to the Canoe Club at the Smith's Ferry section of the river to start the usual stunts and maneuvers. The huge crowd was thrilled with the performance but, unbeknownst to anyone, the real drama was yet to come. Returning to its anchorage above the dam about 5:00 P.M., Pride's plane, 2238, went into a tailspin at 400 feet in the midst of a left spiral turn near the Holyoke Ice House. It fell like an arrow and buried its nose section in the water, while Pride and his assistant pilot, Chief Machinist Mate Charles Milford, climbed out on the wing and then to the tail. In the crash the gravity fuel tank was pushed into the hot engine causing the wreck to burst into flames. Both men, fearing an explosion, continually ordered all craft which came to their rescue to keep away. Once the fire had subsided, they were taken ashore by a rowboat where Milford was treated for lacerations and Pride was found to be uninjured.[21]

All the excitement on the river was not over though, for spectators came in boats and canoes with knives and axes to chop away parts of the wooden framework as souvenirs. As this was going on some gasoline in the water re-ignited frightening two young boys who, in panic, jumped out of their boat just above the dam but were quickly pulled out of danger. The next day the Liberty engine was recovered from fourteen feet of water using a chain fall on an overhead beam that straddled two wooden rafts. It was then lowered onto the top deck of a small river ferry and brought dockside where a flatbed wagon, drawn by horses, delivered it to a local repair garage.[22] There the engine was carefully packed for shipment under the supervision of Ensign Pride and Chief Milford who had returned to duty and would accompany it back to Chatham. Once again ten recruits signed up for the Navy but, this time, only four selected aviation!

The schedule listed a performance for early Saturday evening and another after dark over Riverside Park in Agawam; so, Burk, seeing that his men were not hurt, flew down in 1189 from Holyoke to fulfill the commitment as best as one plane could. He came roaring over the crowd at a low altitude and thrilled all 15,000 on-lookers by his solo exhibition, culminating in a "reverse controlled bank" with the wings almost perpendicular to the ground. He then leveled off for a perfect landing and glided to a stop near the steamboat wharf. The night performance featuring powerful searchlights for the illumination of the air activity was canceled, as Burk had noticed smoke occasionally emitting from his motor and wanted it checked out as a precaution.[23] Sunday morning he was joined by Lieutenant (jg) Hudson in 2241 which had been having its own power plant overhauled at Holyoke and had not flown since arriving on Friday. The two

As the Chatham flying boats made their way up the Connecticut River into Western Massachusetts, overnight lodging for the men was arranged at convenient locations along the riverbank. The photo above is the Holyoke Canoe Club where the men stayed while at the 1919 Holyoke Water Carnival. The photo below is the Springfield Yacht Club which served as their headquarters when they were recruiting in that city. *Photos from the Author's Collection.*

then made additional passes over the park dropping literature and concluded with a bombing demonstration on targets placed in the river. They moored for the night at Riverside and left for Springfield Monday morning where they used the Springfield Yacht Club as their new base of operations.

Shortly after arriving, the planes performed their leaflet drop. Then Burk flew back to Holyoke to help with transportation arrangements for the recovered engine. Hudson, in 2241, made only one local trip in the afternoon carrying a professional photographer aloft to take air views of downtown State Street, the municipal buildings, and the library. When Burk returned, both officers agreed all further flying would be canceled as fuel was getting low and the local supply was limited. Despite being abbreviated, the Springfield stop was encouraging as a great many would-be recruits applied for enlistment, but several were turned down for physical condition or age. Eight had met the qualifications and were sent to Chatham to begin their tour of duty.[24]

Back to Chatham

The planes started Tuesday on their return home, stopping first at Hartford for gasoline. After filling their tanks, the log of the lead plane showed they departed at 1:34 P.M. and were over Wethersfield at 1:39; Rocky Point at 1:44; Middletown at 1:55; Higganum at 1:57; East Haddam at 2:03; Deep River at 2:07, and at 2:16 landed at Saybrook. They stayed at the mouth of the Connecticut River for only 20 minutes then took off in the direction of Cape Cod. The support vessels, which had never left New London, returned to Boston.[25]

Up the Merrimack

On the afternoon of August 19, after a full week of diversion for the men, the planes were once again in the air now headed north to Newburyport at the mouth of the Merrimack River. The third phase of the recruiting plan had begun and this time it was Lieutenant Burk, Lieutenant (jg) Hudson, and Ensign Flood in the pilot seats. Leaving Chatham about noon, all three experienced turbulence in the upper air and fog at sea level which doubled the usual flying time of the 120 mile flight to 2 hours and 10 minutes. With no let-up in weather conditions, publicity flyovers were impossible and, consequently, the aviators recruited for the rest of the day on the riverbank with their planes as a backdrop. All stayed overnight at the American Yacht Club.

In the sunshine of Wednesday morning the three took off at 10:15 A.M., performing spirals and glides for those who had already jammed the waterfront, then showered the area with leaflets as had been expected. Upon completing this, Burk flew to Haverhill to identify a future landing sight, while Hudson and Flood staged air shows over Salisbury and Plum Island for the crowds on the beaches. The three soon regrouped over the river and headed for Haverhill where they made several "bombing runs" and came down at the rear of the post office, the place that had been selected. The other pilots were made aware of the exact landing location by a member of the advance party who, anchored at the spot in a motorboat, waved a large red flag on a stick to be easily seen from above.[26]

When landing, the last plane touched down with such an impact that it cracked its hull forcing the pilot to beach on the Bradford side of the river to avert sinking. Examination showed the required repairs were beyond the capabilities of those present; thus, Chief Carpenters Mate Albert L. Buzzell and Quartermaster 1st Class Charles W. Frank were dispatched from Chatham with their tools and a supply of special replacement wood. Local assistance was also obtained, and no flights were made on the 21st as all hands were required to move the damaged craft onto land. The following day it rained. Five recruits had enlisted at Haverhill before the two operable aircraft left early on the 23rd for Lawrence, the next port of call along the Merrimack. The other, once repaired, was ordered back to Chatham.[27]

The Curtiss HS-2L flying boat 2241 anchored just off the beach with Strong Island in the background. *Photo courtesy of Robert S. Hardy and the Chatham Historical Society.*

Upon greeting Lawrence with a bombing show about 10:30 A.M. Saturday morning, they landed on the river off McFarlin Court. After lunch several more flights were made including one over O'Sullivan Park where, that afternoon, the New England welterweight title fight was being held in a ring set up at the ball field. The match was billed as Army versus Navy and pitted a Lawrence native, Tommy "Kloby" Corcoran against Eddie Shevlin of Roxbury. Corcoran was the champion of the 26th Division in that weight class, while Shevlin was the same for the First Naval District.

The flight over the outdoor ring occurred before the main event began, but the grandstand, bleachers, and playing field were filled with 12,000 spectators waiting for the opening bell. Corcoran knocked out Shevlin in the ninth round, and not only won the title, but also a ride in an HS-flying boat which he thoroughly enjoyed "even though it was a Navy plane".[28] Recruiting and flights continued at Lawrence until their departure for Lowell on Tuesday, August 26.

Living inland, far up the Merrimack, the residents of Lowell had never expected to see anti-submarine patrol planes fly overhead, let alone have them land in the downtown section of the river. It all came true though on the 26th at 2:00 P.M. when the HS-2's circled several times, then gently set down to moor near the Pawtucket Boat House above the dam. It was standard practice at these river cities where a man-made dam existed to land well above it, as such a barrier always created an artificial lake providing calm water and ample room to maneuver on the surface.

The Lowell Sun described the arrival and the excitement of the people with these words on page one which was typical of the exuberance the press had shown at all the stops along the Merrimack:

> "The big feature of the visit of two seaplanes to Lowell this afternoon and their subsequent landing on the Merrimack river just above the Pawtucket dam was not the flight itself, but the pell-mell, headlong attempt of several hundred children and grown-ups to cover the distance between Merrimack Street and the falls in nothing flat. It was a wild race and slow moving pedestrians never had a chance before this human avalanche of expectant sight-seers. But if the sidewalks were turned into cinder paths, the street pavements were racing ovals. The Grand Prix paled in comparison to the honking array of automobiles which fought for the pole in the thrilling race to the landing grounds. No big conflagration, accident or circus parade had caused such a spontaneous outpouring of children and they legged it to the river as if their very lives depended upon getting somewhere in the least possible time. The flight itself was a distinct novelty to thousands of the city people who were drawn from houses, shops and stores as the big bombers sailed overhead. The roar of the 12-cylinder Liberty motors was first heard over the down town section at 2:00 o'clock. The pilots drove their ships in wide circles over the city three times and as the clouds were hanging low, flew at an altitude of about 400 feet. Their wide, gray wings were like clusters of brilliants as the sun occasionally flashed on the canvas and the entire exhibition was perfect."[29]

On Wednesday, the 27th, one of the two developed a broken gas line, and Burk was forced into another solo performance in order to complete the leaflet drops scheduled for the morning. At 12:00 noon Mayor Thompson suited up on the dock and acknowledged the cheers of the crowd as he took his seat next to Burk, anxious to get his flight in before the weather changed. Affixing their goggles they took off over the new Pawtucket bridge and followed the river as far as the Vesper Country Club, skirted the city, and eventually crossed from the Centralville section back to the starting point. His flight lasted only 15 minutes because of the clouds approaching in the distance. Fortunately, the rains held off for a short while allowing Chief Faxon to escort the Mayor to his next stop, the steps of the Sun Building, to release a pigeon. The mayor wrote a thank-you note to the Commanding Officer at Chatham for sending the planes, then watched the feathery messenger soar away to deliver it.[30] By the next day the broken gas line of the second plane was fixed, so both left at 12:45 P.M. flying back to Newburyport and, upon reaching that town, turned northeast toward Rockland, Maine. This was a deviation from the original schedule and was brought about by the intervention of Assistant Secretary of the Navy Roosevelt. It did not involve recruiting.

The previous week a major corporate move had occurred in the fishing industry, whereby the huge East Coast Fisheries of New York absorbed the Rockland based Great Eastern Fisheries and its neighbor, the Lawrence Canning Company. East Coast then indicated it would consolidate its operations to make Rockland the major northeastern processing center and create as many as 500 new jobs for the area. It also announced a modern steam trawler fleet would be homeported locally, and that this would lead to the construction of a huge $2 million ice manufacturing and refrigeration plant on the waterfront. The city fathers were ecstatic, and a holiday was planned to coincide with the arrival of the first steam trawler which was due on August 28.[31]

Congressman Case, whose district included Rockland, wanted to make this occasion a most memorable one, so he wired his friend, Franklin Roosevelt, asking if a naval escort could be provided to accompany the first trawler into the harbor. What he was hoping for was one of the small Navy patrol ships stationed at Machias, but what he got was beyond his expectations. The reply to his telegram request is quoted herewith from the Rockland Courier-Gazette of August 26, 1919:

> Washington, D.C.   August 22
>
> To Congressman William W. Case - Rockland, Maine
>
> "Replying to your telegram of August 21st. The
> Commandant of the First Naval District has been
> authorized to direct seaplanes to participate in
> celebration of August 28th, if practical."
>
>   Roosevelt

The Chatham flying boats arrived over Rockland at 3:15 P.M., soon after the new 160' steam trawler, *Pelican*, had tied up at Tillson Wharf from her maiden voyage. On board were 200,000 pounds of haddock and cod, the largest catch ever brought into that port. The planes, 1189 piloted by Lieutenant Burk and 1915 with Ensign Hudson, had been scheduled to meet the vessel off Owl's Head Light but were delayed by the weather on their trip from Lowell. That they were late did not seem to matter as the cannery's whistle was still blowing, the church bells were still ringing, the bands were still playing, and the parade had not yet started at the time they arrived. The aircraft immediately circled the city and put on a flying display that proved immensely popular with the crowd of 15,000 who had come to the celebration.[32] The events of the day were so newsworthy they were recorded on movie film by Pathe News for distribution to theaters nationally.[33]

The pilots and crews, six men in all, stayed for two days making friends while fielding many questions about the Navy and its aviation section. Then, on Saturday at 12:30 P.M., both planes left for Portland only to have 1189 develop engine trouble which forced it to set down at the quiet little fishing village of New Harbor. 1915 continued on to Portland and came to anchor between Grand Trunk Wharf No. 8 and the dock of the Portland Company. Coming ashore,

The quiet fishing village of New Harbor, Maine where Lieutenant Burk was forced to land in HS-1L 1189 with engine trouble on August 30, 1919. *Photo from the Author's Collection.*

Hudson had no trouble locating the advanced recruiting party which had driven over the road from Lowell with the usual literature. Not knowing when Burk would be arriving in 1189, all agreed that Hudson should commence the recruiting fly-overs as a single plane operation and drop the promised leaflets to the thousands watching from the streets, parks, and rooftops.

On Sunday, August 31, with Burk still in New Harbor, Hudson invited a representative of Portland's newspaper, the Daily Eastern Argus, to go for a 30-minute flight which was quickly accepted. The reporter came to the dock at 3:30 P.M. as agreed, donned his bulky flying suit, put on his leather helmet, and was rowed out to 1915 at its anchorage. The crowd cheered heartily as the plane quickly skimmed along the water and became airborne near Bug Light. The trip continued out over the Quarantine Station on House Island, then over Great Diamond Island to Falmouth Foreside, and back to Portland Harbor via a big circle over the business district, most of it flown at 1300 feet. It was a great ride for the reporter who really enjoyed himself and wrote a long account of his adventure that was featured on page one of the September 1st edition. Another highlight of the day was the releasing of carrier pigeons at Monument Square which more than satisfied the spectators who had gathered once the time of the birds' departure became known.[34]

Monday was a day of surprises. First, Burk in a fully repaired 1189 arrived in Portland from New Harbor about 1:00 P.M., took on a supply of fuel, and left one-half hour later for Boston to keep a scheduled 3:00 P.M. arrival at the Charlestown Navy Yard. Although both planes were expected to be there at that hour to start a flying exhibition, Burk had to go alone as now the other plane, 1915, would not start. Diagnosed as having a faulty carburetor, it was not fixed until September 4th when Hudson flew direct to Chatham, as he was too late to participate in any part of the Boston activities.[35] Despite mechanical setbacks, Maine had been a pleasant experience for the aviators, and they looked forward to someday returning to complete their original itinerary in the north country, by calling at various ports along the Penobscot as far up as Bangor.

A Thank You to Provincetown

Another pleasant experience soon followed at Provincetown where the welcome home festivities for its servicemen took place on September 18. On that day local church bells started peeling at 8:00 A.M., followed by sporting events in the morning, a mammoth parade after lunch, and then speeches to all those gathered on the town hall lawn. At the conclusion of the activities, two hydroplanes appeared from the direction of Chatham and circled the tall Pilgrim Monument several times, while their crews threw cigarettes, tobacco, and candy to the townsfolk. This was the air station's way of saying "Thank you" for the assistance that Provincetown had so often rendered when the flyers and their planes were in need. The aerial participation was attention getting but, for once, it was not the high point. The most impressive moment came during the memorial service in the harbor when a fishing schooner, laden from bow to stern with flowers, sailed out into the bay to scatter them on the ocean surface in memory of those local naval veterans who were not returning.[36]

Recruiting With the NC-4

While the recruiting initiative using HS-1's and HS-2's had come to an end, a more elaborate one was about to start, featuring the NC-4 which had not flown since crossing the Atlantic in May. The big flying boat had been returned from Europe on the deck of a ship, was put on exhibition in Central Park for two weeks, and then was scheduled to go to the Smithsonian Institution as a permanent display. The Naval policymakers however, aware of the crowds that were flocking to Central Park, revised their thinking and decided to have the famous plane fly a recruiting mission before they retired it from active service.

On July 30, it was shipped to Rockaway to undergo a six-week overhaul prior to commencing a tour that would cover the principal cities of the East Coast and the Gulf of Mexico, beginning at Portland, Maine. To create further interest, the plan was to have as many as possible of the original group fly it again and speak at the various stops on behalf of naval aviation.[37]

The NC-4 left Rockaway on September 25 at 11:10 A.M. with a crew of seven plus six passengers and a small dog. Included in those flying the aircraft were four crewmen who had made the transAtlantic crossing. These were Lieutenant Commander Read, once again acting as Commanding Officer and navigator; Lieutenant Hinton, pilot; Ensign Rodd, radio officer, and Chief Machinist Mate Rhoads, engineer. The passengers were sailors joining the *USS Isabel (PY-10)*, a large converted yacht designated as "mother ship" for the NC-4, and now on its way from Boston to Portland to begin its new assignment. Little is known of the dog except that it was loved by the crew.

At Portland

Over Great South Bay on Long Island, about 35 miles east of Rockaway Point, the aviators became aware something had struck one of the propellers; so, Read ordered the flying boat to land. Investigation showed that an air-driven fan used to power the radio had become detached in flight and had blown through one of the spinning propellers. Although blade damage was found to be negligible, the radio would no longer function. The NC-4 then continued on up the coast coming close to Chatham. Here two local planes were to join up, fly as its escort

Above: An artist's conception of the NC-4 in flight under ideal conditions. The airfoil lines of the flying boat create a graceful picture. *Illustration courtesy of the National Archives, Washington, D.C..* **Below:** The NC-4 on display in Central Park after completing its record-setting transAtlantic flight. It attracted such crowds in New York, the Navy decided to fly it for recruiting purposes along the entire East Coast. The sign reads: ``A cruise in the Navy is a liberal education. Apply at 34 East 23rd Street.''*Photo from the Author's Collection.*

northward, and then remain in Maine a couple of days to assist with recruiting. The rendezvous never happened due to fog in the area and a lack of radio communications, so the big plane went on to Portland alone, landing at 3:01 P.M. near Fort Gorges at Hog Island Ledge. The Chatham planes, 1189 with Lieutenant Burk and 1915 with Ensign Pride, arrived the following morning and anchored next to the NC-4 which had previously been brought into the inner harbor.[38]

Female Passengers

The recruiting plan called for the NC-4 to remain at anchor, and all flights made over the area were to be flown by the two planes from Chatham. That afternoon both made three ascensions, going off each time in pairs, flying in formation, and thrilling their passengers with breathtaking views. The first trip featured an interesting variation to the program when the mayor's daughter, Katherine Clarke, and her friend, Helen Havener, became the first females in New England to accept such an invitation. On the next run, the Governor of Maine, Carl Milliken, was taken aloft, while in the other was a noted motion picture photographer, Mr. R. A. Vine of the Mastercraft Photoplay Corporation. The final trip honored two other dignitaries, and at its conclusion the 1189 and 1915 moored for the night between Grand Trunk Pier No. 8 and the Portland Company's wharf. It was estimated that 15,000 people visited the waterfront to view these aircraft as well as to admire the *USS Isabel* which had tied up across the end of nearby Pier No. 2.[39]

On to Boston

Shortly after 2 o'clock Saturday afternoon, the three planes which attracted so much attention Thursday and Friday left for Boston, while a large crowd standing on the wharves witnessed their departure. The two smaller ones went up first and were followed a few minutes later by the NC-4. The flight was made in about one hour and a half, and, when the three appeared over Boston, the entire port resounded with the shrieks of steam whistles and the clanging of the ships bells.[40]

The site that was selected for the Boston viewing was that part of the Reserve Channel where the Army Base Pier meets the bridge at the end of Summer Street. Once the planes landed in the outer harbor, naval launches towed them to their mooring buoys, while the many onlookers lining both the pier and the bridge cheered a boisterous welcome. The three crews were later taken to the City Club which became their headquarters for the duration of their stay. No recruiting flights were scheduled as each take-off and landing required the harbor to be shut down, and Boston was deemed too busy a port to have to accommodate such frequent interruptions to marine traffic.[41]

While the men of the NC-4 were being honored with banquets and receptions, the members of the Chatham detachment were educating the steady line of spectators who were being freely admitted to the Army Base. The local recruiting office in the Cornhill Building noted that enlistments were up by 20 each day while the planes were there. This was quite a tribute to the hard work and sincerity of the airmen from Cape Cod.

On Wednesday, October 1, the Boston visit ended about 9:45 A.M. as Commander Read gave the word to tow the NC-4 out to its take-off point for New Bedford. About an hour later, at 11:10 A.M. to be exact, the largest plane ever seen locally soared over the city and landed safely in New Bedford Harbor, completing the second leg of its Portland-to-New Orleans journey. Trailing it were 1189 and 1915 which would continue to provide escort service as far as New Haven. The airmen were driven to the Wamsutta Club for a formal luncheon, as spectators covered the river area to get a close look at the big flying boat secured to the dock of the New Bedford Yacht Club. In mid-afternoon the three aircraft departed for Providence, followed the coastline to Newport, and proceeded up Narragansett Bay to the State Pier in the heart of the city.[42]

The NC-4 moored in New Bedford harbor with the flight crew preparing to come ashore for the festivities.
Photo courtesy of the Old Dartmouth Historical Society.

Several hundred people were waiting on the various wharves as the NC-4 appeared at 3:30 P.M., circled above them, and proceeded to land about 300 yards downstream. The harbormaster's boat immediately brought it to its assigned berth at the State Pier where the mother ship *Isabel* was already moored, having arrived two hours earlier from Boston via the Cape Cod Canal. For some reason it was difficult trying to secure the plane and a full 30 minutes passed before Read was satisfied that the docking lines were in an effective arrangement.

Once again several receptions and festivities were scheduled so none of the usual celebrity flights were planned. Instead, the following morning, a big parade was held throughout the downtown section which ended with a luncheon at the Narragansett Hotel. The afternoon was taken up with arranged golf matches at the Wannamoisett Country Club, and departure for New Haven occurred the next day, October 3, at 2:06 P.M. .

While in Providence, Read, in conjunction with the Providence Journal, had arranged for a radio demonstration to be given from the cockpit of the NC-4 on its way to Connecticut. To accomplish this an aerial had been strung between two flagpoles on the Journal Building with a wire connecting it to a receiver on the second floor. There, two amplifiers were directed out a window to the crowd jamming Eddy Street. Tuned to a frequency on which the NC-4 was transmitting, all of Read's messages to the *Isabel* and to the naval base at Newport could be heard, including a final one at 3:30 P.M. which reported "Off Fisher's Point! Can see New Haven clearly! Will have no difficulty landing!"[43] These were the first wireless messages ever received in Providence. The big flying boat reached New Haven safely at 3:55 P.M. but with only one escort. The other arrived a short time later having lost its way in the fog over Long Island Sound.

New Haven

The NC-4 flew above New Haven for several minutes so everyone could see the plane in flight. Then it glided down gracefully to land in the harbor about a mile inside the breakwater. The mother ship *Isabel* had already arrived at the Hamilton Street Dock, and mooring buoys were placed near it for the flying boat to anchor. While a local charter vessel took the big plane in tow, the escorts continued circling and soon they too touched down, once the featured attraction had been safely secured. After a weekend full of formal and informal tributes, including a memorable one held at Yale, Read and his crew took off from New Haven on Monday, October 6, at 4:00 P.M. for Philadelphia.[44] Both the HS-2's, however, stayed the night then left for Chatham early in the morning having faithfully shepherded the NC-4 from Maine to Connecticut. The naval air station at Cape May was to inherit the escort duty once Read reached the New York-New Jersey line.

The HS-2L was such a favorite with the aviation personnel that some pictures of it, like the one shown above, were made into postcards after approval by the censor. *Photo from the Author's Collection.*

135

The successful transAtlantic flight of 1919 also gave rise to the ``NC-4 MARCH'' written by the noted composer F.E. Bigelow to honor this extraordinary achievement. *Photo from the Author's Collection.*

Above: A group of HS flying boats lined up at anchor at the Chatham Naval Air Station sometime during the early part of 1919. **Below:** An HS-2L being moved around by a small power workboat. *Photos from the Author's Collection.*

Above Left: An R-9 approaching the beach with Strong Island in the background. Pictured in the foreground is a dolly that was used to haul planes up the ramp and into the seaplane hangar. **Above Right:** A close-up view of HS-2L 1918 seated on one of the Naval Air Station's dollies. *Photos from the Author's Collection.* **Below:** On many occasions, Coast Guardsmen from the various Cape Cod Life Saving Stations went to the aid of Chatham pilots who were down at sea and in distress. *Photo from the collection of William P. Quinn, Orleans, Massachusetts.*

Surf Boat Drill.

Chapter Nine

Non-Operating Status

In July of 1919 the Naval Appropriations Act of Fiscal 1920 was passed reducing to six the number of seaplane stations that could be kept in operation. Congress did not specify which six locations should stay open, but left that for the Navy to determine based on what its long range plans and programs entailed. Several weeks later the Chief of Naval Operations announced that Rockaway, Anacostia (a former Army Base in Washington, D.C. taken over recently by naval aviation), Hampton Roads, Key West, Pensacola, and San Diego were to remain active, while Montauk and Miami would close immediately. Chatham and Cape May would continue to operate, but only with blimps, and these stations would be reclassified as lighter-than-air facilities. They were to supplement a new mammoth lighter-than-air base now under construction at Lakehurst, New Jersey, designed to house a rigid airship the British were building for the United States.[1]

Blimp Base

In the fall the Secretary of the Navy, to bring about further economies, ordered every regional ground school closed seeing them as duplicative, inefficient, and costly. He directed that all future technical instruction for enlisted men would be consolidated and take place at the huge Great Lakes Naval Training Station in Illinois.[2] Chatham, with most of its planes dismantled, its mechanics school gone, and its recruiting assignment completed, now saw its personnel reduced to about 100 officers and men.

Then, in early October, word was received that the B-18 had been reassigned and was to be shipped to the naval air station in San Diego. This was done as ordered on October 21, leaving the base with only one B-class blimp in storage and questions about the future. The aircraft maintenance card of the B-18 indicates the shipment was received in California on December 15 in need of extensive repairs. This came as no surprise. Much of the wartime equipment was beginning to show wear, but spending money to replace it was not foremost in the minds of the naval planners.

Another change occurred at Chatham on October 13. Lieutenant Commander Chase received orders to report to the Army Air Service Training Station at Arcadia, Florida (Carlstrom Field) for instruction in land planes, one of only 18 naval pilots so selected. Designated to be his replacement in command was a lighter-than-air officer, Lieutenant Arthur D. Brewer (Naval Aviator 103). He had been serving as the Squadron Commander of the base's lighter-than-air division since his return in December from the Naval Air Station at Paimboeuf in France. Brewer was a proven leader and a skilled pilot. He had been commended by the French Government as one of the crew that set a continuous flight record of 26 hours, 34 minutes on April 27, 1918 while escorting three Allied convoys through a heavily mined war zone area.[3]

Above: A close-up view of a C-class blimp's gondola and twin engine propulsion unit. Note the Mark IV bomb in its rack on the port quarter beneath the port engine. *Photo courtesy of the National Archives, Washington, D.C.* **Below:** Some of the landings were better than others! *Photo courtesy of Robert S. Hardy and the Chatham Historical Society.*

Brewer Assumes Command

For the first time in the station's history, a grand ball was planned to wish the former skipper Godspeed, and to welcome Lieutenant Brewer to his new position. It was held in the Knights of Columbus building which was elaborately decorated for the occasion with pine branches set against a display of colorful international signal flags. One end of the hall had a space reserved for the honored guests called the "Captain's Cabin", while at the other end was the stage upon which a Boston jazz orchestra played their lively brand of music. Lieutenant Brewer was "piped aboard" at 9:10 P.M. as the entire assemblage stood at attention until he, his staff, and all their escorts were seated. Commander and Mrs. Chase were unable to attend because of last minute changes in their travel orders, but his farewell message was read expressing the enjoyment and satisfaction he had received from his most recent tour of duty. A collation was served and dancing continued until midnight. The committee chairman then announced, to the cheers of all, that a similar such night of sociability would be held in the same place on November 25 but with a Thanksgiving motif.[4] It was becoming apparent that morale was improving at the air station in spite of the down-sizing throughout the Navy.

C-10 Assigned

Chatham now was a lighter-than-air station with a dirigible officer in command, but it had never been assigned one of the large C-class blimps. Thirty blimps of this class had originally been ordered but with the end of the war the last twenty were canceled. The last one built by the B. F. Goodrich Company was C-10 and it was still in Akron, Ohio, now fully repaired from damage suffered during its trial flight of December 16, 1918. On October 9, 1919 it was designated for Chatham and sent by rail in two separate shipments at two different times. The gondola car arrived on November 14 and the envelope came about three weeks later in mid-December. Uncrating and assembly commenced as soon as both components were at the air station, but in the assembly process it was found that neither the rudder nor the stabilizers were included in either delivery. Subsequent checking determined that they were now apparently lost and probably would have to be made anew, as spares also could not be located at this time.

The C-10 contained 180,000 cubic feet of hydrogen in an envelope 192 feet long, 43 feet wide and 46 feet high. It had a maximum speed of 60 mph produced by two 125 hp Hispano-Suizo engines but usually cruised at 45 mph to get greater range and more effective submarine spotting. The gondola was of streamline design 40 feet in length and 5 feet in width with steel outriggers extending five additional feet out each side to carry the engines. This suspended car, specifically built for the C-class blimps by the Burgess Company of Marblehead, had seating for six, although only four men were actually needed as the operating crew. It was constructed with four equally spaced open cockpits, but just the forward two had double seating in a side-by-side arrangement. The first held the coxswain, controlling the rudder for course alterations. The second contained the pilot regulating the valves for altitude changes. Next to each was an empty seat available for a passenger, or an observer or a machine gun operator in wartime. Cockpits three and four were single seaters, the third being for the mechanic who monitored the engines, and the fourth for the radioman with the wireless equipment.[5] Additionally, outside the fuselage opposite the rear seat position, were two racks, one on either side capable of holding a total of four Mark IV bombs.

Relaxation

Also in mid-November, to keep morale moving in a positive direction, the welfare committee sponsored an Armistice Day dance at the Mill Hill Pavilion in West Yarmouth. Good attendance was assured as Mill Hill was a favorite spot in spite of it being some distance away. This did not inconvenience the base personnel at all. A custom had developed that sailors who needed a ride should stand in front of Smith's Drug Store on Main Street and be patient. Locals driving by during the day would stop and give them lifts, while in the evening those townsfolk having touring cars would come and wait there until their vehicles were filled.[6]

The old Mill Hill Pavilion in West Yarmouth. It offered the air station personnel an opportunity to meet local residents and vacationers for dining, dancing and general socialization. *Photo courtesy of Donna Lumpkin, Chatham, Massachusetts.*

A further boost came at this time when it became known that a sizeable up-to-date movie theater would be built at the station, and that construction would start before the end of the year. This coincided with the announcement that Howard Gamble had been appointed to fill the newly created position of Welfare Director at Chatham, having responsibility not only for the theater, but for the former K of C and YMCA clubrooms as well. With a lesser number of men stationed at the base, both organizations had previously ceased operations, and the local clergy were now taking care of all the sailors' religious needs. The Y's Secretary, George Voltz, had already left the area and had relocated to Maine to assist newly arrived Canadian immigrants in making the transition to their new country.[7] The following article from the Harwich Independent's edition of December 24, 1919 is quoted in its entirety as it explains the scope of Gamble's assignment and summarizes his qualifications:

"Howard E. Gamble, General Secretary at the Chatham Naval Station has been promoted by receiving the appointment of Welfare Director at the station, a distinct honor to his remarkable ability and record. He is editor of Fly Paper, and a successful baseball and football coach for the station teams. In the future Mr. Gamble will have entire charge of the athletic, welfare and entertainment work of the station, have two separate buildings used as club rooms, and an up-to-date theatre now under construction."

Outlook Turns Bleak

With the last of December came the end of the first full year of peace, and with that peace had come a steady reduction both in naval personnel and in shore locations. Numberwise, not only had all the Class 5 reservists been released from active duty, but the entire Coast Guard roster, which had been absorbed for the duration, was now back under the Treasury Department. As for facilities, the air station at Montauk was no longer active, and the flight school at Bay Shore had been shut down permanently. Nearer to home, the section bases at Provincetown, Nantucket, and Fairhaven were closed while the former Marconi Wireless Station was once again operating under private ownership.

Chatham had survived the first full year of peace but, since its redesignation as a blimp base, most of the heavier-than-air pilots and crews had been transferred elsewhere, further reducing the base's complement and importance. With Congress continually seeking ways to cut back appropriations for the Armed Forces, the future of Chatham was questionable.

The new year, 1920, started off without any major status changes, but a positive note was soon injected by the people of Chatham. At the annual town meeting, $2500 was appropriated as the town's share towards the construction of the remaining portion of the road to the air station not built in 1918. This indicated to many that the residents and local officials were comfortable the Navy would retain the site indefinitely.[8]

As for the base, the B-19 was operating when winter weather permitted and kite balloons, A-725, A-726 and A-2756 were available if needed, but they were kept deflated inside the hangar. The long awaited parts for the C-10 still had not arrived and most all of the planes remained disassembled. The officers mess had never been reinstated. As a consequence, most were living off the premises including the Commanding Officer, Lieutenant Brewer. However, to the delight of all, the new station theater, named after Admiral Sampson of Spanish-American War fame, was now completed and showing first-run movies every Monday and Friday evenings.[9] In general though, the winter was a quiet period with frequent heavy storms causing time to pass all too slowly. It was not until spring that activity really started to pick up again.

To further equip the newly designated blimp base, the envelope of B-2 was shipped from Key West to Chatham where it arrived on March 4, 1920. The B-2 was manufactured by Goodyear and assigned to Key West on January 20, 1918 to perform standard offshore patrol duty. It held up well in the southern climate, logging 233 hours before being wrecked in February of 1919, when a connecting rod malfunctioned causing a motor failure. This blimp never flew again and was stricken from the Navy list several months later on November 17. However, parts of the bag still had sufficient strength and elasticity to be of use, so the whole envelope was placed in storage instead of being discarded. Orders came through from Washington on January 7, 1920 to send it as spare fabric to the Cape in case patches were needed for those already there.[10]

A Navy B-class blimp flying over the Chatham Naval Air Station in the summer of 1919. Lt. A.D. Brewer, USNR, Pilot. *Photo from the Author's Collection.*

Blimps were such a rarity during the war that Chatham personnel photographed them from every angle at every opportunity to show those at home the latest innovation used in the search for the long-ranging U-boats. *Photos from the Author's Collection.*

Also in March, Chief Quartermaster Hans Christensen received orders to proceed to the Naval Air Station, Rockaway for further transfer to the Naval Rigid Airship Detachment at Howden, England. He was to report there for training relative to becoming a rigger on the ZR-2, the Navy's designation for the British R-38 which was then under construction for the United States.

As alluded to earlier, shortly after the successful transAtlantic flights of the R-34, Washington had negotiated with the British to build a similar but larger rigid airship for our Navy, because we were at that time lacking in expertise and the necessary equipment. The contract was for one 708 feet long, with a capacity for 2,000,000 cubic feet of hydrogen, and powered by five 350 hp engines. In conjunction with signing the contract, and almost simultaneously, ground had been broken for the new lighter-than-air facility at Lakehurst, New Jersey to serve as its home port. By the beginning of 1920, both of these projects were well underway. Attention was then focused on assembling and training a very select group of men to fly it.

A directive was circulated by the Navy Department seeking a crew consisting of 18 gas engine mechanics who had previous lighter-than-air experience; twelve riggers familiar with fabric, cordage, valves, cable splicing and the use of hydrogen; six quartermasters qualified to perform the duties of dirigible coxswain; and two radio electricians. From all the candidates who applied for the highly desired positions only those with the highest qualifications and superlative recommendations were accepted. It was no wonder that everyone at Chatham was elated when Christensen, their leading petty officer in the lighter-than-air division, was selected, indicating that he was one of the best in the Navy.[11]

The Commanding Officer of the training detachment and prospective CO of the ZR-2 was Commander Louis H. Maxfield, a man also well known at Chatham, for he had been officer-in-charge of the 9-plane welcoming flight that greeted Wilson in Boston in early 1919. The whole project, however, would end in disaster August 24, 1921. On its fourth and final trial flight before being accepted by the Navy, it exploded in mid-air over the English city of Hull, killing 44 of the 49 on board. Included among the fatalities was Commander Maxwell but Christensen was spared as he was not assigned to fly the final trial.[12]

Then on March 17, a gala St. Patrick's Day dance was held for the FLY PAPER fund at the Chatham Pavilion. Featured was the well known Blue and White Banjo Orchestra of New York City which attracted one the largest crowds ever. The men could no longer complain about social life on the Cape, as the dance continued almost non-stop until 2:00 A.M., closing with a sentimental rendition of everyone's favorite, "Home Sweet Home". Encouraged by success, another such event was planned for May 5th at the same location.[13]

James F. Shade

Finally that month, one of the more highly publicized lighter-than-air pilots re-enlisted in the Navy and was assigned to Chatham. James F. Shade, before coming to the Cape, had accumulated a total of 1800 hours in the air. This was just one of several remarkable feats in a flying career that had been quite out of the ordinary. He had originally joined in 1901 at the age of 14 and served with the fleet for sixteen years, building a reputation of being an expert mechanic.

At our entry into the war, he was detached from his ship and sent to shore duty at the Pensacola Naval Air Station. There, as a chief petty officer, Shade was placed in charge of a ground crew which one day let a free balloon get away while they were passing it along the deck of a barge that contained the Navy's only floating hangar. He grabbed the "concentration" line and rose in the basket to about 14,000 feet. At that point the rip pane came off, the gas escaped, and the balloon fell rapidly, about 4,000 feet. Shade, with great presence of mind, was then able to shake out the flapping sides into the encircling net, converting the collapsed balloon into a giant parachute. He rode it down to within 100 feet of the ocean surface and then jumped the final distance into the water. When picked up by a speedboat from the air station and asked if he felt injured, he replied, "Hell no! Give me a cigarette!"[14]

He next qualified as a blimp pilot and was promoted to Warrant Officer on November 22, 1917 with the designation of Naval Aviator 551. He then left the service in March of 1919 and went to work in Akron as a civilian instructor with the Army, teaching student pilots the art of flying airships. During this period of employment he created a national sensation on May 24 by touching down a 169' training blimp, the A-4, in a flat space only 30' long by 30' wide on the roof of Cleveland's Hotel Statler. Once the gondola car was on the specially constructed platform, two of his five passengers disembarked and, in accordance with a previously scheduled plan, took the elevator downstairs where one spoke at a dinner meeting being sponsored by the Society of Automotive Engineers. All five were involved airship and balloon men, planning to start a commercial, interstate, blimp service using various tall buildings as pick-up and discharge points for travelers and freight.[15] Shade proved that rooftop platforms were feasible, but the idea never developed further.

Two months later, in July, he again made the papers by piloting a blimp to the Methodist's 100th Annual Convention in Columbus, Ohio and taking one of the ministers aloft to preach from the open car, while the craft hovered above the delegates.[16]

Missing the military style of life, Shade, a bachelor, re-enlisted in the Navy in March of 1920 as a Quartermaster 1st Class (qualified in dirigibles) and was assigned to Chatham. His background and exploits were written up in a lengthy FLY PAPER article before he reported for duty, and the personnel of the air station waited with anticipation to see what additional excitement he would cause while stationed with them.

Status Change

But Shade never really had a chance to become involved in any Cape adventures, for something took place in mid-April which many believed would never happen in their lifetime. The Commanding Officer received orders from the Department of the Navy to place the Chatham Naval Air Station in a non-operating status as soon as practical, but no later than May 15. The orders further stated that Lieutenant William B. Green from the Bureau of Navigation would be visiting shortly to review the procedure and to present a timetable. It was he who had come to Chatham in 1919 and initiated the successful recruiting mission for naval aviation in New England.[17]

Green arrived and informed Lieutenant Brewer that all enlisted personnel would be transferred to other naval air locations, mostly to Rockaway and Hampton Roads, while officers would be reassigned individually to various duty stations around the country. He also advised that the B-19 was to be shipped to Rockaway and the C-10, once operational, would go there as well, but it was to be flown down by its crew. In addition, the kite balloons, at some point, were to be inspected thoroughly and sent to other sites once the results of the inspection determined their status. As for the seaplanes and boats, they would be left in storage at Chatham, but most motor vehicles would be kept in a state of readiness at the Charlestown Navy Yard in Boston. Equally important, to insure that the air station could be fully operational within forty-eight hours, a guard detail of ten enlisted men plus one officer would be retained to look after the property. These men would also tend the pigeons who could not be housed elsewhere and still be expected to provide trustworthy service in the future.[18] Lieutenant Green then conducted an all inclusive inspection and reported to the Chief of Naval Operations on May 4th that he found the base and its equipment in "excellent condition".[19]

Implementation of the various orders commenced immediately with kite balloons A-2756 and A-725 being reassigned on May 4th to NAS Hampton Roads. The former was shipped in good condition while the latter was stricken from the records upon arrival there because of excessive mildew. In even poorer condition was A-726 and it was condemned at Chatham on May 11 with the bag being sent to the New York Navy Yard for disposal. Its fittings and its basket, however, were considered re-usable and went to the Naval Aircraft Factory in Philadelphia until needed. Also on May 4 the faithful B-class blimp, B-19, was deflated and shipped to Rockaway while the C-10 was flown there without incident four days later, after the missing parts were received and installed. Further, the only R-9 still at the station, 943, was sent to the Naval Aircraft Factory as well, for any reactivation of the site would not involve this now obsolete model.

Lastly, the ambulance, the cars, and the trucks that were designated to leave were driven over the road to Charlestown, and the May 5th FLY PAPER dance was canceled as there would no longer be a station newspaper. The final edition came out on May 1st in which Brewer paid homage to the Town of Chatham, saying the naval personnel over the years would always remember it as a special place that was "Small, but real".[20] The same descriptive feeling could also be applied to the Chatham Naval Air Station by those who served there throughout its existence. It was officially placed in a non-operating status at 12:00 Noon on May 15, 1920.

The blimp C-10 arriving at NAS Rockaway. Note the sandy landing area at Rockaway as opposed to the grassy surfaces at Chatham where the C-10 was formerly assigned. *Photo courtesy of the National Archives, Washington, D.C.*

Chapter Ten

The Final Months

Staffing for the guard detail was one of the other major issues and, when the status change was announced, a great many of the station personnel volunteered to remain. The Executive Officer, Lieutenant Sheehan, was surprised with the number of requests, some even from sailors who had been frequent complainers. However, in spite of his familiarity with the applicants, he was to have no input into the selection process. He had received his new assignment and was to be replaced by Lieutenant Percy H. Bierce.

The Guard Detail

Bierce was a thirty-year veteran of the regular Navy and a "mustang", serving his first twenty-six years as an enlisted man in the fleet and his last four as an officer at Cavite in the Philippine Islands. With the departure of Lieutenant Brewer to head up all lighter-than-air operations at Rockaway, Lieutenant Bierce became the officer-in-charge of the base under its new configuration, and he selected Chief Machinist Mate Edward R. Faxon as his second in command. Also chosen from the station's final roster were Russell E. Holcomb, Quartermaster 1st Class (pigeonman); Mervyn W. Jewell, Seaman 2nd Class (bugler); George W. LaRock, Seaman; Carl E. Nelson, Seaman; and Williard E. Nicholas, Seaman. Four others came from elsewhere including the cook.

They had been left a one-ton Ford pick-up truck, an Excelsior motorcycle with side car, and several bicycles for transportation. The buildings available to them were the officers quarters, the enlisted mens quarters (old), the administration building, the mess & recreation building, the heating plant, and the garage. All others had been secured with the water shut off, the radiators and pipes drained, and the screens removed from the windows.[1]

One of their earliest assignments was to pump 7,000 gallons of aviation gasoline into 55-gallon drums and ship it to NAS Rockaway by rail. However, as there were no drums at the station, the men had to wait several weeks until Rockaway sent up the necessary empties.[2] This was just one of many annoyances the guard detail would face while being held responsible for the general upkeep of the base.

Only Pigeons

By fall of 1920, Chatham had taken on an atmosphere of desolation. Although the station was still intact, the life and energy had left when the aviation personnel, who at one time numbered in the hundreds, had been re-assigned and replaced with a token fire watch. The 47-structure installation on the 40.2 acre site, which had cost $7,000,000 to build,[3] was now home to one non-flying officer, ten enlisted men, and over 100 carrier pigeons with varying degrees of homing experience.

The continued training of these birds became difficult, as the usual methods of getting them to distant release points were no longer available. All blimps, balloons, and Sea Sleds had been sent to other facilities, and the three planes left at the station were in dead storage for lack of pilots. Yankee ingenuity and the motorcycle came to the rescue by adapting the side car's chassis with a metal framework, thus allowing the pigeons to be taken in wicker baskets to places like Gloucester and Lowell to resume their practice flights.

The old air station continued to be manned in this limited fashion but, as general deterioration began to set in, it was becoming apparent that it could not go on indefinitely in a non-operating status unless additional monies were forthcoming.

Helping Children

One positive happening did occur though in mid-summer when a surgeon from Boston, who was not part of the Navy, received permission through the combined efforts of the local Visiting Nurse Association, the school nurse of Chatham, and Lieutenant Bierce, to re-open and use the dispensary for one specific weekend. Ten children who had been waiting to have either their adenoids or tonsils removed were brought to the base on Saturday, July 31, and the surgery was performed according to schedule.[4] This eliminated the need for a several day stay in the city where parental visitation would have been both difficult and costly. All surgical procedures were successful and the young patients returned to their homes on Monday, August 2, eager to tell their relatives and friends about this unique but difficult experience.

Dr. Minnie Buck

Also that year, the Harwich Independent reported in its December 15th edition that a civilian dentist had been appointed to look after the dental needs of the few remaining sailors. The selection was well received as Dr. Minnie Buck, besides being competent, was a loyal supporter of the base from the beginning and had placed ads in nearly every issue of FLY PAPER. She was also one of the few female dentists of that era, and probably the only one ever named to serve a naval pigeon training facility as that was now Chatham's designated function.

Free Balloon Alert

Finally, at the close of 1920, Chatham, as well as other naval stations in the New England area, were alerted, as happened once before, to be on the look-out for a missing balloon. This time it was not an unmanned kite type but a free balloon, a sphere of rubberized fabric without engine or tether, containing 35,000 cubic feet of hydrogen with a basket suspended beneath it to carry the crew. Its purpose was to train future lighter-than-air pilots how to maintain control of a blimp that had suffered a loss of engine power while flying. In this instance, three officers had boarded one of these training balloons on December 13 at the Rockaway Naval Air Station on Long Island for a flight to upstate New York, roughly following a course to the northwest of the Hudson River. They were the pilot, Lieutenant Louis A. Kloor (Naval Aviator 2437), plus two other Lieutenants, Farrell and Hinton, both classified as observers although not qualified balloonmen.[5]

The trip started in a routine manner at 1:00 P.M. but, when nothing was heard from the craft by the next day, advisories were sent to certain locations north and east of its projected track. At Chatham, the guard detail began a sky watch, and the loft was manned continually in case a pigeon from the flight might inadvertently come to the Cape. The Chatham watch was in vain, however, as the prevailing winds continued northwesterly, taking the balloon up as far as

Moose Factory, a remote Indian settlement at the southern end of St. James Bay in upper Ontario Province. The three men were finally found four days later in poor condition by a Cree, out checking his traps. Taken to the tribe's village, they were nursed back to health and properly outfitted to withstand the frigid temperatures that existed so far north. They were also taught how to snowshoe before starting on their guided trek back to civilization. Twenty-nine days after departing Rockaway, the airmen finally reached American authorities at the border town of Mattice, Ontario. The theory that the pigeons might come to the Chatham loft could never be developed as the balloon crew, while lost in the dense Canadian wilderness, ate the three of them to supplement the meager rations that had been supplied at the time of take-off![6]

Basketball

For the men of the guard detail the duty was one of constant frustration, trying to maintain the property in a reasonable condition with such a small force. They soon joined a local basketball league to gain some positive diversion in the off-duty hours, although it required all five that were not on watch to show up and participate. Off to a slow start, the sailors improved gradually. By late January of 1921 their morale received a big boost as they defeated a better organized Hyannis Town Team as well as their arch rival, the Radio Corporation of America, by substantial margins. RCA was a newcomer to the league also, having just recently taken over the near-by long-range ship-to-shore wireless facility that had been manned by the Navy throughout the war.[7]

Container Corrosion

On May 21, 1921, a typical example of deterioration was uncovered when an inspection was made of the chemicals used to make hydrogen gas. In storage were 26,700 lbs. of caustic soda (sodium hydroxide) in 500 lb. and 100 lb. drums and 14 tons of ferro silicon in 100 lb. drums. Many of the containers had been gathering rust but now it was noticed that some had begun to corrode. As a consequence of this, the officer-in-charge was instructed to ship all of the drums containing chemicals to NAS Rockaway as soon as possible, where the contents which were still stable could be placed in immediate use.[8]

Birds Transferred

The air station's status remained about the same until November when the second in command, Chief Faxon, was re-assigned to Hampton Roads, Virginia and was not replaced. Also that month the Knights of Columbus, in response to their request, received permission to dismantle and remove the vacant K of C building.[9] This was followed in January of 1922 with orders to close down the entire pigeon operation and transfer the birds to the Gould Island section of the Naval Torpedo Station at Newport.[10] The base on Nickerson Neck had now been reduced to almost total insignificance, and the townspeople felt it was just a matter of time before its abandonment was announced.

Condemnation Proceedings

While Chatham was continuing to unravel as a component of the naval establishment, the

Secretary of the Navy began to focus on the ownership of the land on which it was built. The Navy had acquired title to the property by eminent domain, and the funds were provided through the Urgent Deficiency Act of 1917. All parties acknowledged that the taking was necessary for national defense, but payment had never been made as a price could not be agreed upon. The difference was substantial; the government had offered to negotiate in the area of $150 to $250 per acre while the owners maintained that $2000 to $3000 was a more appropriate range.[11] Now, with the war long since over and the base virtually closed, the Navy looked to resolving this situation as quickly and fairly as possible.

On March 28, 1921, the Secretary of the Navy requested the Attorney General of the United States to commence condemnation proceedings in the Federal District Court at Boston, and the actual petition was filed April 25 in the Clerk's office. This was the legal mechanism used to place a fair valuation on the whole parcel, to determine who the owners were, and to establish how much acreage each one represented. Preparing the case for trial was time consuming however, as the title abstracts and the plot plans were difficult to understand. This was caused by some of the old boundary markers being obliterated during the construction phase, as well as by the Navy filling in certain coves and other waterfront areas to make additional solid ground. In reality the 36.7 acres acquired in 1917 had become 40.2 acres at the time of the 1921 survey.

The case was finally brought to trial on May 23, 1922 and went to the jury on June 7. After nine hours of deliberation the verdict was returned valuing the original tract at $50,335 or just a little over $1370 per acre. Each owner's apportionment, including interest of $3380.06, was as follows:[12]

Franklin B. Nickerson	31,837.13
Heirs of Eunice Kennedy	1,778.61
C. Ashley Hardy	11,204.51
George F. Willett	1,494.01
Philip G. Harris	144.07
Gertrude R. Gilmore, Edward G. Hall, Philip G. Harris, et al	7,256.73
	$53,715.06

The government immediately appealed the decision to the Circuit Court in Boston which, after due deliberation, affirmed the finding brought forth by the jury. Payment was eventually made in April of 1925 with additional interest assessed to cover the further delay.

While the value of the land was being litigated, other events were happening that continued to bode dark days ahead for Chatham. In February of 1922 the Navy announced that the air station was to be placed in a closed status at the end of the year, and a survey would be made of all its equipment and other miscellaneous materials. Those articles that were not needed or could not be used elsewhere would be identified and put up for sale. Commander Albert A. Baker, head of the public works department at the Charlestown Navy Yard and Lieutenant Elmer S. Robinson were appointed to make the inventory and to do it as soon as possible.[13]

Auction Planned

A complete list was submitted to the First Naval District headquarters and to the Bureau of Aeronautics where each determined, within its jurisdiction, what was to be retained. The most valuable items found by the Bureau were 46 Liberty engines which were ordered sent to the Naval Aircraft Factory in Philadelphia for overhaul and storage. As the Bureau of Supply and Accounts had not responded to the Commanding Officer's long-standing request to provide storage crates for these, it was decided to dismantle immediately two of the temporary buildings on the property, and use the wood to build some crates that were suitable for shipping purposes. Other articles kept were certain heavy machine tools for the new naval air facility at Pearl Harbor, 75 tons of bituminous coal for the radio station at North Truro, and 48 35-gallon HS-2L gasoline tanks for the naval aviation storehouse in Gloucester City, New Jersey.

Next, a civilian employee of the Navy's Central Sales Office in Washington, Joseph N. Bryant, was sent to Chatham on April 24 to commence the disposal process of the remainder. Bryant created a 48-page itemized catalog which described each offering in detail, and set June 29, 1922 at 11:00 A.M. at the base as the time and place a sealed-bid auction would take place. The catalog and the bid forms were given a wide geographical distribution.

The goods to be sold ranged from three HS-flying boats that had been stored in one of the hangars since 1920 (1189, 1915 and 2241), to seven used basketball jerseys with the letters NAS on the front. In between were 1376 group listings representing several thousand actual items.[14]

Planes are Bought

The highest bidder for each of the three planes was Robert W. Dewey of New York City who, under the terms of the sale, had until November 22 to remove them from the air station. By November 1 he had shown no visible effort to pursue this, so the Navy made a follow-up contact and learned that he had just chartered a boat to have them delivered to him.

Dewey then had each trucked separately, once it was crated, to Stage Harbor and loaded on board Captain Zeb Tilton's well-known coastal schooner, the *Alice S. Wentworth*. Allowed a short extension of the deadline, the last of the three planes went on its sea voyage south in mid-December.[15]

A solitary figure on a lonely beach appears not to notice one of the last landings of an HS-2L at Nickerson Neck prior to final lay-up. *Photo from the Author's Collection.*

Other Results

Also submitting winning bids were:[16]

John F. Burke, Brighton, MA	blocks & tackles boatswain's gear
L. Grossman & Sons, Quincy, MA	storage batteries recreation equipment galvanized piping
Roy E. Litchfield, Hingham, MA	rugs & carpeting 25' flagpole miscellaneous items
Charles Tunick, Brooklyn, NY	mess & galley gear (crew)
P. H. Bierce, Chatham, MA	mess gear (wardroom)
W. H. Snow & Sons, Orleans, MA	paints and oils

But not all of the items in the catalog were purchased. Some were never bid on and others received such low offers that they were rejected by the Navy. As the station was still scheduled to close at the end of the year, a final but much smaller auction was held on November 22, 1922 to liquidate what remained. This one featured the carry-over from the June 29 sale, but also included those furnishings and articles from the buildings the guard detail had been occupying.[17] What was left at the end of the day was junked.

In between these two auction dates, at the end of September, the radio compass function on Fox Island ceased operating and the equipment was dismantled. The heating unit was shipped to the compass station at North Truro, the rectifier for charging batteries went to the compass station at Prices Neck, Rhode Island, and the rest of the parts were stored at the Charlestown Navy Yard.[18]

Closed

At the end of the year 1922, the First Naval District, against the hopes of many, carried out its scheduled closing of the Chatham Naval Air Station. Contrary to rumors that were circulating around town, there was to be no last minute reprieve. This meant then the elimination of the guard detail and the end of Naval occupancy. The last entry in the station's log was made at 4:00 P.M. on December 31, 1922 and signed by Lieutenant H. P. Rahbusch, who had replaced Lieutenant P. H. Bierce as officer-in-charge. It read as follows:

"THIS STATION CLOSED AS PER COMMANDANT'S PREVIOUS INSTRUCTIONS."[19]

Chapter Eleven

Afterlife

Although the Navy had vacated the air station, it still held title to the property and was well aware that a presence was needed to oversee the vacant buildings to prevent vandalism. This was solved by the appointment of a watchman to live on the premises and to report to the Superintendent of Yards and Docks at the Charlestown Navy Yard.

Civilian Caretaker

The newly appointed resident caretaker was Daniel Mahoney who moved into Building #48, the former gate house, as his new permanent residence on January 1, 1923.

The first years were quiet ones for Mahoney, as most of the activity that took place involved inspectors coming down from Charlestown. Periodically these officers would arrive to view conditions at the base and determine what repairs were needed to maintain the three hangars, as well as to keep the caretaker's quarters livable. They would then submit their recommendations to the Bureau of Yards and Docks, only to have the files show that little or no action was ever taken. With such limited funds available, there was no reporting at all on the needs of the other buildings. Mahoney was allowed, however, to construct a lean-to at the gate house to shelter his automobile, using spare pieces of lumber which he found scattered around the base.

Also by this time interest had waned in retaining the YMCA "hut"; so, permission was granted the "Y" on December 18, 1924 to remove it.[1] The previous year the two 100' non-operating radio towers had been disassembled and, being still useful, were shipped to the Navy radio station at near-by North Truro.[2]

Owners Paid

Then, in April of 1925, the government finally issued payment checks to the former owners of the property. The actual amounts paid out on April 21 totaled $58,335, as additional interest was included to compensate for the further delay. Each reimbursement payment increased accordingly and the final figures are shown below:[3]

Franklin B. Nickerson	$34,387.41
Heirs of Eunice Kennedy	2,085.12
C. Ashley Hardy	12,251.65
George F. Willett	1,615.82
Philip G. Harris	156.46
Gertrude B. Gilmore, Edward G. Hall, Philip G. Harris, et al	7,838.54
	$58,335.00

Buildings Purchased

With the ownership issue settled and the real estate title no longer clouded, Washington started to direct some attention once again to Chatham, with the idea of leasing it out on a long-term basis, or even selling it to a qualified buyer. In order to know the structural conditions then in existence, the Bureau of Yards and Docks ordered that a detailed survey of every building still standing be made by the First Naval District with their recommendations on what should be done with each one. This was completed and, after a period of study, the Bureau concurred with the District's suggestions to dispose of the following:[4]

# 1-pump house	#40-carpenter shop
5-enlisted mens quarters (old)	41-photo laboratory
6-administration building	43-mess hall (new)
7-mess and recreation building	44-barracks
10-machine shop	46-radio house
13-water tank - 20,000 gal.	47-scrub house
15-boat house	49-motor testing shed
32-aviation storehouse	52-radio school
34-laboratory.	

These were purchased as a package deal at the end of April in 1927 by the Saint Lawrence Trading and Supply Company of New York City (Mr. A. Ruderman, President) which bought then for salvage purposes. According to the terms of the sale, the buildings were to be demolished and removed from the premises along with all their contents within a six-month period.[5]

As the first 17 buildings sold relatively fast, the Commandant of the First Naval District proposed to the Chief of the Bureau of Yards and Docks on May 3 that an additional six be declared surplus, as they were of little value. He felt it was advantageous to proceed with this now, as the buildings were steadily deteriorating and, the longer the wait, the lower the price. Further, being small, they might not even attract a buyer by themselves. Yet on the positive side, the company that had bought the others had shown some interest in acquiring more since it currently had its men and equipment on the premises. The units involved were:

# 9-garage	#33-oil reclaiming plant
11-storehouse	45-storehouse
17-magazine	50-boiler house

Shortly afterwards, the proposal was approved and the structures were sold, as anticipated, to the Saint Lawrence Trading and Supply Company under terms similar to those they had agreed to in their prior purchase.[6]

The two one hundred foot radio towers originally at NAS Chatham were moved to the Navy's wireless station at North Truro in 1923 after the air station was decommissioned. *Photo from the Author's Collection.*

Some Recycling

One of the unsold buildings on the property (Building #38, the dirigible storehouse) was later acquired by George Bearse who had it dismantled and reconstructed at the site of his automobile dealership in Chatham to increase the amount of protected new car storage.[7] The lumber from the others was stacked and sold locally to a variety of buyers including, in the spring of 1928, the Chequessett Inn of Wellfleet for repairing its bath houses and cottages. Another supply went to an individual who planned to build a boatyard on Mill Pond.[8] Earlier, the Town of Chatham acquired the station's fire siren and had it installed in the spire of the Methodist church. According to the Harwich Independent of February 22, 1928, the siren was wired to the local telephone office from where it was activated when needed.

As the structural survey was being conducted, an updated inventory was being made of all remaining furnishings, fixtures, and equipment to keep Boston current on what was still available. When this list was finalized it covered thirty typewritten pages and ranged from waste baskets to electric generators. Of these items, the Bureau of Yards and Docks reserved a certain amount of galley equipment for the Charlestown Navy Yard; an oil engine, alternator, and exciter for shipment to the radio station at Guantanamo Bay in Cuba; about a dozen motors with switchboards for Boston; a few screens plus some items of furniture for the radio station at North Truro; and three filing cabinets and a numbering machine for the Bureau itself in Washington. In addition, the entire auxiliary lighting system was to be removed from Building #9, the garage, and shipped to the Guantanamo Bay Naval Base for installation. All other fixtures and furnishings were to be offered for sale.[9]

Ostridge Remembered

While all this demolition and disposal was in progress at the air station, a solemn remembrance to Lieutenant (jg) Charles L. Ostridge was taking place off Cape Cod. On August 31, 1927, 500 Legionnaires left Boston on the liner *Martha Washington* bound for an American

Above: The Goodyear blimp *Mayflower* which broadcast the America's Cup Races off Newport, Rhode Island in the late summer and early fall of 1930. **Below:** The Goodyear blimp *Defender* which carried paying passengers out to observe the Cup Races of 1930. Both the *Defender* and the *Mayflower* were allowed by the Navy to use the Chatham Naval Air Station as a back-up facility if needed. Both landed at the Air Station and utilized the hangar on the night of September 13, 1930. *Photos from the Author's Collection.*

Legion Convention in Paris. Included was a contingent of veterans from Ostridge's home town of Watertown, Massachusetts who had known him since boyhood.

By pre-arrangement with the vessel's Captain, the liner was stopped at sea at the nearest possible point to Chatham, while a memorial service was held by those on board. All other activity on the ship came to a halt as a eulogy was given, prayers were offered, and flowers were strewn upon the waters in memory of their comrade who was killed just off shore in 1919. At the conclusion of the ceremony, and coincidentally at sundown, "Taps" was sounded by the traditional solitary bugler. The voyage to France was then resumed.[10]

Attempt to Lease

By 1927, all the planes were gone and all the buildings were sold except the three hangars and the gate house. In May of that same year, the First Naval District began a lengthy process of searching for someone to lease the property for a five-year period. The hangars were still standing because the Bureau of Aeronautics wanted them available to use in case of some unforeseen circumstance, even though funds were not being supplied for their upkeep. The Bureau also felt that the base should preferably be leased for an airport, a seaplane base, or an aircraft factory so that the Navy could take it over at very little cost and without delay in case of a national emergency.[11]

The First Naval District began by contacting real estate brokers in Chatham and the surrounding towns with the idea of obtaining prospects who might be interested in receiving information and viewing the property. A total of 34 firms and individuals were eventually identified and sent appropriate literature, which indicated that bids would be opened by the Navy Department on September 22, 1929. Of the 34 sent out, only four requested bid forms. These were:

> Aviation Business Bureau, Inc., 72 Wall Street, New York City -- manufacture of flying boats and amphibians.
>
> Spurr Aeronautical Products, Inc., 68 Devonshire Street, Boston -- manufacture of airplanes and possible use of the Station as a seaplane base.
>
> Harold Tuttle, Chatham, Mass. -- airport.
>
> Gilmore & Co., 24 Federal Street, Boston -- airport.

No bids were ever submitted.[12]

Commercial Blimps

At the same time that the Navy was trying to lease out the air station, the Goodyear Company was developing a small fleet of improved lighter-than-air craft for experimental and training purposes. It was during these flights in 1925 that Goodyear first realized the advantages

The commercial blimp *Neponset* which operated out of Chatham in the summer of 1930. It was one hundred thirty eight feet in length with two pusher-type, 83 horsepower engines that drove it at speeds up to 65 mph. The luxurious passenger cabin area featured deep wicker chairs and large windows of shatter-proof glass for comfortable panoramic viewing. *Photo courtesy of the Walpole Historical Society.*

a blimp would have as an advertising vehicle; so over the next four years, six were produced with the company name displayed on each side. During the summer of 1929 one of these, the *Mayflower*, was dispatched to New Bedford for four months with scientists from M.I.T. on board it conducting advanced radio research. It would actually remain around southeastern Massachusetts much longer than scheduled and be docked at a small hangar (140' x 60' x 58') at Round Hill, the spacious waterfront estate of Colonel E. H. R. Greene in South Dartmouth, Massachusetts.[13]

Then, in 1930, the *Mayflower* was invited to take part in the America's Cup yacht races being held for the first time in Block Island Sound off Newport. The blimp was to carry aloft a broadcasting crew with all the equipment that was needed to describe the action live to the nation.[14] The final races would occur in September, preceded by practice trials in July and qualifying heats in August.

Goodyear felt this was also an excellent opportunity to utilize the flagship of their fleet, the *Defender*, to carry paying passengers out to observe the racing events, and to further expose the company name to those along the shore. But that meant it would have two airships in the area during the summer and only one small hangar; so, the Navy was contacted about the possible availability of Chatham. Goodyear asked that it be allowed occasional use of the facilities during July, August and September in exchange for making the hangar habitable.[15] This was a very generous offer for, in addition to a badly leaking roof, multiple broken windows had given access to hundreds of starlings who carpeted the floor with guano up to a foot thick in some places.[16] The Navy quickly agreed to the proposal and instructed Dan Mahoney, the

160

caretaker, to advise the First Naval District each time one of their blimps landed at the old air station.

On July 16, 1930, Mr. Mahoney, not being too familiar with the airship industry, sent the following report in a routine manner to Boston as instructed:

> "The Goodyear blimp *Neponset* arrived from Round Hill at 8:00 A.M. and was berthed in the hangar at 11:00 A.M. today. A ground crew of a dozen men are sleeping in the hangar and eating in restaurants. The dirigible hangar doors were opened last evening by 15 men aided by a large truck after about three hours labor."[17]

The First Naval District was astounded! Goodyear did not have a blimp named *Neponset*. Follow-up conversations with Mr. Mahoney only compounded the mystery when he told them it did not have the name "Goodyear" on it but apparently was promoting some type of roofing materials.

Investigation showed that the *Neponset* was owned by the New England Airship Corporation of New Bedford, a new business entity incorporated under the laws of the Commonwealth of Massachusetts on April 26, 1930. On May 17, 1930 it purchased a blimp from the Goodyear Tire & Rubber Company which was the first one ever sold to a non-military buyer. Its intention was to operate an airship for commercial marketing promotions and to give rides to paying passengers. New England Airship soon obtained an advertising contract with a well known roofing manufacturer, Bird & Son of East Walpole, Massachusetts. It displayed that company's trade style on the sides of the craft while it visited country fairs and the like, offering recreational flights.[18] Now with the yacht races off Newport, New England Airship had decided to operate in the Southeastern Massachusetts area for at least the summer. It had an agreement with Goodyear to dock at Round Hill, sharing that facility with the *Defender* and the communications blimp *Mayflower*. Goodyear did not look upon this as competition, but rather encouraged their participation, hoping to have New England Airship become successful and thereby open up a whole new industry that would buy their blimps in the future.

When the pilot brought the *Neponset* down at Chatham on July 16 for minor repairs, he did so in good faith. He believed his company had emergency docking rights there under a broad permission granted by the Navy to Goodyear. He was totally unaware that naval approval had been extended only to the airships operated by the manufacturer. By the time repairs were completed on the 21st, however, all parties had met and reached an agreement that allowed New England Airship to have the same privileges that Goodyear enjoyed, even for a longer period of time. It also authorized the new company to store a spare engine and extra cylinders of helium in the hangar in case of a need at a later date.[19] Chatham's caretaker now had two separate operators on which to report arrivals and departures; Goodyear for the July, August and September yachting events, and New England Airship from July until the end of November when the college football season ended. Mr. Mahoney was to have little to report, however. Goodyear used Chatham only on September 13 when both *Mayflower* and *Defender* were berthed in the hangar, while New England Airship landed several times during the summer but not after September 7.[20] It is interesting to note that Goodyear's International Listing of Principal Airship Docks for 1930 contained 22 operational locations around the world, one of which was Chatham, identified as owned by the United States Navy with a functional hangar of 250' x 66' x 100'.[21]

The following year, 1931, there were no international yacht races in the area, but the use of the landing field and dirigible hangar was again sought by the New England Airship Corporation. This time they proposed to lease the big hangar for the entire summer, instead of having permission to occupy it only in emergencies. The Commandant of the First Naval District recommended approval, but Washington wanted to lease the whole facility on a 5-year basis and had some concern that a temporary deal might effect other negotiations. There is no indication if their blimp ever used Chatham that summer but, in 1932, the Chief of the Bureau of Aeronautics recommended to the Chief of Naval Operations (CNO) that the dirigible hangar be sold, dismantled, and removed from the air station. This was approved and the hangar, Building #3, was taken down and carted away, though not until the spring of 1933.[22]

Also in 1932 two small usage requests from other interested parties were granted but resulted in only limited activity at the site. One allowed two amphibians from the EDO Aircraft Corporation of College Park, Long Island to land on July 23 and taxi onto the concrete pad in front of the hangar for the week-end, while the occupants vacationed locally.[23] The other permitted Chatham Post #253 of the American Legion to use the station grounds for holding parade practices every Sunday afternoon from September 30 until Armistice Day.[24]

The annual inspection for 1934 was made on October 3, and the inspecting party found the grounds in fair condition. A notation was made in the report that a special work detail, which recently had been sent from the public works office of the First Naval District in Boston, had cleared the underbrush in a satisfactory manner and had boarded up the windows of Building #43, the newer of the two seaplane hangars. It also made mention that Building #17, the magazine, had been sold to the Saint Lawrence Trading and Supply Company in 1927 but, as it was never removed, it had come back under government control by default. The inspectors found the magazine's wooden frame in fair condition but that the doors and hinges were badly rusted and very loose.

Building #17 – The magazine at the isolated end of the overgrown landing field in 1947. *Photo courtesy of the National Archives – Northeast Region (Boston).*

1935 Inspection

On November 7, 1935, the most inclusive inspection report of this whole period was filed and, to obtain a clear understanding of what the air station was like in the mid-to-late 1930's, it is quoted here in its entirety:[25]

"Annual Inspection of Public Works and Public Utilities
U. S. Naval Air Station, Chatham, Mass.

Station inspected on 28 October 1935
This station is out of commission.
Police Protection: There is a civilian guard resident on the station for the protection of Government property.

Fire Protection: The only water available is from two small wells furnishing water for domestic purposes and water from the ocean. The 600 feet of hose is old and in poor condition. There are four galvanized pails with water at the quarters and two at the hangars. The six small Pyrene hand fire extinguishers are in poor condition.
Extinguishers will be provided.
Grounds: The grounds are in fair condition. Concrete floors and foundations of buildings sold and disposed of remain in place.

Roads: Roads are in fair condition.
Sewerage Systems: Septic tanks are still in place but are not in use.

Water Supply: There are two wells with small pitcher pumps one about 150' from the quarters, Building No. 48, with scant flow and water unfit for drinking and the other well one-third of a mile from quarters with water that is good.

BUILDINGS:

Building No. 42: Seaplane hangar. The roof of this building is poor and leaks badly. Exterior walls are fair to poor. A number of panes of glass are broken. Doors are in poor condition, supports of some being cracked in places.
The concrete ramp has disintegrated below high water.

Building No. 16: Seaplane hangar. Roof is in poor condition and leaks extensively. Frame of building is in fair condition.
The wood platform and ramp are in bad condition. The ramp below high water mark has disappeared. The underpinning of the platform and what remains of the ramp are in fair condition.
Building No. 48: Quarters. Building is in fair condition. Exterior

walls and interior need painting. There is no flushing system for water closet in these quarters.

Building No. 17: Magazine. This building is in fair condition.

Boundary Fence: Wire fence for greater part has fallen down and posts are in bad condition.

Gasoline Tanks: The tanks at Building No. 16 and on the site of Building No. 3, remain in place.

Waterfront Structures: Pier. All that remains of this pier are the wooden piles off shore.

Distributing Systems: The fresh water and salt water distributing systems are in place but not in use and are in doubtful condition.

Lighting System: Light is furnished to the station by the Cape & Vineyard Electric Company and service is satisfactory.

In view of the policy not to maintain the structures at Chatham, no repairs are recommended and accordingly, no estimates of cost of repairs accompany this report."

The years 1936 and 1937 were quiet years during which the deterioration not only continued but accelerated, as funds for repairs and maintenance were still not made available. On June 5, 1937, the Commandant of the First Naval District recommended to the CNO that the property at Chatham be offered to the Department of the Interior for development as a national park. Nothing came of this although it seemed a practical way to rid the Navy of a long-standing liability and, at the same time, put some of the unemployed to work at government expense on a WPA-type beautification project. It was unfortunate because lessees and buyers of airports were somewhat scarce at the height of the Depression.

Hangar Collapses

Exactly two weeks later, the smaller and older of the two seaplane hangars, Building #16, collapsed. The Commandant at Boston, in his report to the Chief of the Bureau of Yards and Docks, describes in detail what happened:

"The two remaining trusses of hangar building fell at 7:45 a.m. today (19 June 1937), carrying down what remained of the roof, and throwing the east end (doors) out on the platform, destroying frame work on which the doors slide on, and a section of the north wall caved in. As the building stands now three walls are standing, and the roof on the west end is hanging, all looking wobbly, and in a precarious condition. About sixty panes of glass were broken today."[26]

The buildings remaining were now reduced to three; the larger seaplane hangar, the magazine, and the gate house which the caretaker was occupying.

Reserve Drills

Near the close of 1937, the Commanding Officer of Unit 5, Section 5 of the Naval Communication Reserves, composed of 22 local enlisted men, requested use of the remaining hangar, Building #42, as a drill hall.[27] This was approved on January 4, 1938 with the understanding that arrangements for each drill would be made in advance with the caretaker, and that no smoking or small arms practice would take place inside the structure. These conditions were acceptable, and drills were conducted for the next several months on a regular basis. Then on August 16, caretaker Mahoney was transferred to the Charlestown Navy Yard in a further cost reduction move and was not replaced.[28] The Unit Commander, Ensign Samuel Freedman, seized this opportunity and requested that the armory, as well as the headquarters function of his unit, be allowed to relocate into the now unoccupied gatehouse. He further asked that an enlisted reservist be permitted to live in the building, rent free, in exchange for serving as a part-time watchman for the property.

While the small reserve unit was training at Chatham, geopolitical events were happening across the Atlantic which would have a lasting impact on just about every nation in the world. Germany, now controlled by Adolph Hitler, had been quietly building up a highly effective war machine with weapons and tactics that had been perfected in the Spanish Civil War. Hitler, a former army corporal in The Great War, had created a dictatorship which, by flexing its military muscle, had brought about the bloodless annexation of Austria, then the Sudetenland, and finally the rest of Czechoslovakia by June of 1939.

War in Europe

Poland was the next step in his territorial expansion, but the Polish outright refused to become a part of the new Third Reich. After a final ultimatum for a peaceful occupation went unanswered, German forces invaded Poland at dawn on September 1, 1939. Two days later both Great Britain and France came to Poland's assistance by declaring war on Germany.

President Roosevelt, to advise the world where the United States stood on this sudden crisis in Europe, issued a Proclamation of Neutrality on September 5 and then directed the Navy to establish an armed neutrality patrol along the Atlantic seaboard. Naval planners responded by formulating a complete coverage grid for the coast to track any belligerent submarine, aircraft, or surface vessel that might be found entering the off-shore shipping lanes or approaching eastern ports.

Patrol Bases Designated

Planes as well as ships were to be featured in this patrol; so, geographically appropriate air facilities had to be designated, even if some that were selected might be just of a temporary nature. The first list, promulgated on November 4, included Chatham which was to be reactiviated for flying boat usage only.[29] Although it would be expensive to rebuild, the primary consideration was to establish satisfactory locations as quickly as possible to get the patrol into the air.

There were two other First Naval District bases on the list as well: the Squantum Naval Reserve Air Station in Quincy, Massachusetts and the Quonset Point Naval Air Station in Newport, Rhode Island.[30] Both of these were created in the 1920's, both had adequate runways in addition to seaplane aprons, and both were currently operational in one way or another. The three together would insure sufficient security for the New England area. Then the announcement came that the planes to be used would be the Consolidated PBY Catalinas, the new single-wing twin-engine flying boats which dwarfed anything flown by the Navy during World War I. Sixteen of these were be to assigned to Chatham.[31]

Once the decisions from Washington became known within the naval establishment, officers more familiar with the old base on the Cape questioned the feasibility of its reactivation. Not only was costly construction involved, but now with big flying boats coming, extensive dredging would be required, possibly on a regular basis because of the continually shifting sand bars. Also a fog analysis of the Pollock Rip Lightship's daily weather logs did not help to support Chatham as a viable choice either.

Chatham Eliminated

When these other influences were brought to the attention of the Chief of Naval Operations, he reconsidered the inclusion of the old air station and ordered that it be dropped from the list. This left the Bureau of Aeronautics with 16 unassigned planes, so 8 of them were sent to Squantum and 8 to Quonset Point to augment their original allotments. The money that had been set aside for the construction of new buildings on the Cape site was redirected to expand the fuel storage capabilities of the Naval Air Station at Norfolk, Virginia.[32] Chatham was not to be reactivated, although the government continued to own the land.

Post World War II

After World War II had ended, the Navy once more focused attention on the former air station at Chatham and this time turned the long vacant property over to the War Assets Administration (WAA) on May 7, 1946 for disposal. The WAA, as required by the Surplus Property Act of 1944, first offered the site as a public airport to the state, then to the county, to the town, and finally to the adjacent town of Orleans but no interest was shown. Next an appraiser, Benjamin F. Teel of Centerville, was selected by competitive bid and on July 28, 1947 he submitted his fair value estimate of $13,738.00, itemized as follows:

Frame building at entrance		$ 638.00
Magazine		(no value)
Easterly section of land 10 acres @ $300.		3000.00
Southerly " " " 15 acres @ $500.		7500.00
Northerly " " " 8 acres @ $100.		800.00
Meadow and marsh land 6 acres @ $ 50.		300.00
Fox Hill 3 acres @ $500		1500.00
Total		$13,738.00
Total established fair value of		
Land, Buildings & Improvements		$13,738.00[33]

Sold

At the same time that the disposal process was going forward, the WAA was receiving inquiries on when offers would be accepted from private parties. All names and addresses of those interested were kept on file and, once the appraisal was approved, information was mailed advising that bids would be opened on November 20, 1947 at the Army Base in South Boston. To further publicize the date, large 5" x 7" notices were placed in both the Boston Globe and the Cape Cod Standard Times starting on October 21. By the deadline date, five offers had been received including one from a former pilot at Chatham, A. M. Pride, who had made the Navy his career and was now a Rear Admiral.[34] When the envelopes were unsealed there were two high bidders, a John Cronin and a Sidney Horowitz, each of whom had submitted a bid for the exact amount of the appraisal. A drawing by lot was then held between these two on December 1st and Mr. Horowitz of New Hyde Park, New York became the buyer for $13,738.00.[35] The actual real estate closing occurred on June 16, 1948. Thus it was that the old air station property finally left government control after 31 years, but the site remained undeveloped under the new private ownership. Then on March 23, 1956 the entire 40.2 acres were purchased by a local building contractor, Frederick W. Crowell. It was his company that gradually transformed the parcel into what is now one of the most beautiful waterfront residential areas on Cape Cod.[36]

Building #48 – Originally the gate house and later the quarters of the custodian, it is shown here abandoned in 1947. *Photos courtesy of the National Archives – Northeast Region (Boston).*

A view of the Naval Air Station site as it appeared from aloft after the base was sold. Note the concrete slabs indicating where the buildings once stood. *Photo from the Author's Collection.*

An aerial view of Nickerson Neck taken during August in the year 2000. There is little evidence left of the Chatham Naval Air Station, but in the foreground, the cement ramps are still visible on this highly developed waterfront property. *Aerial Photograph by William P. Quinn, Orleans, Massachusetts.*

A special Naval Aviation enlistment poster used in the Chatham aerial recruiting campaign of mid-1919. *Courtesy of the National Archives, Washington, D.C.*

Appendix A
Lighter-than-air at Chatham

Kite Balloons

Number	From	To	Disposition
A-725	3/20/18	5/4/20	To NAS Hampton Roads
A-726	3/20/18	5/11/20	Condemned at Chatham
A-2756	8/24/18	5/4/20	To NAS Hampton Roads

B-class Blimps

Number	From	To	Disposition
B-7	3/12/18	6/5/18	Wrecked
B-12	3/26/18	12/1/18	To Akron
B-18	1/25/19	10/21/19	To NAS San Diego
B-19	1/27/18	5/3/20	To NAS Rockaway
B-20	11/28/19	1/25/19	Wrecked

C-class Blimps

Number	From	To	Disposition
C-10	11/14/19	5/8/20	To NAS Rockaway

Appendix B

Planes at Chatham

R-9's

Number	From	To	Disposition
A-913	3/15/18	7/13/18	Wrecked
A-914	3/15/18	7/11/18	Wrecked
A-915	3/15/18	8/15/18	Wrecked
A-916	3/15/18	6/21/18	Wrecked
A-931	4/1/18	4/17/18	Wrecked
A-932	4/1/18	11/9/18	To NAF Philadelphia
A-943	12/18/18	5/11/20	To NAF Philadelphia
A-965	4/15/18	10/4/18 *	To NAF Philadelphia
A-967	4//17/18	10/4/18 *	To NAF Philadelphia
	1/21/19	1/11/20 **	Stricken - worn out
A-991	5/9/18	10/4/18 *	To NAF Philadelphia
A-992	5/12/18	11/1/18	To NAF Philadelphia
A-993	5/10/18	8/3/18	Wrecked
A-994	5/10/18	10/4/18 *	To NAF Philadelphia

* Flown to Naval Aircraft Factory in special 4-plane flight.
** Served in two separate tours of duty at Chatham.

HS-1's

Number	From	To	Disposition
A-1693	6/23/18	10/11/18	Wrecked
A-1694	6/26/18	9/17/18	Wrecked
A-1695	6/25/18	7/3/19	Hull donated to Gloucester
A-1696	6/28/18	10/1/18	Wrecked
A-1189	4/1/19	6/29/22	Sold at public auction
A-1321	4/1/19	*	*

*Aircraft Record Card incomplete.

HS-2's

Number	From	To	Disposition
A-1847	7/25/18	7/22/19	Stricken - worn out
A-1848	7/25/18	10/26/18	Wrecked
A-1849	7/25/18	7/22/19	Stricken - worn out
A-1850	7/25/18	7/22/19	Stricken - worn out
A-1851	7/25/18	7/22/19	Stricken - worn out
A-1852	7/25/18	9/28/18	Sank while under tow
A-1853	7/25/18	12/27/18	Wrecked
A-1854	7/25/18	5/7/19	Wrecked
A-1855	7/25/18	9/14/19	Wrecked
A-1856	7/25/18	4/25/19	Lost at sea - crew not found
A-1915	8/12/18	6/29/22	Sold at public auction

Appendix B (Cont'd.)

HS-2's (Cont'd.)

Number	From	To	Disposition
A-1916	8/12/18	5/19/19	Wrecked
A-1917	8/12/18	2/8/19	Wrecked
A-1918	8/12/18	5/11/19	Stricken - worn out
A-1456	11/23/18	12/17/18	Wrecked
A-1457	11/23/18	12/29/18	Wrecked
A-2237	10/24/18	7/22/19	Stricken - worn out
A-2238	5/3/19	8/9/19	Wrecked
A-2241	5/3/19	6/29/22	Sold at public auction

A panoramic view of the Chatham Naval Air Station showing Fox Island to the left with the dirigible hangar behind it and the ``double'' seaplane hangar to the right. *Photo courtesy of Robert S. Hardy and the Chatham Historical Society.*

Appendix C

Buildings at Chatham

Building Number	Description	Building Number	Description
1	pump house	32	aviation storehouse
2	hydrogen buildings	33	oil recycling plant
3	dirigible hangar	34	laboratory
4	officers quarters	35	hydrogen cylinder storehouse
5	enlisted mens quarters	36	blower house - north
6	administration building	37	blower house - south
7	mess & recreation building	38	dirigible storehouse
8	heating plant	39	storehouse
9	garage	40	carpenter shop
10	machine shop	41	photo laboratory
11	storehouse	42	seaplane hangar
12	hospital	43	mess hall
13	water tank - 20,000 gal.	44	barracks
14	septic tank	45	storehouse
15	boat house	46	radio house
16	seaplane hangar	47	scrub house
17	magazine	48	gate house
19	temporary building	49	motor testing shed
21	temporary building	50	boiler house
22	temporary building	51	gasoline pump house
23	temporary building	52	radio school
29	gas holder - 100,000 cu. ft.	53	septic tank
30	pigeon house	54	filter bed
31	radio tower	55	sewage pump house

Note: #18, 20, 24, 25, 26, 27, & 28 were never assigned. The K of C and the YMCA buildings were identified by name only.

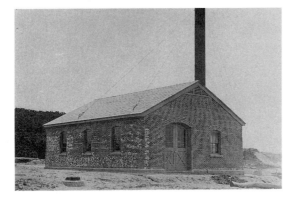 

Above left: Building #50, the boiler house which supplied heat to the buildings located between the main gate and the dirigible hangar. **Above right:** The two coal-fired furnaces housed in Building #50. A second but similar heating system served the buildings in the area of the seaplane hangars. *Photos courtesy of the Boston National Historical Park.*

Appendix D

Pilots at Chatham *

Lighter-than-air

Name	Naval Aviator Number	Name	Naval Aviator Number
Bark, Earl B.	707	Haskell, Merrill	1752
Brewer, Arthur D.	103	Houghton, Arthur R.	859
Breyman, Charles H.	700		
Briscoe, William C.	1070	Lange, Karl L.	547
		Littleton, Covington S.	1555
Eastman, Gardiner P.	1579		
Erdman, Albert W.	1562	Medusky, William J.	1100
Evans, Albert W.	696	Moora, Charles S.	1759
Franzheim, William A.	1197	Shade, James F.	551
Griffin, Walter B.	544	Whitney, John R.	1084

Heavier-than-air

Name	Naval Aviator Number	Name	Naval Aviator Number
Anderson, Gordon B.	1826	Corey, Russell B	553
Andrews, Junius F.	413	Cormack, William S.	1089
Ashley, John W.	281		
		Drew, Harold D.	1362
Backus, Clinton D.	355	Durfee, Thomas	415
Bailey, Morris H.	313		
Bamrick, Edward J.	1289	Eaton, Phillip B.	60
Baron, Frederick J.	1511		
Bates, Chester A.	1510	Ferrone, Frank N.	1047
Bergin, Thomas M.	232	Flood, John C.	921
Bransome, Edwin D.	286	Fox, George W.	2279
Brennan, Edward P.	406		
Brown, Waldo H.	458	Gallivan, Thomas J	1512
Buchanan, John S.	276	Galloupe, Chauncy A.	423
Burk, Frank L.	481	Gardiner, Charles M.	1831
Cassidy, Robert V.	1072	Hall, Charles A.	2489
Chase, Nathan B.	37	Hartley, Francis	(no number assigned)
Chute, James L.	1453	Haynes, Philip L.	2608
Clayton, Henry C.	360	Hicks, Frederick B.	729
Coatsworth, Caleb J.	1005	Hines, John W.	338
Collins, John A.	1664	Holton, Richard A.	877
Corcoran, Lawrence M.	1426	Hoopes, Thomas T.	1094

Appendix D (Cond't)

Heavier-than-air (Cond't)

Name	Naval Aviator Number	Name	Naval Aviator Number
Howard, John C.	1949	Rouleau, Louis T.	453
Hudson, Alfred W.	490	Rounds, Edward W.	1290
Husted, John G. W.	970		
		Sargent, Howard C.	372
Jencks, Stephan H.	684	Schiff, Herbert	916
Jennings, Allyn R.	455	Sheehan, John M.	484
Jordan, Robert	924	Shields, Edward M.	452
		Shields, William L.	2695
Krouse, Samuel H.	960	Shilling, Willian J.	951
		Smith, Ralph E,	938
Lingard, Eric A.	540	Smith, William P.	644
Lonnquist, Theodore C.	2963	Staniford, Robert J.	967
Marschat, Richard A.	1027	Terhume, Edward A.	1444
McKitterick, Edward H.	39	Thomas, Reginald D.	207
Montgomery, George S.	300	Tobin, Gregory J.	1268
Ostridge, Charles L.	231	VanDusen, Frederick C.	937
Parsley, Clyde L.	1989	Walker, William J.	1167
Pride, A. Melville	1119	Welch, Everett P.	997
		Weston, Carlyle	928
Reber, Earl E.	2696	Woolsey, William E.	934
Richmond, Isidor	918	Worthington, Jacques P.	2758
Robinson, Glen E.	1255		

*Only pilots issued an official naval aviator certificate are listed.

Appendix E

In Memoriam

The following men met their death while stationed at the Chatham Naval Air Station:

Junius F. Andrews, Ensign - killed July 13, 1918 in crash of R-9 No. 913.

Joseph D. Yanacek, Quartermaster 3rd Class - died September 19, 1918 from pneumonia due to Spanish flu.

William J. Corbett, Chief Electrician (RO) - died September 20, 1918 due to exposure and partial immersion.

Eric A. Lingard, Ensign - died October 29, 1918 from pneumonia due to exposure and partial immersion.

John S. Buchanan, Lieutenant - lost at sea April 25, 1919 while on a flight in HS-2L No. 1856.

John C. Howard, Ensign - lost at sea April 25, 1919 while on a flight in HS-2L No. 1856.

Bernard Tornes, Electrician 1st Class - lost at sea April 25, 1919 while on a flight in HS-2L No. 1856.

Charles L. Ostridge, Lieutenant (jg) - killed May 19, 1919 in crash of HS-2L No. 1916.

Herbert Hartenstein, Quartermaster 1st Class - killed on May19, 1919 in crash of HS-2L No. 1916.

May they rest in everlasting peace.

An aerial view of the Chatham Naval Air Station, after it closed showing the boat house and the seaplane hangars. Built into the roof of the ``double'' hangar to the left of the picture can be seen a fifteen foot observation tower, forty-six feet above ground level. *Photo courtesy of the National Archives, Washington, D.C.*

Notes

Introduction

[1] Publication No. 1, Historical Section, U.S.N.: *German Submarine Activities on the Atlantic Coast of the United States and Canada* (Washington: Government Printing Office, 1920). pp. 17-22.

[2] DCNO (Air), *U.S. Naval Administration in World War II*; Part 7, "Aviation Shore Establishments, 1911 - 1945" (Typewritten) pp. 70 - 72. (On microfilm at the National Museum of Naval Aviation, Pensacola, FL).

[3] Adrian O. Van Wyen, *Naval Aviation in World War I* (Washington; Government Printing Office, 1969), p.8.

[4] DCNO (Air), *U.S. Naval Administration in World Ward II*; Part 7, "Aviation Shore Establishments, 1911 - 1945" (Typewritten) pp. 70. Also Ralph D. Paine, *The First Yale Unit* (Cambridge: Riverside Press, 1925) 2 vols.; Vol. 1, p.88.

Chapter One - The First Months

[1] National Archives, Washington: Record Group 45, Box 704; Folder 3. "History of the U.S. Naval Air Station, Chatham, Mass." (Typewritten) pp. 1-2. Hereafter cited as "History, NAS Chatham".

[2] Harwich Independent, October, 31, 1917. Also Barnstable Patriot, November 5, 1917.

[3] All reports and correspondence of the period use the designation "dirigible hangar" for the structures housing lighter-than-air craft even though the Navy did not have a rigid airship in service or under construction at any time during the war.

[4] Hingham Journal, January 18, 1918

[5] David Seidman, "Damned by Faint Praise." *WoodenBoat* magazine. June, 1991. Also Mystic Seaport Museum Manuscript Collection, Mystic, CT. The magazine article covers the building of the various Sea Sled models while the museum holds most of the company's administrative and production records.

[6] The arrival of each assigned plane, blimp and kite balloon at Chatham as well as its identification number, the date it ended its service there and its "Trouble Report", are recorded on individual Aircraft Maintenance Cards held at the Naval Historical Center, Washington Navy Yard, Washington, D.C..

[7] National Archives, Washington: Record Group 45, Box 477. "Naval Records Collection - First Naval District; Naval Air Detachment."

[8] ibid

[9] Personal papers of Ensign Brown made available to the author by his son, Paul G. Brown.

[10] Barnstable Patriot, April 8, 1918. Also Harwich Independent, April 19, 1918.

[11] Nantucket Inquirer and Mirror, April 20, 1918 and May 4, 1918.

[12] ibid, May 4, 1918.

[13] National Archives-Northeast Region (Boston). Record Group 26, Box 866; Pamet River LSS log, May 9, 1918. Also Box 512; Highland LSS log, May 9, 1918.

[14] National Archives, Washington: Record Group 72, Box 72. ltr; R. W. White, Ensign to Chief of Bureau of Steam Engineering, May 4, 1918. Also Record Group 72, Box 138. ltr; Sanitation Officer, First Naval District to Bureau of Medicine and Surgery, June 14, 1918.

[15] Nantucket Inquirer and Mirror, June 8, 1918.

[16] Hull Beacon, June 21, 1918.

[17] National Archives-Northeast Region (Boston). Record Group 26, Box 99; Cahoons Hollow LSS log, June 19,1918.

[18] Area charts drawn by Ensign Brown and made available to the author by his son, Paul G. Brown.

[19] Lieutenant Charles W. Mathews, USN, "Patrolling and Patrol Stations on the Western Atlantic", *History of the U.S. Navy Aviation During the World War*. Washington: Navy Department, Historical Section. n.d. (typewirtten) p. 11. Hereafter cited as "Patrolling and Patrol Stations".

[20] "allo" was the tern used by the French and adopted by the Americans to signify an enemy submarine or an unidentified contact was in the area.

[21] "Patrolling and Patrol Stations", p.213. Also National Archives, Washington: Record Group 72, Box 138. ltr; Commanding Officer, Chatham to Chief of Naval Operations (Aviation) dated June 8, 1918.

[22] Gloucester Daily Times, June 11, 1918.

[23] Boston Post, July 11-13, 1918, Boston Globe, July 11-13, 1918.

[24] Boston Post, July 13, 1918.

[25] National Archives-Northeast Region (Boston). Record Group 26, Box 814; Old Harbor LSS log, July 13, 1918.

[26] Samuel Eliot Morison, *The Ropemakers of Plymouth*. (Boston: Houghton Mifflin Company, 1950), p. 116.

[27] Nantucket Inquirer and Mirror, June 8, 1918.

[28] Barnstable Patriot, June 10, 1918.

[29] "History, NAS Chatham", pp. 39-40.

[30] Harwich Independent, June 19, 1918.

[31] National Archives, Washington. Record Group 72, Box 95. Order Form; Bureau of Construction and Repair to Inspector of Aeroplanes, Fullmer-Clogg Company, July 17, 1918.

[32] Admiral William S. Sims, USN, *The Victory at Sea*. (New York: Doubleday, Page & Company, 1920), p. 400.

33 Erich Groner, *Die deutschen Kriegsschiffe 1815-1945*, Vol. 1. (Munich: J. F. Lehmanns, 1966). These characteristics apply to all the converted boats except U-155 (ex-Deutschland) which differed in several essentials.

Chapter Two - U-boat on the Prowl

[1] Robert M. Grant, *U-boat Intelligence 1914-1918*. (Hamden, CT: Archon Books, 1969). p. 189 The author makes use of old German naval records captured in 1945 which indicate the Commanding Officer was Kapitanleutnant Richard Feldt and not Kapitanleutnant von Olderburg as previously believed.

[2] Although this barge was identified as No. 403 in write-ups at the time of the attack, the barge captain's son, Arthur S. Peterson, was quoted as saying it was misidentified and the actual designation of his father's barge which was sunk was the No. 703. See Margaret Koehler, "The Day the Submarine Shelled Orleans"; *Cape Cod Compass* Vol. 28; June 1976. p. 77.

[3] When the fires eventually burned themselves out, the smouldering hull of the Perth Amboy was towed to Vineyard Haven on the island
of Martha's Vineyard and docked. Later it was towed to New York and totally rebuilt. In 1936 the tug was bought by the Moran Towing Co. and renamed the Nancy Moran. In 1943 it was taken over by the War Shipping Administration in Washington and loaned to the British Ministry of War Transport. The Nancy Moran (ex-Perth Amboy) sank in a collision May 30, 1946 on a voyage from Southhampson to Gravesend.

[4] New England Aviators Publishing Committee, *New England Aviators 1914-1918*. 2 Vol. (Boston: Houghton Mifflin Company, 1919) Vol. 2, p. 330.

[5] National Archives, Washington: Record Group 72, Box 138. ltr; P. B. Eaton to Commandant, First Naval District, July 25, 1918.

[6] Robert M. Grant, *U-boat Intelligence 1914-1918*. (Hamden, Ct: Archon Books, 1969), pp. 155-156, 189.

[7] "Patrolling and Patrol Stations", p. 40.

[8] Ralph D. Paine, *The First Yale Unit*. 2 Vol. (Cambridge, The Riverside Press, 1925). Vol. 1, p. 202.

[9] ibid: Vol. 1, p. 252.

[10] National Archives, Washington: Record Group 72, Box 138. ltr; Chief of BuOrd toCNO, August 22, 1918.

[11] Henry J. James, *German Subs in Yankee Waters*. (New York: Gotham House, Inc., 1940). pp. 85-86.

[12] Sandwich Independent, August 8, 1918.

[13] Named after the designer, Captain Caquot of the French Army. See *Aircraft Yearbook-1920*, p. 137.

Chapter Three - Flight Activity Intensifies

[1] New Bedford Times, July 23, 1918.

[2] Halifax Chronicle (Nova Scotia), July 23-24, 1918.

[3] "History, NAS Chatham", pp. 40-44.

[4] Nantucket Inquirer and Mirror, July, 27, 1918.

[5] New Bedford Times, July 23, 1918.

[6] Nantucket Inquirer and Mirror, July 27, 1918.

[7] National Archives-Northeast Region (Boston). Record Group 26, Box 679; Monomoy Point LSS log, July 23-24, 1918.

[8] Barnstable Patriot, August 5, 1918.

[9] "History, NAS Chatham", p. 3.

[10] Kautz Family YMCA Archives; c/o University of Minnesota Library, 2642 University Avenue, St. Paul, Minnesota 55114.

[11] "FLY PAPER" Vol. 1. No. 7. October 31, 1919, p. 2.

[12] Captain William A. Maguire (ChC) USN, *Rig for Church*. (New York: The Macmillan Company, 1942). p. 44.

[13] Boston Globe, August 1, 1918.

[14] *Fore River Log*, July, 1919. pp. 9, 12-13. Also Boston Globe, August 5, 1918.

[15] *Fore River Log*, September, 1918. p. 3. Also Boston Globe, August 7, 1918.

[16] National Archives-Northeast Region (Boston). Record Group 26, Box 160; Chatham LSS log, August 7, 1918. Also Box 661; Monomoy LSS log, August 7, 1918.

[17] Harwich Independent, July 24, 1918. Also a letter from Camp Quanset's owner/operators, Bruce and Ann Hammatt, to the author dated September 30, 1997 telling of the propeller.

[18] National Archives-Northeast Region (Boston). Record Group 26, Box 717; Nahant LSS log, September 8-15, 1918.

[19] National Archives-Northeast Region (Boston). Record Group 26, Box 766; Nauset LSS log, September 11-18, 1918.

[20] National Archives-Northeast Region (Boston). Record Group 26, Box 866; Pamet River LSS log. September 12, 1918. Also Box 512; Highland LSS log, September 12, 1918.

[21] "History, NAS, Chatham", p. 21.

[22] Cape Ann Shore, July 31, 1920. P 7.

[23] ibid, July 31, 1920. p. 7.

[24] "History, NAS Chatham", pp. 25-28.

[25] Gloucester Daily Times, November 2, 1918.

[26] Ensign Brown wrote an account of the incident at the time it occurred and a copy was made available to the author by his son, Paul G. Brown.

Chapter Four – A Busy October

[1] "History, NAS Chatham", p. 4.

[2] ibid, p. 4.

[3] ibid, p. 5.

[4] ibid, pp. 22-25.

[5] National Archives-Northeast Region (Boston). Record Group 26, Box 446; Gurnett LSS log, October 23-24, 1918. Also Old Colony Memorial, November 1, 1918.

[6] William Washburn Nutting, *The Cinderellas of the Fleet*. (Jersey City, NJ: The Standard Motor Construction Co., 1920). p. 174.

[7] ibid, p. 67.

[8] ibid, p. 77.

[9] "History, NAS Chatham", pp. 28-38.

[10] Barnstable Patriot, December 15, 1919.

[11] Harwich Independent, November 6, 1918.

[12] Akron Beacon Journal, November 9, 1918. Also NA/NER-26, Box 814; Old Harbor LSS log, November 10, 1918.

[13] "History, NAS Chatham", p. 15.

14 National Archives, Washington. Record Group 72, Box 138. Ltr, Commanding Officer, Chatham to Commandant, First Naval District, July 10, 1919.

Chapter Five – Chatham by Departments

[1] "History, NAS Chatham", pp. 5, 10.

[2] "Patrolling and Patrol Stations", pp. 57-61.

[3] "History, NAS Chatham", p. 13.

[4] National Archives, Washington. Record Group 72, Box 96. Report by A . D. Brewer, December 3, 1919.

[5] National Archives, Washington. Record Group 72, Box 96. ltr; N. B. Chase to Bureau of Steam Engineering, June 26, 1919.

[6] "History, NAS Chatham", pp. 13, 59.

[7] "Patrolling and Patrol Stations", pp. 59-60.

[8] National Archives-Northeast Region (Boston). Record Group 26, Box 814; Old Harbor LSS log, May 23, 1918.

[9] Lieutenant Norman R. Van Der Veer, USN, *The Bluejacket's Manual*, Sixth Edition 1918. pp. 431-432.

[10] David H. Quinn, ed. *Flying Officers of the U.S.N.. 1917-1918*. (Washington: Naval Aviation War Book Committee, 1919). pp. 71-72.

[11] Provincetown Advocate, September 19, 1918.

[12] Old Colony Memorial, Apeil 16, 1920.

[13] Department of the Navy, Bureau of Ordnance. *Naval Ordnance Activities, World War 1917-1918*. (Washington: Government Printing Office, 1918). p. 140.

[14] "Patrolling and Patrol Stations", p. 130.

[15] Christopher Chant, ed. *How Weapons Work*. (Chicago: Henry Regnery Company, 1976). p. 42.

[16] Department of the Navy, Bureau of Ordnance. *Naval Ordnance Activities, World War 1917-1918.* (Washington: Government Printing Office, 1918). p. 146.

[17] ibid, p. 147.

[18] National Archives, Washington. Record Group 72, Box 96.

[19] National Archives, Washington. Record Group 024. "Naval Air Station log book: Chatham." Daily log for July 22, 1919.

[20] "History, NAS Chatham", p. 6.

[21] Hingham Journal, December 7, 1917.

[22] Cape Cod Community College, Nickerson Memorial Historical Library. Oral History: *Report of Harold Tuttle, Chatham.*

[23] Lieutenant J. F. Neuberger (MC) USN, *Medical Aspects of Naval Aviation.* Reprinted in booklet form from the July 1921 edition of *The Military Surgeon.* p. 10.

[24] Town of Chatham Death Records - 1918. Town Clerk's office, Chatham Town Hall.

[25] Harwich Independent, September 25, 1918.

[26] National Archives, Washington. Record Group 72, Box 138. ltr; P. B. Eaton to Commandant, First Naval District, May 9, 1919.

[27] National Archives, Washington, Record Group 024. "Naval Air Station log book: Chatham." Daily log for January 20, 1920.

[28] Lieutenant Norman R. Van Der Veer, USN, *The Bluejacket's Manual,* Sixth Edition 1918. pp. 21-22.

[29] National Archives, Washington. Record Group 72, Box 138. ltr; Commanding Officer, Chatham to Commandant, First Naval District, July 10, 1919.

Chapter Six – The Armistice and Celebrations

[1] Boston Globe, November 11, 1918.

[2] ibid, November 11, 1918.

[3] ibid, November 12, 1918. (The Little Building still exists at the corner of Tremont and Arlington Streets. Today it houses only commercial tenants.)

[4] Boston Globe, November 11-12, 1918.

[5] ibid, November 13, 1918.

[6] ibid, November 13, 1918.

[7] Old Colony Memorial, November 15, 1918.

[8] Boston Globe, November 12, 1918.

[9] Harwich Independent, November 27, 1918.

[10] Boston Globe, November 17, 1918.

[11] Harwich Independent, November 27, 1918.

[12] Boston Globe, November 29, 1918.

[13] Daily Eastern Argus, December 4, 1918.

[14] ibid, December 6, 1918.

[15] Harwich Independent, January 8, 1919.

[16] ibid, January 8, 1919.

[17] Old Colony Memorial, December 17, 1918.

[18] ibid, January 31, 1919.

[19] Boston Globe, January 14, 1919. Also NA/NER-26, Box 839; Orleans LSS log, January 14, 1919.

[20] Old Colony Memorial, January 31, 1919.

[21] ibid, February 21, 1919. Also Hull Beacon, February 24, 1919.

[22] Roy A. Grossnick, ed, *Kite Balloons to Airships - The Navy's Lighter-than-Air Experience.* (Washington: Government Printing Office, 1986). p. 8.

[23] Barnstable Patriot, March 3, 1919.

[24] Providence Journal, February 22-25, 1919. The pilot in command of this flight was Ensign James L. Gillon (Naval Aviator 416).

[25] National Archives, Washington: Record Group 45, Box 477. "Naval Records Collection - First Naval District; Naval Air Detachment."

[26] ibid, March 3, 1919.

[27] Boston Globe, February 27, 1919.

[28] ---------------- *History of the 101st United States Engineers A.E.F. 1917-1918-1919.* (Cambridge: Volunteer Committee of the Regiment, 1926). p. 316.

[29] William J. Robinson, *Forging the Sword, The Story of Camp Devens.* (Concord, NH: The Rumford Press, 1920). p. 164.

[30] ---------------- *History of the 101st United States Engineers A.E.F. 1917-1918-1919.* (Cambridge: Volunteer Committee of the Regiment, 1926). p. 322.

[31] Nantucket Inquirer and Mirror, May 3, 1919.

[32] National Archives-Northeast Region (Boston). Record Group 26, Box 160; Chatham LSS log, April 12, 1919.

[33] Nantucket Inquirer and Mirror, March 8, 1919.

[34] Newport Daily News, April 12, 1919.

[35] National Archives-Northeast Region (Boston). Record Group 26, Box 839; Orleans LSS log, April 12, 1919.

[36] National Archives, Washington. Record Group 71, Box 93. ltr: Bureau of Supplies and Accounts to Bureau of Yards and Docks, April 23, 1919. Also ltr; Bureau of Ordnance to Supply Officer, Navy Yard, Boston, May 1, 1919.

[37] Old Colony Memorial, May 2, 1919.

[38] Boston Globe, May 2, 1919.

[39] ibid, May 1, 1919.

[41] New Bedford Times, April 29, 1919.

[42] Providence Journal, April 30, 1919.

[43] National Archives, Washington. Record Group 45, Box 477. Daily Summary of Patrol, April 29, 1919. Also Fall River Daily Globe, April 30, 1919 and May 1, 1919.

[44] New Bedford Times, April 24, 1919.

[45] Providence Journal, May 4, 1919.

Chapter Seven – Post War Activity

[1] Chief Machinist Mate Edward R. Howard, who had been stationed at Chatham, was originally designated to go as engineer. However during the engine tests on May 7th of the NC-4 at Rockaway, his hand was severed at the wrist by a spinning propeller which necessitated his being replaced. "Patrolling and Patrol Stations", p. 37.

[2] Edward Rowe Snow, "Former Chatham Residents Assisted in First Transatlantic Flight 50 Years Ago"; *Lower Cape Cod Chronicle*: May 8, 1969. p. 2.

[3] Cape Cod Times, May 4, 1986.

[4] Personal interview on January 27, 1998 with Gladys and Donna Lumpkin, daughter and granddaughter of George Goodspeed.

[5] Barnstable Patriot, May 10, 1919.

[6] Richard K. Smith, *First Across*. (Annapolis: Naval Institute Press, 1973). p. 90.

[7] New Bedford Times, May 19, 1919.

[8] Harwich Independent, May 21, 1919.

[9] National Archives-Northeast Region (Boston). Record Group 26, Box 839; Orleans LSS log, May19-21, 1919. Also Gloucester Daily Times, May 20, 1919.

[10] ---------------- "Naval Airship C-5 Makes 1100-mile Flight" *Aviation and Aeronautical Engineering*: June 1, 1919. pp. 475-476.

[11] Report distributed by the Associated Press and carried by an unidentified newspaper dated May 19, 1919. Clipping is part of the Jerome C. Hunsaker scrapbook in the Institute Archives at the Massachusetts Institute of Technology.

[12] ---------------- "Official Story of the C-5 Dirigible's Record Flight to Newfoundland" *Aerial Age Weekly*: June 16, 1919. p. 683.

[13] Richard K. Smith, *First Across*. (Annapolis: Naval Institute Press, 1973). pp. 94-95.

[14] New Bedford Times, May 16, 1919.

[15] Richard K. Smith, *First Across*. (Annapolis: Naval Institute Press, 1973). p. 96.

[16] Old Colony Memorial, July 11, 1919. Also Harwich Independent, July 23, 1919.

[17] "FLY PAPER" Vol. 1, No. 3. August 9, 1919. p. 2.

[18] "FLY PAPER" Vol. 1, No. 8. November 24, 1919. p. 1.

[19] During the war these initials were jokingly said to stand for U Shall Never Reach France.

[20] National Archives, Washington. Record Group 24. Bureau of Navigation Circular Letter dated November 21, 1918.

[21] National Archives, Washington: Record Group 45, Box 478. Daily summary of Chatham flight activities.

[22] National Archives, Washington: Record Group 72, Box 138. ltr; P. B. Eaton to Commandant, First Naval District, July 25, 1918.

[23] ibid.

[24] Barnstable Patriot, May 7, 1919.

[25] National Archives, Washington: Record Group 72, Box 138. telegram; Commanding Officer, Naval Air Station, Chatham to Office of Operations, Washington, dated February 14, 1919.

[26] National Archives, Washington: Record Group 72, Box 138. Inspection report, Naval Air Station, Chatham, May 5, 1919.

[27] "FLY PAPER" Vol. 2, No. 2. May, 1920. p. 10.

[28] "FLY PAPER" Vol. 1, No. 3. August 9, 1919. p. 2.

[29] ibid, p. 1.

[30] Barnstable Patriot, October 7, 1918.

[31] ibid, January 13, 1919.

[32] ibid, January 13, 1919.
[33] Boston Globe, September 9, 1919.
[34] Patrick Abbott, *Airship, The Story of the R-34 and the First East-West Crossing of the Atlantic by Air.* (New York: Charles Scribner's Sons, 1973). p. 78.
[35] Edward Jablonski, *Atlantic Fever.* (New York: The MacMillan Company, 1972). pp. 60-61.
[36] Patrick Abbott, *Airship, The Story of the R-34 and the First East-West Crossing of the Atlantic by Air.* (New York: Charles Scribner's Sons, 1973). p. 104.
[37] Incident related to the author by Robert Hardy, retired American Airlines pilot, lifelong resident of Chatham and longstanding member of the Chatham Historical Society.
[38] Gloucester Daily Times, July 3, 1919.
[39] ibid, July 3, 1919.
[40] ibid, July 5, 1919.
[41] ibid, July 5, 1919.
[42] New Bedford Standard Times, July 21, 1949.
[43] New Bedford Times, July 5, 1919.

Chapter Eight – Recruiting Around New England

[1] "FLY PAPER" Vol. 1, No. 3. August 9, 1919. p. 1.
[2] New London Day, August 5, 1919.
[3] "FLY PAPER" Vol. 1, No. 3. August 9, 1919. p. 4. Also New London Day, August 5, 1919.
[4] New London Day, August 5, 1919.
[5] Boston Globe, July 24, 1919.
[6] New Bedford Times, July 22-23, 1919.
[7] ibid, July 28, 1919.
[8] ibid, July 29, 1919.
[9] ibid, July 29, 1919.
[10] Sandwich Independent, August 6, 1919.
[11] Salem Evening News, August 1, 1919.
[12] Boston Advertiser, August 2, 1919.
[13] Salem Evening News, August 2, 1919.
[14] ibid, August 4, 1919.
[15] Lynn Daily Item, August 4, 1919.
[16] "FLY PAPER" Vol. 1, No. 3. August 9, 1919. p. 4.
[17] New London Day, August 5, 1919.
[18] The Middletown Press, August 7, 1919.
[19] Hartford Daily Courant, August 9, 1919.
[20] ibid, August 9, 1919.
[21] Holyoke Daily Transcript, August 11, 1919. Also Springfield Union, August 10-11, 1919.
[22] Holyoke Daily Transcript, August 11, 1919.
[23] Springfield Union, August 11, 1919.
[24] ibid, August 12, 1919.
[25] New London Day, August 13, 1919.
[26] Newburyport Daily News, August 20, 1919.
[27] Haverhill Evening Gazette, August 20-21, 23, 1919.
[28] Boston Globe, August 24, 1919. Also Lawrence Eagle, August 25,1919.
[29] Lowell Sun, August 26, 1919.
[30] ibid, August 27, 1919.
[31] The Camden Herald, August 29, 1919.
[32] Daily Eastern Argus, August 29, 1919.
[33] Rockland Courier-Gazette, August 29, 1919.
[34] Daily Eastern Argus, September 1, 1919.
[35] ibid, September 2, 5, 1919.
[36] Boston Globe, September 19, 1919.
[37] New Bedford Times, July 30, 1919.
[38] Bangor Daily News, September 26, 1919. Also Daily Eastern Argus, September 26-27, 1919.
[39] Daily Eastern Argus, September 27, 1919.
[40] ibid, September 27, 1919.
[41] Boston Globe, September 28, 1919.
[42] New Bedford Times, October 2, 1919. Also Providence Journal, October 2, 1919.
[43] Providence Journal, October 3-4, 1919.
[44] New Haven Register, October 2, 4, 7, 1919.

Chapter Nine – Non-Operating Status

[1] DCNO (Air), *U.S. Naval Administration in World War II*: Part 7, "Aviation Shore Establishments. 1911-1945" (Typewritten) p. 204.

[2] ibid, p. 204.

[3] Reginold Wright Arthur, *Contact! Careers of U.S. Naval Aviators Assigned Numbers 1 to 2000*: (Washington, The Naval Aviator Register, 1962). p.534.

[4] "FLY PAPER" Vol. 1. No. 7. October 31, 1919. p. 2.

[5] *Aerial Age Weekly*, August 25, 1919. pp. 1095, 1098.

[6] Cape Cod Community College, Nickerson Memorial Historical Library, Oral History; *Report of Harold Tuttle, Chatham.*

[7] Kautz Family YMCA Archives, c/o University of Minnesota Library, 2642 University Avenue, St. Paul, Minnesota 55114.

[8] *Town of Chatham Annual Report - 1920*. "Appropriations Voted" p. 73.

[9] "FLY PAPER" Vol. 2, No. 1. April 1920. p. 12.

[10] Aircraft Maintenance Card for B-2.

[11] "FLY PAPER" Vol. 2, No. 1. April 1920. p. 12.

[12] Boston Globe, August 25, 1921.

[13] "FLY PAPER" Vol. 2, No. 1. April 1920. p. 2.

[14] ibid, p. 3. Also Akron Beacon Journal, June 9, 1919.

[15] Cleveland Plain Dealer, May 24, 1919.

[16] "FLY PAPER" Vol.. 2, No. 1. April, 1920. p. 3.

[17] "FLY PAPER" Vol.. 2, No. 2. May, 1920. p. 10.

[18] ibid, p. 10.

[19] National Archives, Washington. Record Group 72, Box 96. memorandum; Lieutenant William Green to Chief of Naval Operations. May 4, 1920.

[20] 'FLY PAPER' Vol. 2, No. 2. May, 1920. p. 10.

Chapter Ten – The Final Months

[1] National Archives, Washington. Record Group 72, Box 96. memorandum; Lieutenant William Green to Chief of Naval Operations, May 4, 1920.

[2] National Archives, Washington. Record Group 72, Box 96. ltr; Bureau of Supplies and Accounts to Supply Officer, NAS Chatham, June 6, 1920.

[3] Cape Cod Standard Times, September 30, 1940.

[4] Harwich Independent, August 11, 1920. Also *Town of Chatham Annual Report - 1920*. "Report of School Nurse" p. 108.

[5] Harwich Independent, January 19, 1921.

[6] ibid.

[7] Barnstable Patriot, January 24, 1921.

[8] National Archives, Washington. Record Group 143, Box 1355. ltr; Supply Officer, Navy Yard, Boston to Bureau of Engineering, May 14, 1921.

[9] National Archives, Washington. Record Group 71, Box 93. ltr; Chief of Bureau of Yards and Docks to Commandant, First Naval District, November 21, 1921.

[10] Barnstable Patriot, November 28, 1921.

[11] Barnstable Patriot, June 12, 1922.

[12] National Archives-Northeast Region (Boston). Record Group 181, Boxes 169-170. *United States of America v. Certain Lands in Chatham, County of Barnstable, Franklin B. Nickerson et al*. "Amended Final Decree" April 21, 1925.

[13] Barnstable Patriot, July 31, 1922.

[14] National Archives, Washington. Record Group 143, Box 1357. Catalog of Sales, Chatham Naval Air Station, June 29. 1922.

[15] Interview with Robert S. Hardy. Also Barnstable Patriot, November 27, 1922 and December 4, 1922. Also National Archives, Washington. Record Group 143, Box 1359. Bureau of Supplies andAccounts, General Correspondence; 1913-1925.

[16] National Archives, Washington. Record Group 143, Box 1357. ltr; Commandant, Navy Yard, Boston to Bureau of Supplies and Accounts, July 12, 1922.

[17] National Archives, Washington. Record Group 71, Box 95. Catalog of Sales, Chatham Naval Air Station, November 1, 1922.

[18] National Archives, Washington. Record Group 72, Box 96. ltr; Commandant, Boston Navy Yard to Bureau of Engineering, October 18, 1922.

[19] National Archives, Washington. Record Group 024. Chatham Naval Air Station log, December 31, 1922.

[1] National Archives, Washington. Record Group 71, Box 93. ltr. Chief of Bureau of Yards and Docks to A. E. Hoffmire, Secretary, YMCA, December 18, 1924.

[2] National Archives, Washington. Record Group 71, Box 258. Inspection of the Naval Air Station, Chatham, April 23, 1924.

[3] National Archives-Northeast Region (Boston). Record Group 181, Boxes 169-170. (Hereafter cited as NA/NER-181). United States of America, District of Massachusetts Civil Docket #1984. *United States of America v. Certain Lands in Chatham, County of Barnstable, Franklin B. Nickerson et al.* "Amended Final Decree" April 21, 1925.

[4] NA/NER-181, . ltr; Commandant, 1st Naval District to Bureau of Yards and Docks, May 3, 1926.

[5] NA/NER-181. ltr; St. Lawrence Trading & Supply Co. to Commandant, 1st Naval District, May 28, 1927. Also ltr; Commandant, 1st Naval District to Secretary of the Navy, September 1, 1927.

[6] NA/NER-181. ltr; Commandant, 1st Naval District to Bureau of Yards and Docks, May 3, 1926. Also ltr; Commandant, 1st Naval District to Secretary of the Navy, September 1, 1927.

[7] Interview with Robert S. Hardy.

[8] Clipping in possession of the Chatham Historical Society. Also Arthur Vanderbilt "The Two Year Defense". *Cape Cod Compass*, 1986 Part Two. p. 85.

[9] NA/NER-181. memorandum; P.J.. Searles, Acting, to Commandant, 1st Naval District. August 2, 1926.

[10] Boston Globe, September 1, 1927.

[11] NA/NER-181. ltr; Commandant, 1st Naval District to Secretary of the Navy, September 16, 1929.

[12] NA/NER-181. ltr; Commandant, 1st Naval District to Secretary of the Navy, September 16, 1929. Also ltr; Commandant, 1st Naval District to Judge Advocate of the Navy, October 24, 1929.

[13] Hugh Allen, *The Story of the Airship*. (Akron, The Goodyear Tire & Rubber Co., 1931 edition). p. 20.

[14] ibid, p. 20.

[15] NA/NER-181. ltr; Ernest Lee Jahncke, Acting Secretary of the Navy to W.E. Young, Goodyear Tire & Rubber Co., July 16, 1930. Also write-up of telephone conversation between Captain Abele, Assistant Commandant and Captain W.R. Furlong of Naval Operations, July 19, 1930. p. 2.

[16] Interview with Robert S. Hardy.

[17] NA/NER-181. ltr; Daniel Mahoney, Policeman to Public Works Officer, Navy Yard, Boston. July 16, 1930.

[18] NA/NER-181. ltr; Goodyear Zeppelin Corporation to Commandant, 1st Naval District, July 24, 1930. Also Bradstreet's Report, New England Airship Corporation, June 19, 1931. p. 2.

[19] NA/NER-181. ltr; Commandant, 1st Naval District to Daniel Mahoney, Caretaker, July 28, 1930.

[20] NA/NER-181. ltr; Daniel Mahoney, Policeman to Public Works Officer, Navy Yard, Boston. September 15, 1930.

[21] Hugh Allen, *The Story of the Airship*. (Akron, The Goodyear Tire & Rubber Co., 1931 edition). p. 75.

[22] NA/NER-181. ltr; Chief of Bureau of Aeronautics to Chief of Naval Operations, September 7, 1932. Also Inspection Report of the Chatham Naval Air Station, October 16, 1934.

[23] NA/NER-181. ltr; Commandant, 1st Naval District to EDO Aircraft Corporation, Long Island, N.Y., July 20, 1932.

[24] NA/NER-181. ltr; Commandant, 1st Naval District to Commander, Chatham Post #253 American Legion, September 30, 1932.

[25] NA/NER-181. Inspection Report, November 7, 1935.

[26] NA/NER-181. ltr; Commandant, 1st Naval District to Chief of the Bureau of Yards and Docks, June 29, 1937.

[27] NA/NER-181. ltr; Commandant, 1st Naval District to Commanding Officer, Unit 5, Section 5, U.S. Naval Communications Reserves, January 4, 1938.

[28] NA/NER-181. ltr; Assistant Secretary of the Navy (Shore Establishments) to Commandant, 1st Naval District, September 20, 1938.

[29] NA/NER-181. Telegram, November 15, 1939.

[30] NA/NER-181. ltr; Chief of the Bureau of Aeronautics to Chief of the Bureau of Yards and Docks, November 13, 1939.

[31] ibid.

[32] ibid.

[33] National Archives-Northeast Region (Boston). Record Group 270, Box 54. Appraisal, July 28, 1947.

[34] ibid. Pride would eventually retire as a four-star Admiral, the highest rank attained by any man ever to be stationed at Chatham.

[35] ibid. memorandum; C.D. Rockwell, Acting Chief, Non-industrial Sales Branch. subject - Bid Opening, December 1, 1947.

[36] Barnstable County Registry of Deeds, Barnstable, MA. Book 944, p. 518. Date of Recording June 22, 1956.

BIBLIOGRAPHY

Books

Abbott, Patrick, *Airship - TheStory of R-34 and the First East-West Crossing of the Atlantic by Air*.
    New York: Charles Scribner's Sons, 1973.

Allen, Hugh. *The Story of the Airship*. Akron: The Goodyear Tire & Rubber Co., 1931 edition.

Allen, Hugh. *The Story of the Airship*. Akron: The Lakeside Press, 1943 edition.

Althoff, William F. *Sky Ships - A History of the Airship in the United States Navy*. New York:
    Orion Books, 1990.

Arthur, Reginold Wright, ed. *Contact! Careers of U. S. Naval Aviators Assigned
    Numbers 1 to 2000*. Washington: The Naval Aviator Register, 1962.

Beyle, Noel W. *The Target Ship in Cape Cod Bay*. Eastham, MA: First Encounter Press, 1978.

Byrd, Rear Admiral Richard E., USN. *Skyward*. New York: Blue Ribbon Books, 1938.

Clark, William Bell. *When the U-boats Came to America*. Boston: Little, Brown and Company, 1929.

Department of the Navy, Operations-Aviation Planning and Information Section.
    Practical Rules for Flying and Miscellaneous Instructions for Student Naval Aviators.
    Washington: Government Printing Office, 1918.

Department of the Navy, Bureau of Ordnance. *Navy Ordnance Activities World
    War 1917 - 1918*. Washington: Government Printing Office, 1920.

Department of the Navy, Historical Section, Publication No. 1. *German Submarine
    Activities on the Atlantic Coast of the United States and Canada*.
    Washington: Government Printing Office, 1920.

Department of the Treasury. *Instructions for United States Coast Guard Stations*.
    Washington: Government Printing Office, 1916.

Doyle, James Madison, comp. *A History of the U.S.S. Mount Vernon*. Brooklyn:
    The Brooklyn Daily Eagle, 1918.

Duetsch, Captain Robert A., USN/ *The Defender's History - A Historical Account of Naval Air
    Station, South Weymouth, Mass*. Weymouth: South Weymouth Naval Air Station, 1997.

Egan, Maurice Francis and Kennedy, John B. *The Knights of Columbus in Peace
    and War*. 2 vols. New Haven: The Knights of Columbus, 1920.

Faurote, Fay L., ed. *Aircraft Year Book - 1919*. New York: Manufacturers Aircraft
    Association, 1919.

Grossnick, Roy A. ed. *Kite Balloons to Airships - The Navy's Lighter-than-Air Experience*.
    Washington: Government Printing Office, 1986.

History of the 101st United States Engineers A.E.F. 1917 - 1918 - 1919.
    Cambridge: Volunteer Committee of the Regiment, 1926.

Horne, Charles F. and Austin, Walter F. eds. *Source Records of the Great War*.
    7 vols. Indianapolis, IN: American Legion, 1923. Volume 6: 1918 - *The Year of Victory*.

Howe, M. A. DeWolfe. *Memoirs of the Harvard Dead in the War Against Germany*.
    5 vols. Cambridge: Harvard University Press, 1921.

Jablonski, Edward. *Atlantic Fever*. New York: The MacMillan Company, 1972.

James, Henry J. *German Subs in Yankee Waters*. New York: Gotham House, 1940.

Kerrick, Harrison S. *Military and Naval America*. New York: Doubleday, Page and Company, 1916.

Knappen, Theodore M. *Wings of War*. New York: G. P. Putnam's Sons, 1920.

Litchfield, P. W. *Industrial Voyage* (The author's career at Goodyear). Garden City, NY:
    Doubleday & Company, 1954.

Maguire, Captain William A., (ChC), USN. *Rig for Church*. New York: The MacMillan Company, 1942.

Mathews, Lieutenant Charles E., USN. "Patrolling and Patrol Stations on the Western
    Atlantic". In *History of U.S. Navy Aviation During the World War*.
    Washington: Navy Department, Historical Section. n.d. (Typewritten)

Books (Cont'd.)

Mayo, Katherine. *"That Damn Y"*. Boston: Houghton Mifflin Company, 1920.

Miller, Blaine. *Navy Wings*. New York: Dodd, Mead & Company, 1937.

Millholland, Ray. *The Splinter Fleet*. New York: The Bobbs-Merrill Company, 1936.

Moffat, Captail Alexander, USNR, (Ret.). *Maverick Navy*. Middletown, CT:
              Wesleyan University Press, 1976.

Molson, K. M. & Shortt, A.J.. *The Curtiss HS Flying Boats*. Annapolis: Naval Institute Press, 1995.

Monbleau, Marcia J. *Home Song Chatham*. Chatham, MA: Chatham Historical Society, 1995.

Morison, Samuel Eliot. *The Ropemakers of Plymouth - A History of the Plymouth
              Cordage Company 1824-1949*. Boston: Houghton Mifflin Company, 1950.

Morse, Edwin W., gen. ed.. *America in the War*. 5 vols. New York: Charles
              Scribner's Sons, 1922. Vol. 3: *Our Navy in the War*, by Lawrence Perry.

Neuberger, Lieutenant J. F. (MC), USN. *Medical Aspects of Naval Aviation*. Reprinted
              in booklet form from the July 1921 edition of *The Military Surgeon*.

New England Aviators Publishing Committee. *New England Aviators 1914-1918*.
              2 vols. Boston: Houghton Mifflin Company, 1919.

Nutting, William Washburn. *The Cinderellas of the Fleet*. Jersey City, NJ: The
              Standard Motor Construction Co., 1920.

Oman, Rear Admiral Charles M. (MC), USN. *Doctors Aweigh - The Story of the United
              States Navy Medical Corps in Action*. New York: Doubleday, Doran and Company, Inc., 1943.

Paine, Ralph D. *The First Yale Unit*. 2 vols. Cambridge: The Riverside Press, 1925.

Quinn, David H., ed. *Flying Officers of the U.S.N. 1917-1919*. Washington: Naval
              Aviation War Book Committee, 1919.

Robinson, William J. *Forging the Sword - The Story of Camp Devens*. Concord, NH:
              The Rumford Press, 1920.

Rossano, Geoffrey L., ed. *The Price of Honor*. Annapolis: Naval Institute Press, 1991.

Sheely, Lawrence D., ed. *Sailor of the Air*. Tuscaloosa: University of Alabama Press, 1993.

Smith, Richard K. *First Across*. Annapolis: Naval Institute Press, 1973.

Snow, Edward Rowe. *A Pilgrim Returns to Cape Cod*. Boston: Yankee Publishing Company, 1946.

Snow, Edward Rowe. *Great Atlantic Adventures*. New York: Dodd, Mead & Company, 1970

Turnbull, Archibald D. and Lord, Clifford L. *History of United States Naval Aviation*.
              New Haven: Yale University Press, 1949.

Van Der Veer, Lieutenant Norman R., USN. *The Bluejacket's Manual*. New York: The
              Sherman Company, 1918 (sixth edition).

Van Wyen, Adrian O. *Naval Aviation in World War I*. Washington: Government Printing Office, 1969.

Van Wyen, Adrian O. and Pearson, Lee M., eds. *United States Naval Aviation
              1910-60*. Washington: Government Printing Office, 1961.

Periodicals

Gerr, Dave, "The Hickman Sea Sled: The Best High-Speed Hull Ever?" *Boatbuilder*.
              September/October. 1988. pp. 6-11.

Koehler, Margaret. "The Day the Submarine Shelled Orleans." *Cape Cod Compass*
              Vol. 28; June, 1976. pp. 79-85.

Lacouture, Captain John, USN. "NAS Chatham." *FOUNDATION* (Published by the
              Naval Aviation Museum.) Fall, 1988. pp. 70 - 76.

Mros, Richard. "Attack on Orleans." *Cape Cod Life*. April/May, 1987. pp. 38 - 45.

Seidman, David, "Damned by Faint Praise". *WoodenBoat* magazine. June, 1991. pp. 46 - 57.

Periodicals (Cont'd.)

Vanderbuilt, Arthur. "The Two Year Defense." *Cape Cod Compass*. Summer/Fall, 1986
        (Part Two). pp. 79 - 85.
(----------------). "Destroyer McDermut Sponsored By Mrs. E. G. Grace." *The Fore River Log*.
September, 1918. p. 3. (Published monthly by the Bethlehem Steel Corporation for the employees of
their Fore River Yard in Quincy and their Victory Yard in Squantum.)
(----------------). "A World's Record at Fore River." *The Fore River Log*. July, 1919. pp. 9, 12 -13.
(----------------). "We Christen the Neponset." Bird's Neponset Review. June, 1930.
        pp. 1 - 5. (Published monthly by Bird & Son, Incorporated of East
        Walpole, Massachusetts for their employees and for their dealers.)
(----------------). "Good Will Tour of the Neponset." Bird's Neponset Review. August, 1930. pp. 1 - 2.

Newspapers

Connecticut

Hartford Daily Courant	New Haven Evening Register
Middleton Evening Press	New London Day

Maine

Camden Herald (Weekly)	Rockland Courier-Gazette (Weekly)
Daily Eastern Argus (Portland)	

Massachusetts

Barnstable Patriot (Weekly)	Lowell Sun
Boston Post	Lynn Daily Item
Boston Globe	Nantucket Inquirer and Mirror (Weekly)
Fall River Daily Globe	New Bedford Evening Standard
Gloucester Daily Times	New Bedford Times
Harwich Independent (Weekly)	Newburyport Daily News
Haverhill Evening Gazette	Old Colony Memorial (Plymouth)(Weekly)
Hingham Journal (Weekly)	Provincetown Advocate (Weekly)
Holyoke Daily Transcript	Salem Evening News
Hull Beacon (Weekly)	Sandwich Independent (Weekly)
Lawrence Eagle	Springfield Union

Nova Scotia

Halifax Chronicle	Halifax Herald

Ohio

Akron Beacon Journal	Cleveland Plain Dealer

Rhode Island

Newport Daily News	The Providence Journal

Other Sources

Libraries - Academic

Cape Cod Community College Library -"The Cape Cod History Collection".
Guggenheim Aeronautics and Astronautics Library at MIT.
Harvard College Archives.
Massachusetts Institute of Technology Archives.

Libraries - Public

Boston Public Library
Holyoke Public Library
New Bedford Public Library
New London Public Library
Portland Public Library

Museums

Glenn Curtiss Museum - Hammondsport, NY
Mystic Seaport Museum - Mystic, CT
Owls Head Transportation Museum - Owls Head, ME
San Diego Aerospace Museum - San Diego, CA

Historical Organizations

Cape Ann Historical Association (Gloucester)
Chatham Historical Society
Nantucket Historical Association
Old Dartmouth Historical Society (New Bedford)
Quincy Historical Society
Walpole Historical Society
Western Front Association

United States Government

Boston National Historical Park - Charlestown, MA
Library of Congress - Washington
National Archives - Washington
National Archives - College Park, MD
National Archives - Northeast Region (Boston) - Waltham, MA
National Museum of Naval Aviation - Pensacola, FL
Naval Historical Center - Washington
Smithsonian Institution; National Air and Space Museum – Washington